PEN...

AR...

ASTROLOGY: THE EVIDENCE OF SCIENCE

Much of Percy Seymour's work has been motivated by two convictions. The first is that the large-scale structure and dynamics of the universe are intimately bound up with life on earth and the structure of atoms. The second, an inevitable consequence of the first, is that astronomy is relevant to our day-to-day lives.

These beliefs have led him into many different branches of astronomy, and to consider the links between astronomy and the other sciences. After studying physics at Manchester University, he spent three years working out the structure of the magnetic field of the Milky Way. He then taught physics and astronomy in schools for a few years. As Senior Planetarium Lecturer at the Greenwich Observatory he introduced a series of lectures linking astronomy with the sciences and other subjects in the school curriculum – from geography and history to art and literature. His interdisciplinary approach to astronomy led him to explore the roots of astrology and the impact of navigation on the history of astronomy. He is currently Principal Lecturer in Astronomy at the University of Plymouth, where he continues to link astronomy with other disciplines, both in his teaching and in his research. His books include *Adventures with Astronomy, Halley's Comet, Cosmic Magnetism* and *The Paranormal* (Arkana 1992). Some of them have been translated into several languages. He is married and has one son.

Percy Seymour

ASTROLOGY:
The Evidence of Science

ARKANA
PENGUIN BOOKS

To Dianna

PENGUIN BOOKS

Published by the Penguin Group
Penguin Books Ltd, 27 Wrights Lane, London W8 5TZ, England
Penguin Books USA Inc., 375 Hudson Street, New York, New York 10014, USA
Penguin Books Australia Ltd, Ringwood, Victoria, Australia
Penguin Books Canada Ltd, 10 Alcorn Avenue, Toronto, Ontario, Canada M4V 3B2
Penguin Books (NZ) Ltd, 182–190 Wairau Road, Auckland 10, New Zealand

Penguin Books Ltd, Registered Offices: Harmondsworth, Middlesex, England

First published by Lennard Books 1988
This revised edition published in Arkana 1990
3 5 7 9 10 8 6 4 2

The extract from *Troilus and Criseyde* in Chapter 2 is reproduced by permission
of the Curtis Brown Group, London, copyright © the estate of Nevill Coghill, and
extracts from the Penguin Classics edition of *The Canterbury Tales* (translated
into modern English by Nevill Coghill, 1979) elsewhere in the chapter are
reproduced by permission of Penguin Books.

Printed in England by Clays Ltd, St Ives plc
Filmset in 10/12pt Sabon

Contents

List of Illustrations

Acknowledgements

First of all, I would like to thank my wife, Dianna, for her interest in my work and the moral support she has given me over the last ten years. Then I would like to thank Professor A. Smithers of Manchester University for taking an interest in my work at a time when the academic community seemed to be generally dismissive of any ideas in this area.

Over the last two years I have been able to meet astrologers at a number of different conferences and share my theory with them. For these opportunities I would like to thank Charles Harvey, President of the Astrological Association, and I would also like to thank him for writing the Foreword to this book. Development of my theory has benefited from discussions with the following people: Simon Best, Editor of *Correlation*, Michael Harding, Professor Peter Roberts of the City University and Michel Gauquelin. I would also like to thank the following people for help either with illustrations or by providing me with information relevant to the project: Gillian Glegg, Jean Jackson, Peter Langdown, Geoff Millward, Ian Norton and Michael Payne. Finally I would like to thank Roderick Brown of Lennard Publishing for encouragement and editorial help through several stages of the project.

Illustration Acknowledgements

I would like to thank the following for their permission to reproduce illustrative material. Although every effort has been made to contact copyright holders, it has not been possible to do so in every case, and I apologize to any that may have been omitted.

Adam Hilger: 12, 13, 15, 16, 17, 18, 19, 20; John Murray: 2, 3, 4, 6; the Slide Centre: 1, 9, 10, 14.

Foreword

The Church refused to look through Galileo's telescope. They *knew* from first principles that Jupiter could not have any moons. The High Church of Modern Science has, in the main, shown itself no less reluctant to examine the evidence for astrology. Astrology is, in terms of the received model, impossible. Therefore those that contend otherwise, or pretend to have evidence, are either deluded or deliberate charlatans who can have no place in intelligent society.

Faced with such a taboo, it is still only the brave scientists who are willing to consider the evidence for astrology, and only the most courageous who are prepared to dedicate their creative energies and reputations to exploring this outcast science. It is to Dr Seymour's great credit that as an astronomer he has firmly clutched the nettle of the evidence for astrology, as those in his discipline are especially antipathetic to the claims of star lore. Having done so, as a true scientist in search of truth, Dr Seymour has felt impelled by that evidence to apply his specialist knowledge of cosmic magnetism in seeking explanations for the phenomena recorded, and to get to grips with its implications.

Indeed, the great importance of this book lies not so much in the lucid and highly readable account that it gives of the growing body of evidence for astrology, valuable though this is, but in Dr Seymour's willingness, as an orthodox scientist, to look beyond the evidence and to formulate a realistic, rigorously constructed theory as to the way in which astrology *could* work. This process of searching for causal connections and of constructing and testing theories that will account for the facts has, as Dr Seymour points out, always been the mainspring of science. As John Addey has repeatedly said, astrology can only benefit from following the procedures of science as far as they can be taken.

Despite its necessarily mechanistic formulation, astrologers will hear in Dr Seymour's theory, in which the whole solar system plays

viii

out the magnetic 'symphony of the music of the spheres' on the nervous system of the individual, echoes of both Kepler's and Addey's thinking, with all its metaphysical implications. The theory's immediate attraction for the orthodox scientist must lie in the fact that it manages to account convincingly for many of the observed phenomena of astrology while at no point stepping outside the current framework of accepted science.

Whether or not Dr Seymour's type of model can eventually be extended to embrace fully the many subtleties of astrological experience remains to be seen. But, as Einstein maintained, 'theories are neither right nor wrong: they are either fertile or sterile'. Thanks to Dr Seymour, we now have a theory that can be tested and debated. For the future of astrology this is fertile ground indeed. It is an essential step in the process of restoring this ancient discipline to its rightful place amidst the fraternity of sciences. What precisely that rightful place may be is still open to conjecture, but no one who reads this open-minded book with a tolerant mind can be left in any doubt that the astrological dimension of science is one that will increasingly challenge our conception of man's relationship to the cosmos. Improbable though it may seem, astronomy and astrology, for so long divided, may even now be on course for a reunion.

Charles Harvey
7 January 1988

Preface to the Arkana Edition

The advent of radio several decades ago introduced many new concepts and phrases into our language. We often talk about 'being on the same wavelength', 'tuning into someone's thoughts' or 'picking up their vibrations'. The basis of all radio communications is the very important principle of resonance.

Resonance makes it possible for a radio telescope to tune into the specific vibrations of hydrogen atoms in the Andromeda galaxy (which is 14 million million million miles away); for us to listen to particular radio stations as we drive along in our cars; and for the Moon to shift a hundred billion tons of water out of the Bay of Fundy in Canada twice a day. It also allows us to identify atoms and molecules by the light waves that they resonantly absorb from the full rainbow spectrum of visible and invisible radiation. If the nucleus of the carbon atom did not have a certain resonant energy level, then the heavier chemical elements could not have been synthesized in the interior of a star, and life as we know it would not have been possible. On a much larger scale, astronomers can explain the gaps in Saturn's rings in terms of resonance between the particles of the rings and the satellites of this planet; and resonance between the planets and the asteroids leads to gaps in the asteroid belt. In the biological world, birds and other animals respond selectively to the sounds made by their own species and those made by their predators and prey as a result of resonance. Thus we see that resonance operates from the very large scale to the very small.

All the detailed calculations that are supposed to show that the Sun, Moon and planets cannot affect life on Earth have ignored the possibility of resonant interactions, although Geoffrey Dean and Arthur Mather in their book *Recent Advances in Natal Astrology* say that 'resonance is an essential consideration in any theory of astrological causation'. The theory I describe in this book is a serious scientific attempt to provide a causal theory based on the known forces of physics. It makes extensive use of the concept of resonance – resonance between the tidal tug, due to gravity, of the planets on the very hot gases trapped in the magnetic fields of the Sun and Earth, and resonance between the resulting fluctuations of the Earth's magnetic field and the electrical activity of the neural network of the foetus.

Although all physical scientists, most engineers and many other scientists from physical chemistry and biophysics are aware of the nature of resonance, all the critics of my book failed, probably as a result of prejudice, to understand this important fact. They used arguments against some vague ideas of how astrology might work, the same arguments that have been trotted out for decades. Most of these arguments are concerned with the weakness of the forces involved. The important point about resonance is that a small fluctuating force can have large consequences if it has the same frequency as the natural frequency of the system to which it is applied. This central and consistently applied principle, as will become clear in the course of the book, invalidates all the arguments lodged thus far against my theory.

Because of the great importance of resonance in so many diverse areas of science, there exists an extremely thoroughly developed framework of mathematics to underpin the basic physical concepts. As stated at several points in the book, it is this mathematical framework that I used in my theory. The full scientific and math-ematical details were presented at the Fifth International Astrological Research Conference held in London in 1986. A few days before the conference I published the details in a monograph, *A Causal Mechanism for Gauquelin's Planetary Effect*, which was quoted as reference 77 in the first edition of this book. As required by law, copies of this monograph were lodged with the copyright records office of the British Library in November 1986, so through the interlibrary loan system it was available to any serious scholar. In April 1987 A. J. Turner, one of my third-year astronomy students at Plymouth Polytechnic (now called Polytechnic South West), presented his final-year project thesis, entitled 'Planetary Effects on the Solar Cycle'. This contains the results of numerical testing of the solar-planetary aspect of my theory and shows that it is consistent with many of the observations relating to the solar cycle. When

Astrology: The Evidence of Science was first published in April 1988, some science writers and journalists phoned or came to see me, and I was able to show them the results of my research and that of Turner.

The severest critics of my book, because they had prejudged the theory, undertook none of the accepted practices of serious scholarship, journalism or science writing. Nigel Henbest, astronomy consultant to the *New Scientist*, has this to say about it in his review for that magazine: 'a string of unsupported speculations, founded neither on known facts nor on physical calculations'.[1] The science correspondent of the *Daily Telegraph*, Adrian Berry, writes that I ignored 'the mathematics of scale, which tells us that the planets are too small and too far away to affect our personalities at birth'.[2] Jacqueline Mitton, editor of the *Journal of the British Astronomical Association*, reviewing the book in her journal, says that 'if Seymour has hit on a genuine mechanism, he will have to do a lot more work on the details of his theory before it becomes acceptable to sceptics'.[3] And Anthony Garrett, a physicist at Glasgow University, writes in the *British and Irish Sceptic*: 'Seymour claims his theory is scientific because it is testable. But there is insufficient information about the theory's mechanism to allow numerical calculations, and therefore no possibility of statistical validation or refutation. This work cannot – yet – be described as a theory; rather it is speculation.'[4]

It is very obvious to me that none of these critics had bothered to follow up any of the references that conflicted with their preconceived ideas, including my own monograph. Their self-righteous claim that they were being 'scientific' in their reviews can be treated with the contempt it deserves. With one exception, they all have scientific training, so they are quite aware of the importance of resonance. I believe that they reject my theory not because they do not understand the basic ideas, but because they are uncomfortable with their application in a context with which they are not familiar. In the case of the *New Scientist*, it is quite clear that it is not the individual concepts of my theory that the reviewer objects to, but the linking of them together in the context of a theory that could explain some aspects of astrology. John Gribbin, physics consultant to the *New Scientist*, says in his book *Beyond the Jupiter Effect* (written with Stephen Plagemann): 'Since nobody yet knows exactly how or why sunspots form, it would be foolish to dismiss these tidal forces [of the planets] out of hand.' A few months after Henbest said, erroneously (as will be shown in the last chapter), in his review of my book that the buffeting of the magnetosphere by the solar wind on most days swamped the lunar daily magnetic variation, the magazine carried an article by Robert Currie on the possible effects of the Moon on crop yields and the American economy. The *New Scientist* has on several occasions run articles on the effects of magnetic fields (even weak ones) on chemical reactions, the effects of changes in the Earth's magnetic field on weather and climate, and also articles (mostly by John Gribbin) on the possible effects of the planets on climate.

There is further evidence that it is the use of these ideas in the context of astrology that these science writers are objecting to. A few days after the appearance of the Henbest review, I wrote a letter to the editor of the *New Scientist*, pointing out that Henbest had completely missed the point about the use of resonance in my theory. For various reasons, the *New Scientist* failed to publish this letter, the substance of which was that Henbest's review contained a glaring logical error. Henbest rightly points out that the planets have varying periods within which they appear to move around the Earth, and that it sometimes happens that Saturn has the average period of Jupiter, while Jupiter has a different period. He then poses the question, 'How is the poor foetus to know which planet causes the latter signal?' My book at no stage claims that the effects of the planetary signals are confined only to birth. I am proposing that each foetus inherits a series of biological pendulum clocks, the natural periods of which are close to the average periods of the planets as they seem to move around the Earth. The theory of resonance shows that one or two cycles are not sufficient to entrain such a clock, but even if the energy imparted by each cycle is small, there is a build-up of this energy over several cycles, provided the energy is fed in at periods that are very close to the natural period of the system. By the very definition of the average period, Saturn will be close to its average period more often than Jupiter, and so babies with a Saturn-type personality will be born under Saturn more often than under Jupiter, which will have only the average period of Saturn on infrequent occasions, and then only for a few cycles. Thus resonance is able to explain Gauquelin's result that more, although not all, babies born under Saturn will have the personality characteristics that are associated with Saturn. Since the work of Gauquelin suggests that the tuning of the neural networks is fine enough to distinguish between the very close average frequencies of planets like Jupiter and Saturn, my theory of resonance very easily deals with Henbest's claim that the solar daily magnetic variation swamps the lunar daily magnetic variation on most days, and that 'a pregnant woman in a modern household will experience much stronger magnetic fluctuations from the washing-machine and the food processor'. The solar daily magnetic variation has a range of periods that are fractions of the solar day and consist of 24, 12, 8 and 6 hours. The basic period of the lunar daily magnetic variation is 12 hours, 24 minutes, and the magnetic fluctuations caused by household equipment have a period of 1/50 of a second, which is one million times greater than that of the solar or lunar daily magnetic variation. Thus the resonance of each period will be markedly different, and none of them could 'swamp' any of the others. If Henbest is trying to use my theory of resonance to demolish my arguments about the planets, he should have seen that it also demolishes his earlier arguments about the Sun, Moon and household equipment.

The editor and letters editor of the *New Scientist* clearly missed this flaw in Henbest's review. Yet the editor was quite willing to use his magazine to promote the very speculative theory of Rupert Sheldrake, which tries to explain form and structure in biology in terms of some amorphous morphogenic field and morphic resonance. It is quite clear that he can cope with resonance when it is used in this vague way in a very speculative theory, but neither he nor his staff can cope with it when used in a rigorous mathematical form in the context of my theory.

It is no accident that I decided to examine the so-called scientific arguments against astrology. I was born in South Africa and lived there for the first twenty-two years of my life. Scientifically and technologically the country is the most advanced on the continent of Africa. The ruling white minority considers it acceptable that they should be in power, because their world view is right and superior to that of the non-white majority. The arguments that they put forward to justify their attitude have the same hallmarks as most of the arguments against astrology put forward by scientists. In their book *The Gemini Syndrome*, R. B. Culver and P. A. Ianna quote the following passage by Abraham Maslow: 'Science is the only way we have of shoving truth down the reluctant throat. Only science can overcome characterological differences in seeing and believing. Only science can progress.' They add: 'The evidence – objective descriptions of nature – is the only basis of truth.' Like many other scientists, they seem unaware of the present crisis in physics, which is well set out by Nick Herbert in his book *Quantum Reality*:

> One of the best kept secrets of science is that physicists have lost their grip on reality. News of the reality crisis hardly exists outside the physics community. What shuts out the public is partly a language barrier – the mathematical formalism that facilitates communication between scientists is incomprehensible to outsiders – and partly the human tendency of physicists to publicize their successes while soft-pedalling their confusion and uncertainties.[5]

Intolerance is as unacceptable in science as it is in other walks of life. Recently the Archbishop of Canterbury criticized religious intolerance. He said: 'Where toleration is in peril, persecution stalks not far behind.' This is also true for science. In his book *The Ascent of Man*, Dr Jacob Bronowski said: 'Science is a very human form of knowledge. We are always at the brink of the known, we always feel forward for what is to be hoped. Every judgement in science stands on the edge of error, and is personal. Science is a tribute to what we can know, although we are fallible. In the end the words were said by Oliver Cromwell: "I beseech you, in the bowels of Christ, think it possible you may be mistaken."' In the television series that the book accompanied, Bronowski was standing in a pond into which the ashes of some four million people had been flushed when he spoke these words, and continued with the following: 'I owe it as a scientist to my friend Leo Szilard, I owe it as a human being to the many members of my family who died at Auschwitz, to stand here by the pond as a survivor and a witness.

We have to cure ourselves of the itch for absolute knowledge and power. We have to close the distance between the push-button order and the human act. We have to touch people.'

PAHS
Plymouth, July 1989

Introduction: Astronomy versus Astrology – the Age-old Debate

That we can think of no mechanism for astrology is relevant but unconvincing. No mechanism was known, for example, for continental drift when it was proposed by Wegener. Nevertheless, we see that Wegener was right, and those who objected on the grounds of unavailable mechanism were wrong.

Carl Sagan

In February 1986 I attended a conference of the Urania Trust at London University's Imperial College. The Trust had been set up to promote research into astrology and its links with other disciplines; most of those attending the conference were either committed astrologers or very deeply and fervently involved in the subject in one way or another. It was obvious that many had a distrust of science and scientists, and my presence as a scientist was unusual. On the final day of the conference, I was allowed 10 minutes to explain *my* theory of astrology.

I started with the following words: 'For an astronomer to take an interest in astrology is rather like volunteering for Indian horse torture, with astronomy as the one horse and astrology as the other. Most astrologers seem to take the attitude that they know astrology works and they do not need scientists to tell them why it works; and most of my astronomical colleagues are quite certain it does *not* work.' I said this because my work had become the recent focus for the conflict between astronomers and astrologers that has its origin in the ancient world. The response from several astrologers at the conference helped to dispel this feeling, and it became clear to me that a larger number were interested in a scientific theory for astrology than I had thought. Since that time, I have been invited to other astrological conferences, and on these occasions I was given the opportunity to talk much more fully about my theory. This book is largely concerned with explaining that theory in detail, with setting it within the context of the histories of astrology and astronomy, and with the continuing, often heated debate between the practitioners of the two disciplines.

Here I want to concentrate on that debate, and on how and why I moved from the astronomy 'side of the house' to formulate the first fully developed scientific theory of astrology.

Astronomy and Astrology: The Essential Differences

'It is quite ridiculous to think that lives and destinies are controlled by the stars. The trouble is that people don't know the difference between astrology and astronomy.'[1] So wrote Patrick Moore, the well-known astronomer, in November 1984. Since my book sets out to discuss the strong links between astronomy and astrology, it is very necessary to be quite clear about the differences between the two subjects, so here I will present some definitions regarding the two.

Astronomy and Its Branches

Astronomy is defined in *The Shorter Oxford English Dictionary* as 'The science which treats of the constitution, relative positions, and motions of the heavenly bodies, including Earth.' With the tremendous increase in knowledge that has taken place over the years, most areas of the subject have become so vast that astronomers specialize in one or more of the branches of the subject. They have begun to study the universe with a variety of different techniques, and these provide natural subdivisions of the subject. Optical astronomy is the branch that uses light to study the universe; radio astronomy uses the radio waves collected by radio telescopes; X-ray astronomy uses special X-ray detectors on board satellites to receive the X-ray messages emitted by various extra-terrestrial objects; infrared astronomy uses special telescopes up very high mountains and similar instruments on board satellites to detect the heat waves given off by many heavenly bodies.

All these branches of the subject receive their specific messages in a coded form that must be decoded. The keys to this code are the known laws of physics, and the branch of astronomy devoted to decoding the celestial messages is astrophysics. Cosmology is the part of astronomy that tries to understand the large-scale structure, evolution and possible origin of the universe. Naturally, these different areas of the subject overlap to some extent, and there has to be a great deal of collaboration between the astronomers who practise the various subdivisions, if we are to understand the nature of the universe and its constituent parts.

At one stage in the history of astronomy and astrology, the two words were used synonymously, but in reality they were never the same, despite the fact that some astronomers also practised astrology at some periods of time. This being the case, we also have to define astrology, and some of its subdivisions.

Astrology and Its Branches

The Dictionary of Astrology by Fred Gettings defines astrology as 'The study of the relationship between the Macrocosm and the Microcosm, which (in materialistic terms) is often defined as the study of the influence of the celestial bodies on the Earth and its inhabitants.'[2] There are different branches of astrology, but one of the most important is natal astrology, which links the positions of the Sun, Moon and planets, as seen against the background stars at the moment of birth, with the personalities and the destinies of individuals. Astrometeorology is concerned with predicting earth-quakes, volcanic eruptions and the weather. Gettings defines horary astrology as 'the astrological art of interpreting specific questions in terms of a chart erected for the moment the question is asked'. Medical astrology is concerned with the diagnosis and treatment of diseases. Electional astrology is the application of astrological principles to the purpose of finding the appropriate times for starting specific activities, for example, marriage.

The Basic Ideas of Astrology

Essential to most branches of astrology are the concepts of the zodiac and the houses (see illus. 1). To understand them, we must imagine that the constellations are plotted on an enormous sphere surrounding Earth, called the celestial sphere. In their apparent motions against the background stars, the Sun, Moon and planets all move through a narrow band of constellations that form the zodiac. This circle of sky around the Earth is divided into twelve sectors, each of 30 degrees, and each occupied by one constellation, or sign, of the zodiac. All these zodiac constellations lie on the ecliptic – the apparent path of the Sun against the background stars. Since the planets are never more than a few degrees from the ecliptic, they also pass through the zodiac constellations.

For purposes of interpretation, the sky both above and below

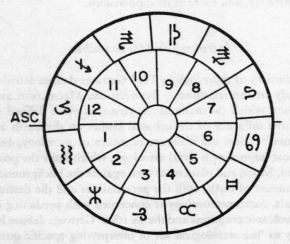

1 The signs of the zodiac (outer circle) and the equal house system (inner circle). The ascendant (ASC) corresponds to the eastern horizon.

the horizon may be divided into twelve further sectors called houses. The sector immediately below the horizon at the moment of birth is called the first house, and the sectors are labelled anti-clockwise. The concepts of houses and signs of the zodiac are embodied in schematic form on a circular astrological birth chart. The outer ring of the birth chart represents the circle of sky that is the zodiac. It is divided into twelve 30-degree sections, each repre-senting one zodiacal sign. The constellation that touches the eastern horizon at the moment of birth is called the ascending sign, and is considered to be of great significance in astrological interpretation. The birth chart circle is also divided into twelve houses, the first house beginning at the degree of the ascendant. The twelve zodiac signs represent types or characteristics of personality, and these are further subdivided into four elements – fire, earth, air, water – and other subdivisions. The twelve houses represent factors of life or the environment. Positions of the Sun, Moon and planets at the moment of birth are marked on this circle.

The Sun-sign of a person is the sign of the zodiac in which the Sun is placed at the moment of birth; the positions of all the planets, Sun and Moon in the sign and houses, the sign of the ascendant, and the angles between the planets all contribute to the astrological inter-pretation of an individual's characteristics, strengths and weak-nesses, and his or her potential for interaction with the external world. The angles between the planets are called the aspects, and they relate to their positions in the sky as seen from Earth. For example, two planets are said to be in conjunction if they appear very close to each other in the sky. They will be in opposition if they are 180 degrees apart; in square if 90 degrees apart, and so on. Certain aspects are considered to be 'difficult', others are 'easy', but interpretation is a complex business, and the particular nature of the planets involved, the signs and houses in which they appear, and the general balance of the chart all have to be taken into account. Interpretation is also a very subjective part of the process. Different astrologers will give varying weights to different parts of the birth chart, and there are also disagreements about how to draw certain parts of the chart. There are a few different house systems, and the use of one rather than another can lead to different interpretations.

John Addey, widely held by many astrologers to be the greatest British astrologer of this century, was very aware of this variety: 'There are disputes . . . about the "right" zodiac to be used; there are pronounced differences between Eastern and Western traditions which are tactfully ignored; the houses are a notorious battleground of disagreement; quite apart from the rival systems there are divergent views about cusps as boundaries or centres of houses; even about the correct number of houses.'[3] I will not become involved here with these disputes, because I am trying only to explain those areas of astrology for which there is some positive scientific evidence. Nevertheless, my theory and any evidence do point the way to the resolution of these differences.

Astrology and the New Planets

At various stages in the history of astrology, it has come under attack from scientists as a result of specific discoveries in astronomy. The most notable attacks are those associated with the discovery of the new planets. Astronomers have pointed out that the discovery of Uranus, Neptune and Pluto must surely upset previous astrological schemes of interpretation. In countering such attacks, astrologers have replied that the discoveries of these planets solve previous problems of interpretation; and claim that empirical evidence collected on the 'new' planets makes it possible to incorporate them into the expanded scheme of horoscopes.

Astronomy and Astrology: The Roots of Conflict

Why did the conflict arise? To begin to answer that, we must look for the first appearance of astrology. A great deal of documentary evidence suggests that astrology had its origins in Mesopotamia, and that the Babylonians and Assyrians were initially its chief practitioners. In particular, many of the outstanding astrologers came from the Chaldean part of the Babylonian Empire, and hence *The Shorter Oxford English Dictionary* tells us that a Chaldean is 'A native of Chaldaea, esp. (as at Babylon) one skilled in occult learning, astrology, etc.; hence generally a soothsayer, astrologer.'

Even at this early stage, there was a resistance to the art of astrology, as many other cultures were suspicious of those who practised it. We see in the Bible the scorn that was cast on its followers:

> Thou art wearied in the multitude of thy counsels. Let now the astrologers, the stargazers, the monthly prognosticators, stand up and save thee from these things that shall come upon thee (Isaiah 47:13)

> Behold, they shall be as stubble; the fire shall burn them; they shall not deliver themselves from the power of the flame: there shall not be a coal to warm at, nor fire to sit before it (Isaiah, 47:14)

These early practisers of astrology were also referred to as mathematicians, and this term occurs later, used by the Roman emperor Diocletian, around AD 300, when he said: 'It is in the public interest that one learns and practises the art of geometry. But mathematical art is damnable: it is absolutely forbidden.'

There were many great thinkers in the ancient world who believed in astrology, but there were also many sceptics. Plato believed in the influence of the stars on terrestrial events, and Aristotle taught that 'this world is inescapably linked to the motions of the world above'. Pythagoras, one of the greatest mathematicians of all time, was a great believer in astrology. Galen, the Greek physician who founded experimental physiology, was interested in the use of astrology in the treatment of diseases.[4] However, Cicero was totally opposed to the ideas of astrology, as was Hippocrates.

The philosopher Carneades raised specific objections to astrology. He pointed out that the son of a king and the son of a slave, born at the same instant, nevertheless had very different fates. He argued that Jews born in different countries had the same national characteristics, even if they did not have the same horoscopes. He asked why it was that those falling in the same battle did not have the same horoscopes. He pointed out that twins, who had more or less the same time of birth, often had very different fates. In their counter-arguments, astrologers pointed out that some of the objections resulted from small variations in the positions of the heavenly bodies, even in fairly short periods of time. Ptolemy, whose work will be discussed in more detail in a later chapter, argued that, in certain events, there were other determining factors that were beyond the power of the stars to alter.[5]

T. G. Cowling, an outstanding mathematical astronomer who, until a few years ago, was a professor at the University of Leeds, sums up the history of this clash between astrology and science: 'The objections remained, to be raised regularly by successive generations of sceptics, and as regularly smoothed over by the generations of believers.' But this is not the whole story, because the objections on the one side, and the defence on the other, have both become more sophisticated with time and have varied from epoch to epoch, culture to culture. So let us continue to examine developments in the argument, calling on the testimony of present-day experts.

Two professional astronomers, R. B. Culver (Associate Professor of Astronomy at the Colorado State University) and P. A. Ianna (Assistant Professor of Astronomy at the University of Virginia) wrote a book in 1979 called *The Gemini Syndrome: Star Wars of the Oldest Kind*,[6] in which they made an effort to discredit all of astrology. In dealing with astrology in the Middle Ages, they argue that there was a significant decline in the empirical approach to science, and that the philosophical approach to the acquisition of knowledge was prevalent. Astronomy did not make much progress, but the interest in astrology remained high. From this they conclude that 'They [the astrologers] had no interest in the theoretical foundations of their craft or in its improvement,' and in support of their views, they quote Otto Neugebauer: 'One may well say that at no stage in the development of astronomy did astrology have any direct influence, beneficial or otherwise, on astronomy beyond the fact that it provided a secure market for treatises and tables and thus contributed to the survival of works which would hardly have reached us.'

Neugebauer is a very respected historian of ancient astronomy. He has spent most of his life doing research on Babylonian, Greek and Egyptian astronomical texts, and his great *A History of Ancient*

Mathematical Astronomy[7] is considered to be the definitive work on the subject, so his statements are not to be taken lightly. However, in order to put these comments concerning astrology in the Middle Ages into a broader historical context, we must look at the work of other scholars, in particular an historian of science, Thomas S. Kuhn. Kuhn has not only been concerned with the internal details of specific branches of the history of science in general, and astronomy in particular, he has also been very influential in developing general theories on how scientific discoveries are made, and how science and scientists interact with society. His book *On the Structure of Scientific Revolutions* has had an important effect on the social sciences and on the philosophy of science.[8] Another of his works, *The Copernican Revolution*, is a remarkable study of the part played by planetary astronomy in the development of Western thought. In it he says:

> The elaborate tables of planetary position and the complex computational techniques developed by planetary astronomers from antiquity to the Renaissance were the main prerequisite for astrological prediction. Until after Copernicus's death these major products of astronomical research had little other socially significant application. Astrology therefore provided the principal motive for wrestling with the problem of the planets, so that astrology become a particularly important determinant of the astronomical imagination.[9]

Cultural Differences in Astrology

'The national and cultural differences in astrological systems are typical. Even within one cultural group there may be competing procedures espoused by one group or another giving quite divergent predictions. The physical sciences stand in sharp contrast to this. For whereas astrology in China may scarcely resemble astrology in the United States, their sciences are quite equivalent.' These are the words of Culver and Ianna in *The Gemini Syndrome*. From this they draw the conclusion that *all* astrology must be untrue. But it

9

seems to me that there are flaws in their argument. Let us take the proposed unity of science: although there are large areas of agreement among scientists about most of the basic principles of physics, there are also large areas of disagreement. This is particularly true in the frontiers of physics and astronomy.

Experience has taught me that in science we should not accept statements unless supported by *evidence*. It has also shown that no matter how often a great scientist has been right in the past, there are also times when he can be wrong. Although most scientists do accept these attitudes, many seem to be willing to suspend their support for these fundamental postulates of science when it comes to examining the evidence for and against astrology.

My search for a scientific theory for astrology led me to see that the ancient Greeks and Babylonians made some very important discoveries concerning the links between life and the cosmos. However, these basic scientific discoveries were developed into a belief system, and many of these subsequent elaborations are not justified by the basic principles. As the basic ideas were developed with time, they were embroidered, and these embroideries were further distorted as other cultures sought to fit their own religious and cosmological ideas into the now highly embellished framework. The desire to make the entire universe an essential part of our life and our environment seems to be as universal as the need for a religious life among all early peoples who inhabited our planet. It is this desire that led to cosmologies in which astrology developed. But it was only in the ancient classical world that the conceptual tools of science and mathematics were sufficiently developed for some progress to be made in sorting out the wheat from the chaff, and even then the process had to continue over the centuries because it was incomplete. We also have to play our part in carrying this work still further. The work of Michel Gauquelin, which will be discussed throughout this book, swept away much of the chaff and revealed very important grains of truth. My work provides a new framework for understanding the meaning of Gauquelin's results, and it also shows that his evidence provides support for more of traditional astrology than he himself thought possible.

Modern Scientific Attitudes to Astrology

In September 1975 the American magazine *Humanist* carried a statement called 'Objections to Astrology', signed by 186 'leading scientists', including eighteen Nobel prizewinners. It read as follows:

> Scientists in a variety of fields have become concerned about the increased acceptance of astrology in many parts of the world. We, the undersigned – astronomers, astrophysicists, and scientists in other fields – wish to caution the public against the unquestioning acceptance of the predictions and advice given privately and publicly by astrologers ... It should be apparent that those individuals who continue to have faith in astrology do so in spite of the fact that there is no verified scientific basis for their beliefs, and indeed there is strong evidence to the contrary.[10]

The astronomer Carl Sagan was invited to sign this statement, but he declined to do so: 'I find myself unable to endorse the "Objections to Astrology" statement – not because I feel that astrology has any validity whatever, but because I felt and still feel that the tone of the statement is authoritarian ... That we can think of no mechanism for astrology is relevant but unconvincing'.[11]

A philosopher of science, Paul Feyerabend, stated *his* disagreement with 'Objections to Astrology':

> The judgement of the 186 leading scientists rests on antediluvian anthropology, an ignorance of more recent results in their own fields (astronomy, biology and the connection between the two), as well as on a failure to perceive the implications of the results they do know. It shows the extent to which scientists are prepared to assert their authority even in areas in which they have no knowledge whatsoever.[12]

The Genesis of My Scientific Theory for Astrology

Before the summer of 1984 I would have agreed with some of the statements made in the 'Objections to Astrology' manifesto. In June of that year an incident occurred that was to start me thinking more seriously about the arguments for and against astrology. The BBC was training a television crew and this involved the production of a short programme. They decided to do one on astrology, so they went about the streets of Plymouth, asking the public questions about their attitudes to astrology. Then they came to ask me about my views on the subject, as a professional astronomer and as Director of the William Day Planetarium of Plymouth Polytechnic. I made it quite clear that although I believed the cosmos could synchronize biological clocks in plants and animals, and the Sun and stars could be used for bird navigation, I did not believe the universe had any links with the personalities of individuals. When asked if I thought that science may well discover such a link at some distant time in the future, I stated that I thought this was very unlikely.

Later, after giving my orthodox replies to their questions, I found myself going over all the arguments against astrology, which I had heard so many scientists make, and which I had paraphrased in my answers. Then, quite suddenly, I found myself questioning these arguments.

I started reading *Astrology: Science or Superstition?* by Hans J. Eysenck and David Nias, both from the Institute of Psychiatry of London University. Their arguments in favour of the research carried out by Michel and Françoise Gauquelin were extremely persuasive. I decided to reread Michel Gauquelin's book *Cosmic Influences on Human Behaviour*.[13] I also read *Recent Advances in Natal Astrology* by Geoffrey Dean,[14] an analytical chemist, science writer and astrologer, and Arthur Mather, a geologist, information scientist and astrologer. Their findings convinced me that there was some evidence in favour of astrology, and they also provided some insights as to how astrological effects might arise. What they did *not* do was develop any testable theories concerning these effects.

However, it was comments made by Eysenck and Nias in their

book on astrology that really started me on the quest for a causal mechanism for Gauquelin's work. What they say is this:

> What are the most likely candidates for the role of 'link' between extraterrestrial events and biological and other phenomena here on earth? The most promising, of course, are sunspots and other disturbances and the various wave and particle emissions caused by them; the possibility that these in turn are affected by the planets involves the whole planetary system in this attempted explanation ... The task of turning such a vague and obviously unspecific hypothesis into a testable prediction is not an easy one, but it seems to us an important one in our unending efforts to understand and control the physical and biological universe. Science should not abdicate its mandate because it fears ridicule by being associated with 'astrology'.

This was the challenge that I took up, and by the end of the summer I had formulated the rudiments of my theory, but it was still not, at this stage, a full scientific theory, one that could lead to testable results. There were still several specific problems to be solved before I could state the theory in terms that would be acceptable to me as a trained theoretical astrophysicist. By the beginning of December 1984 I had made good progress. Then an opportunity presented itself that allowed me to make public my views on astrology.

In 1985 a summary of my work appeared in *Transit*, a magazine of the Astrological Association of England. Soon after, I started a correspondence with Gauquelin in Paris, and later that year wrote on my work for *The Times Higher Education Supplement*. However, at this stage the theory was still just a physical one that had not as yet been formulated in mathematical terms, and all my attempts to improve the situation had been unsuccessful.

It was in the summer of that year that I made my first really important breakthrough. My research soon showed that an initial idea I had had earlier was wrong; but while browsing through journals, it dawned on me that the effect of the Moon on our environment held a vital key to the whole situation, one that had been overlooked by previous researchers. In November of that year I made another breakthrough, this time on the effects of the planets on the sunspot cycle. The third breakthrough came in the summer of 1986. This was concerned with the link between the Earth's magnetic field and personality. The details of these discoveries will be told at appropriate places later in this book.

A Brief Outline of My Theory

For the last few hundred years people have used the magnetic compass to guide them across the sea and land and, more recently, through the air. In doing so, they have made use of the fact that we live on a giant magnet: the Earth itself. Direction-finding using the magnetism of Earth is done with the knowledge that, to a large extent, this field does not change with time, and that there are steady magnetic 'lines of force' stretching from the north to the south of our Earth. These lines of force are not quite as steady as they may seem at first sight. Although they keep their directions for long periods of time, they also vibrate about these directions, rather like telephone wires vibrating in the wind. Some of these vibrations are related to the positions and movements of the Moon, and others are related to the movements and activity of the Sun. The very rapid progress of astronomy and space science, especially over the last thirty years, has revealed that our Sun, some planets, many stars and several galaxies have their own magnetic fields. There is growing evidence that the behaviour of the magnetic fields of the Earth and Sun is bound up with the positions and movements of the planets. My scientific theory is able to explain why this is so. It is as if the whole solar system – the Sun, Moon and planets – is playing a complex symphony on the lines of force of the Earth's field.

In recent years biologists have shown that many life forms, such as bacteria, birds and fishes, can use the magnetic field of Earth to find direction. Some scientists have demonstrated that human beings can also, to a limited extent, find direction using the magnetic field of the Earth and without using a portable compass. Biologists have also shown that vibrations of the Earth's field do have an effect on many forms of life, including humans. It is as if the nervous systems of many different animals can act like aerials through which we can detect some of the vibrations of the Earth's field. According to my theory we are all genetically tuned to receiving a different set of melodies from the magnetic symphony of the solar system. While in the womb our normal sense organs are still developing, so they are less effective in receiving information than they are after we are born. However, the womb is no hiding place from the all-pervading magnetic field of Earth, so the tunes of the magnetic symphony of the solar system that we receive can become part of our earliest memories. It is here that some of the magnetic music of the spheres becomes etched on our brains. When the orchestra of the solar system plays our tune on the magnetic field of Earth at a later stage in life, it evokes these memories, and our response can influence the way we react in a given situation. That gives some weight to a very old astrological saying, 'The stars incline, they do not command.'

The Impact of My Discoveries

Through my discoveries, it is possible to explain the links between the cosmos at birth and personality in terms of the most recent researches in the fields of astronomy, space science, geomagnetism and biology. It is quite unnecessary to invoke undiscovered physical forces or to enlist the help of concepts from the spheres of the occult or the paranormal for those areas of astrology that have stood up to the stringent tests of modern scientific methods. My theory also provides a means of assessing the worth of ancient astrological traditions. It convinces me that the ancient astronomer–astrologers made sound discoveries concerning the links between the behaviour of individuals and the Sun, Moon and planets. With my theory, we can understand how they made these discoveries. It provides a tool for reassessing the various possibilities that have been suggested for the most important celestial manifestation in history: the appearance of the Star of Bethlehem.

Conclusion

My objective in writing this book is to describe the origins and development of my theory, embracing subjects that cover a wide range of areas of specialized knowledge.

The first six chapters, therefore, are devoted to providing the background information against which my theory must eventually be assessed. The origins of the theory are then described, and this leads to suggested uses of it in explaining both cosmic and terrestrial phenomena.

Astrology is a fundamental part of our culture, and it is appropriate that the book should end with a consideration of the influence of cosmic factors in the dominant event of our civilization: the birth of Christ.

I

Getting to Know the Cosmos

Up from Earth's Centre through the Seventh Gate
I rose, and on the Throne of Saturn sate,
And many Knots unravel'd by the Road
But not the Knot of Human Death and Fate

The Rubáiyát of Omar Khayyám

It was a warm night on Christmas Eve. The sky was very clear and the stars were very bright. To my infant mind they also seemed very close. My guide to the sky was my grandfather. He showed me the three stars of the Belt of Orion and referred to them as the Three Kings. He also showed me the Milky Way arching overhead. Although I was only four or five at the time, I had been allowed to stay up late because it was Christmas Eve, and this was the first time that I can remember being introduced to the sky. After that night, my grandfather taught me a great deal about the sky, including how to find the Southern Cross. The clear skies just outside Kimberley, on the edge of the veldt, where we lived, were ideal for the purpose. I was fascinated by what he had to tell me, and, as I grew up, I wanted to know more about astronomy.

The theory of astrology that I have developed unifies astrology with astronomy in a way that has never been achieved in the whole history of these ancient disciplines. However, in order to explain this theory, I have to share with the reader the three-dimensional view of the universe given to us by modern astronomy, and give colour and substance to the black and light picture of the sky that we see with the naked eye, and that was the basis of ancient astrology and astronomy.

Our Earth in Space

We see the universe from an observing platform that is spinning on its own axis and also going around the Sun. The speed of our Earth on its own axis, at the equator, as seen by an astronaut hovering in space, is more than 1,000 miles per hour. At the same time the whole Earth is speeding around the Sun, which is about 93 million miles away from us, at more than 60,000 miles per hour. We are not aware of these enormous speeds because we are chained to the planet by gravity and so are part of this complex dance.

These movements of the Earth have noticeable consequences for us on its surface. The spinning of the Earth causes the Sun to appear to move across the sky, to rise near the east and set somewhere near the west. This spinning also causes the Moon, stars and planets to seem to move across the sky from east to west. The seasonal variations in the points on the horizon at which the Sun seems to rise and set are caused by the way in which the Earth spins on its axis, as well as the motion of the Earth around the Sun.

The Earth is like a gyroscope in space. A gyroscope is a very rapidly spinning body that has one all-important property: if it is far from most other bodies in space, then its axis will always lie in the same direction with respect to the fixed stars. If we had a gyroscope in space and pointed it at a particular star, it would continue to point to the same star as long as it kept spinning. It is this property that makes it so useful for the guidance systems of space probes and why the gyroscope has been adapted to act like a compass on board ships and aircraft. Since the Earth is like a gyroscope, the northern tip of its axis will keep pointing towards one particular spot with respect to the stars for very long periods of time. At the moment this end points very close to the North Star, also known as Polaris or the Pole Star. During the northern summer the north pole of the Earth leans towards the Sun and during the northern winter the north pole is leaning away from the Sun. The result is that we have longer days in the summer and shorter days in the winter. We also receive much less warmth from the Sun (see illus. 2).[1]

The Moon – Our Nearest Celestial Neighbour

The Moon is only a quarter of a million miles from Earth – on average. In a sense, the size of the Moon, about a quarter of the size of the Earth, compared with the sizes of some of the other planets makes it a small sister planet of our Earth. The surface of the Moon is made up of mountains and saucer-like depressions, called craters. It also has large flat areas, the lunar seas, so called because at one time it was thought that this is what they were. We now know that there is no water on the Moon, and that these 'seas' look darker from our Earth because they reflect light rather differently from the rest of the Moon's surface, due to their flatness. The Moon, like all the planets, produces no light of its own; it reflects light from the Sun. Since the Moon is a sphere, only half of its surface will be lit by light from the Sun. At any one time we see

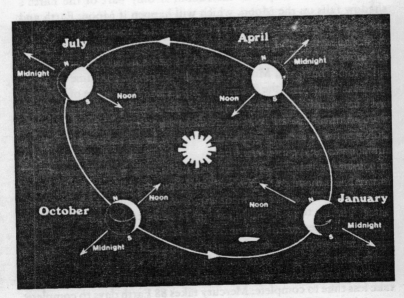

2 A schematic view of a model demonstrating the cause of the seasons.

half of the Moon's surface. If the half lit up corresponds to the half which we see, as happens when the Sun and Moon are almost on opposite sides of the Earth, then we have a full Moon, whereas at all other times the half that we see does not coincide with the half lit up, so we see only part of it illuminated by sunlight. Although the Moon orbits the Earth about once every 28 days, it keeps very nearly the same face turned towards the Earth, so we see little more than half the Moon's face over a period of time.

Eclipses

When the Moon, Earth and Sun are in a straight line, then, in principle, no light should reach the Moon. But since the atmosphere of Earth bends some red light from the Sun towards the Moon, so the Moon, at such a time, will have a dull reddish appearance. This is called a total eclipse of the Moon. If only part of the Earth's shadow falls on the Moon, which will happen if Moon, Earth and Sun are not quite in a straight line, we have a partial eclipse of the Moon.

As seen from Earth, the Moon has the same apparent size as the Sun, so when Earth, Moon and Sun are in a straight line then the Moon will blot out the Sun, and we have a total eclipse of the Sun. If the alignment is not quite perfect, then we have a partial eclipse of the Sun.

The Solar System

Our Earth is one of nine planets orbiting the Sun. There are two planets closer to the Sun than we are – Mercury and Venus. The other six planets are further out from the Sun, and their order in distance from the Sun is: Mars, Jupiter, Saturn, Uranus, Neptune and Pluto (see illus. 3). Those planets closer to the Sun not only have faster speeds, but they also have smaller orbits, which they take less time to complete: Mercury takes 88 Earth days to complete one orbit and Venus 225 Earth days. Mars takes 687 Earth days, Jupiter just under 12 Earth years, Saturn over 29 Earth years,

Uranus 84 Earth years, Neptune 164 Earth years and Pluto 248 Earth years. The varying speeds of the planets and the sizes of their orbits, combined with the movement of our Earth around the Sun, cause the planets to move in very complex ways as seen from the Earth.

Mercury and Venus never get very far from the Sun in the sky, as seen from Earth, and sometimes they will move between us and the Sun, while at other times they will move beyond the Sun. This means that sometimes they will appear to slip very slowly from west to east against the background stars, as the nights go by, and sometimes they will slip from east to west (see illus. 4). A similar phenomenon occurs for the outer planets. Sometimes the Earth will overtake these bodies as it moves between them and the Sun, and then they will seem to slip from east to west against the background stars, whereas at other times they will slip from west to east (see illus. 5). These apparent motions are in addition to the apparent motion of all heavenly bodies from east to west, which, as we have already seen, is due to the spinning of the Earth on its axis.

Ancient astronomers just saw the planets as points of light, whereas we know that the planets are like spheres spinning in space, very similar in some respects to our Earth. More recently, space probes have revealed them in greater detail. In order to set the scene, let us look at the salient features of these objects, starting with Mercury.

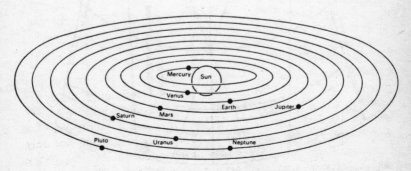

3 A schematic view of our solar system. Sizes and distances not to scale.

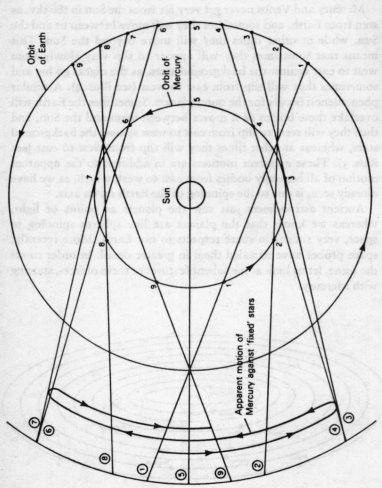

(Distances and orbits are not exact)

Orbit of Earth

Orbit of Mercury

Sun

Apparent motion of Mercury against 'fixed' stars

4 The apparent motion of Mercury, as seen from Earth.

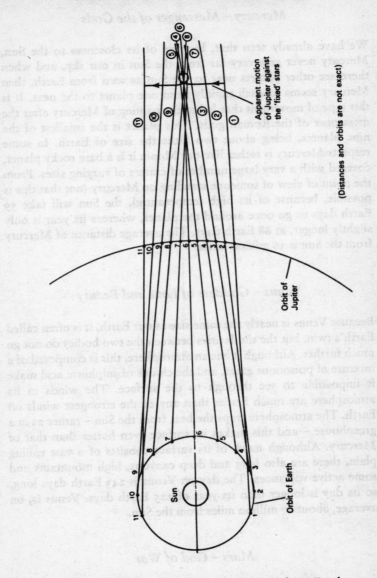

5 The apparent motion of Jupiter, as seen from Earth.

Mercury – Messenger of the Gods

We have already seen that, because of its closeness to the Sun, Mercury never gets very far from the Sun in our sky, and when there are other planets near to the Sun as seen from Earth, then Mercury seems to dash rapidly from one planet to the next. It is this type of movement that led to the naming of Mercury after the messenger of the Roman gods. This planet is the smallest of the nine planets, being about two fifths the size of Earth. In some respects Mercury is rather like our Moon: it is a bare rocky planet, covered with a very large number of craters of varying sizes. From the point of view of someone standing on Mercury (not that this is possible, because of its high temperature), the Sun will take 59 Earth days to go once around the planet, whereas its year is only slightly longer, at 88 Earth days. The average distance of Mercury from the Sun is 36 million miles.

Venus – Goddess of Love and Beauty

Because Venus is nearly the same size as our Earth, it is often called Earth's twin, but the similarities between the two bodies do not go much further. Although it has an atmosphere, this is composed of a mixture of poisonous gases, and the clouds of sulphuric acid make it impossible to see through to the surface. The winds in its atmosphere are much fiercer than any of the strongest winds on Earth. The atmosphere traps the heat from the Sun – rather as in a greenhouse – and this makes its surface even hotter than that of Mercury. Although much of its surface consists of a vast rolling plain, there are also long and deep canyons, high mountains and some active volcanoes. The day on Venus is 243 Earth days long, so its day is longer than its year of 225 Earth days. Venus is, on average, about 67 million miles from the Sun.

Mars – God of War

Mars also has an atmosphere made up of several different gases, but its atmosphere is thinner than that of Venus. The winds in the atmosphere drive the dust of its surface into sand storms, so the air is often filled with these fine particles that give the planet its strange orange colour. The surface of Mars is broken up by very deep and wide canyons, and it also has several volcanoes – one of which is three times higher than Mount Everest. Mars is about half the size of Earth. Its day is about the same as that of Earth – being about 24 hours and 37 minutes of Earth time – and its axis is tilted by almost the same amount as that of the Earth, so it has seasons similar to Earth, although these are longer because it has a year of 687 Earth days. Its average distance from the Sun is about 141 million miles.

Because of some of its similarities to our planet, people have, over the centuries, speculated on the possibility of life on Mars. This speculation was further fuelled by Giovanni Schiaparelli, an Italian astronomer. In 1877 he thought he saw through his telescope long straight lines on the planet, which he then called by the Italian word *canali*, meaning channels. However, *canali* were translated into English as canals. The American astronomer Percival Lowell believed that these canals must have been built by intelligent beings. He argued that the northern ice cap of Mars would melt during the northern summer, and that these canals were constructed to lead water across the planet to the drier areas. He went on to suggest that although these canals were rather thin and not visible through the telescope, he was seeing enriched vegetation along the banks of the canals. Later on, photographs of the planet showed that Lowell was wrong, and that the lines he thought he saw were a psychological effect resulting from the brain making links between some of the surface features of the planet. Automatic space probes that landed on the surface of Mars analysed the surface soil, and as a result scientists have concluded that the possibility of life on the planet is very unlikely.

Jupiter – The Giant of the Planets

Jupiter is more than eleven times the size of our Earth, and this makes it the biggest planet of the solar system. The average distance of Jupiter from the Sun is approximately 483 million miles. The planets Mercury, Venus, Earth and Mars are called the terrestrial planets, because they resemble the Earth in that they are predominantly solid bodies with rocky surfaces. Jupiter, on the other hand, is largely liquid, with perhaps a small rocky core, and surrounded by a very thick cloudy atmosphere. There is a feature in its atmosphere that is called the great red spot because of its ruddy appearance. This is a swirling elliptical body of gas about three times the size of Earth. Because we are really seeing only the upper cloud-cover of the planet, we would not expect the different parts to rotate at the same speed. This is indeed the case. The region on either side of the equator takes 9 hours, 50 minutes to complete one rotation, whereas the rest of the planet takes 9 hours, 55 minutes. Space probes have revealed that there are lightning storms in its atmosphere, and phenomena resembling the Northern Lights have also been detected. Radio astronomers have discovered that Jupiter is a very strong source of radio waves.

Saturn – The Ringed Planet

Saturn is named after the Roman god of farming. With the naked eye it looks very much like the other planets. When Galileo first looked at Saturn with his telescope in the early-seventeenth century, he was puzzled by what he saw. Saturn seemed like a disc with two ears. Gradual improvements in the design of telescopes revealed that Saturn was surrounded by a ring system. The rings are formed from many billions of bits of ice, varying in size from tiny specks to much larger pieces that look like big snowballs, which orbit Saturn much like our Moon circles Earth. Saturn is about ten times the size of Earth, and, like Jupiter, consists largely of liquid and gas, with, perhaps, a small rocky core at the centre. Its day is about as long as 10 Earth hours. The average distance between Saturn and the Sun is 886 million miles.

Uranus – The First 'Modern' Planet

Uranus was the first planet to be discovered by a telescope, so it was not known in the ancient world. It was discovered by the astronomer William Herschel, working in Bath, in March 1781. Herschel was of German origin, but had come to England to work as a musician after deserting from the German army. He built his own telescopes, and with one of these he discovered the planet that was later called Uranus, after the father of Saturn. Although this body had been seen through telescopes by other astronomers on about twenty occasions, they all catalogued it as a star, since none of their telescopes was as good as that of Herschel. Herschel himself wanted to call this planet the Georgian Planet, after George III, then king of England. Some astronomers also suggested that it should be named after Herschel, but in the end it was decided to stick to a classical name.

It takes Uranus about 18 Earth hours to spin once on its axis, but this is not always the length of its day. This is because the axis of Uranus is tilted more than that of any other planet. At one particular point in its orbit, the north pole is directed almost straight towards the Sun, and about 42 years later it is directed away from the Sun. At the points between these two extremes it almost rolls along its path. The planet is believed to consist of a rocky core surrounded by a deep ocean, and is covered by thick clouds of gas. Its average distance from the Sun is about 1,783 million miles.

Neptune and Its Discovery

Irregularities in the orbit of Uranus helped astronomers to discover the planet Neptune. Planets follow a timetable as they move across the sky that can be calculated using Isaac Newton's laws of motion and law of gravity. When Uranus was discovered, they worked out the timetable it should follow, but later observations showed that it did not follow this all the time. Sometimes it was late at a particular 'bus stop' in the sky; it was as if Uranus were hitting a small bump on its path around the Sun. The British astronomer John Couch Adams (1819–92) suggested that this bump was due to another planet tugging at Uranus with its force of gravity. Because Adams knew the position of the 'bus stop' at which Uranus was late, he could work out where in the sky this other planet should be. Unfortunately, the British astronomers with access to the most powerful telescopes did not take this calculation seriously, so they did not search for this planet. Quite independently, another astronomer in France, Urbain Leverrier, carried out a similar calculation and obtained virtually the same result. Leverrier asked Johann Galle, a German astronomer at the Berlin Observatory, to search for the new planet. It was found in 1846 not far from its predicted position in the sky.

Neptune was named after the Roman god of the sea. It has an average distance from the Sun of about 2,793 million miles. Its day is 18–20 Earth hours long. In size it is about four times bigger than our Earth, which makes it about as big as Uranus.

The Search for Pluto

Percival Lowell argued that irregularities in the movements of Uranus and Neptune were caused by another planet still further from Earth. He carried out calculations similar to those of Adams and Leverrier in an attempt to pin-point the position of this new planet, and his work prompted another American astronomer, Clyde Tombaugh, working at the Lowell Observatory, to search for the planet. In 1930 he found the planet now called Pluto, named after the Roman god of the underworld, rather far from its predicted position. But Pluto is too small to cause irregularities in the orbits of Uranus and Neptune, and these bumps in the orbits of the last two planets can now be explained in terms of their interaction with the inner members of the solar system. It was then purely fortuitous that the calculations of Lowell led to a successful search for Pluto.

A day on Pluto is about 6 Earth days long, and the planet is smaller than our Earth. Its physical features resemble some of the moons of Jupiter and Saturn rather than those of the other planets. It has an average distance from the Sun of about 3,667 million miles. Its orbit is more elliptical than that of the other planets, and this means that, on occasion, it gets closer to the Sun than Neptune. This has actually been the case since 1979, and the situation will continue until 1999.

Comets

Some comets are periodic in that they return to our skies after a period of time. For the most part, these periodic comets orbit the Sun in highly elliptical orbits, so they spend relatively short times close to the Sun, when they are moving the fastest and when we can see them, and comparatively long times in the outer reaches of the solar system.

A comet is a potato-like lump, made up mainly of water ice impregnated with other frozen gases and fragments of dust. As a comet gets close to the Sun, the Sun's heat boils off some of this frozen material, and the resulting vapour and gas form an atmosphere around the comet. This atmosphere, the coma, is about a million kilometres wide; the remaining solid material, the nucleus, is a few kilometres across. A stream of very energetic particles coming from the Sun, called the solar wind, blows the gas and dust in the coma into two tails, one of gas and one of dust. Since the solar wind is more effective in blowing the gas tail than it is in blowing the dust tail, the gas tail always points away from the Sun, whereas the dust tail curves away more gently. The tails glow because sunlight is reflected off the dust and gas, and because the solar wind and the light from the Sun release energy from the particles of gas.

Although several spacecraft went to encounter Halley's Comet when it appeared in 1986, *Giotto*, the European spacecraft, went closer to the nucleus than any of the others. It went straight through the coma and took pictures from 900 kilometres, which showed that the nucleus was about 14 kilometres long and about three kilometres wide. It was covered in a very dark, soot-like material.

The Sun and Stars

Our Sun is a star, quite ordinary and like countless others, but so close to Earth that we see it as a hot ball of gas in the sky rather than as a point of light. Studies made by telescopes in many parts of the world have shown that most stars are very large, hot spheres of gas and many are much bigger than our own Sun. Some of them occur singly, others in groups of two or more, and some in large clusters. The distances to the stars are so great that they are measured in light years, one light year being the distance travelled by a beam of light in one year, or about 6 million million miles.

The Milky Way

Look upwards on a very clear night somewhere far away from city lights, and you may see a beautiful, hazy band of light stretching across the sky. This is the Milky Way, made up of a hundred thousand million stars. Some of these are to be found within large clouds of gas, but there is also gas and dust between them. Our Milky Way is like a city of stars with a city centre called the nucleus and spiral highways leading from it. Our Sun is one of the many stars along one highway, about two thirds out towards the edge of the city.

Other Galaxies and the Universe

In the early part of this century, large telescopes in America showed many other galaxies besides our own Milky Way. Galaxies come in many different shapes and sizes, and more than half of all galaxies are grouped into clusters, with the rest scattered in the spaces between the clusters. Distances between galaxies in a cluster are vast (about ten times the size of a galaxy, i.e., about 7 million million million kilometres), but even these distances are small compared with the distances between clusters.

The universe, then, can be seen as a collection of a large number of clusters of galaxies, with some individual galaxies between clusters. Every cluster will contain a large number of galaxies, and each galaxy will consist of a still larger number of stars. Observations have also shown that the other galaxies and clusters are all rushing away from us at vast speeds, which is part of the general expansion of the universe. This expansion is the result of the Big Bang explosion that gave birth to the universe. Abbé Georges

Lemaitre (1894–1966), a Catholic priest, physicist and cosmologist who did very important work on the Big Bang theory of the origin of the universe, describes it brilliantly: 'The origin of the universe can be compared to a fireworks display that has just ended. A few red wisps, ashes and smoke. Standing on a well-chilled cinder, we study the slow fading of suns, and try to recapture the vanished brilliance that gave rise to the origin of worlds.'[2]

Conclusion

It is not possible in a few pages to convey more than the merest outline of the complexity and scale of the cosmic factors that play their part in human existence. Man has, however, directly related himself to the cosmos, and astrology is one expression of that relationship. In the next chapter the influence of cosmic knowledge and belief on religion, history, art and literature is reviewed.

2

The Influence of Cosmic Belief

Astrology is astronomy brought to Earth and applied to the affairs of men

Ralph Waldo Emerson

In this chapter we very briefly examine the effects both astrology and astronomy have had on history, art and literature. My attempts to link astronomy with the subjects of art and literature showed me that as far as cultural symbols were concerned, the influence of astrology was much greater than that of astronomy. It also became clear that the astrological world view was the prevailing cosmology of the people for centuries, and that, more often than not, the more technical details of the astronomical world view current at the time had very little effect on how most people saw themselves in relation to the cosmos. Astrology has had a profound and lasting effect on human history. The belief that the heavenly bodies influence our lives has survived for centuries. Astrology has cut right across geographical boundaries, religious beliefs, social systems and cultural values, with the details varying from one country and age to the next. Although the symbolism of astrology became more elaborate than that of astronomy, astrological symbols, nevertheless, had their roots in earlier astronomical practices. It is therefore necessary to look at some of these aspects of astronomy and to consider their relationship to astrological traditions.

Astrology and Early Christianity

The conflict between astrology and the tenets of Christianity has a long history. In the early Christian Church around the year 200, there existed a certain heretical sect, the Gnostics, who believed that they had superior knowledge of spiritual things and interpreted the sacred writings according to a mystic philosophy. The Gnostics also believed that the ultimate goal of human beings was to attain emancipation from the astrologically dominated material world. One of the followers of this sect, a Syrian by the name of Bardesanes, believed that the motions of the stars governed only the physical world, and that the soul was free to judge between good and evil.

Further assessment of the role of astrology within a Christian context came from Priscillian, a Spanish ascetic who lived in the fourth century. He and his followers, known as Christian Priscillianists, believed that the stars were there to make the will of God manifest to those trained in astrological symbolism.

On the other hand, those in opposition to the assimilation of astrology into Christian thought were widely read and influential. One of the first Christians to attack astrology was St Augustine. His main objection to astrology was that it enslaved people to a predestination controlled by the stars and offered little hope of redemption. 'Christians have many better and more serious things to occupy their time than such subtle investigations concerning the relative magnitude of the stars and the intervals between them.' He pointed out that a calf and a human baby born at the same time did not have very similar lives, although they would have the same birth charts.[1]

A more moderate view was held by Albertus Magnus (1193–1280), a Christian scholar who had an interest in astrology. He believed in free will but stated that an astrologer who was properly trained could, on the basis of the birth chart, make predictions concerning the future life of an infant, but within the constraints allowed by God. Magnus became the teacher of St Thomas Aquinas, so it was not surprising that Aquinas also took some interest in the subject. In fact, St Thomas said that the stars ruled the passions and baser instincts of people, but they could overcome these astrological influences by conquering their passions.

Astrology in India

The astrology of the Greeks was transmitted to India, via Sanskrit translations, some time between AD 100 and AD 300. As a result, the techniques of Indian astrology were very similar to those used by the Greeks. The transmission, however, was of method, of practicalities, divorced from any underlying philosophy of astrology, so the forecasts that were originally intended for the type of society that existed in Greece and Rome were superficially modified to make them more relevant to India. These modifications obviously had to incorporate the values of Hinduism, including the caste system and the Hindu belief in reincarnation, and in order to accomplish this, Indian astrologers elaborated the already complex ideas of Greek astrology. They divided the zodiac equally into twenty-eight *nakshatras*, or lunar mansions, and also introduced further subdivisions of the zodiac.

Astrology in Persia

In AD 226 Ardashir founded the Sasanian Empire, making Persia a major new force in the Middle East, and soon after we find the introduction of Greek astrology into Persia, followed by some astrological modifications from India. The unique contribution of the astrologers of the Sasanian Empire was their development of a theory of astrological history. In other words, they tried to formulate a general theory for trends in history, past and future, in terms of particular astrological configurations.

Astronomy, Astrology and the World of Islam

Celestial phenomena played a part in the religion of Islam in a way that had nothing to do with astrology. First of all, the Islamic religious calendar has always been based on the Moon, as the calendar of the Babylonians was at an earlier stage in history. This meant that Islamic astronomers had to make a careful study of the positions and movements of the Moon. In particular the appearance of the crescent Moon marked the end of the month of Ramadan, which was the ninth month of the Islamic year, when a fast was observed during the hours of daylight.

Second, the followers of Islam had to offer up daily prayers at specific times of the day and face in the direction of Mecca when they prayed. Seyyed Hussein Nasr, of the Arya-Mehr University in Tehran and a world authority on Islamic science, has written: 'The times of the daily prayers have to be determined throughout the year for every geographical latitude and longitude where there are faithful, practising Muslims, and the direction of the prayers facing Mecca has to be determined again for every locality where the prayers are performed.'[2] These problems were solved using astronomical methods, so the Islamic astronomers made numerous contributions not only to astronomy but also to areas of mathematics, such as spherical trigonometry, that were needed in order to put these methods into practice.

Astrology made inroads into the world of Islam from Greek, Indian, and Sasanian sources during the eighth and ninth centuries. Despite strong opposition to the practice of astrology on religious grounds, it nevertheless made a lasting impact on Islamic culture. 'It was, in fact, the profound symbolism inherent in astrology which made its integration into Islamic civilization and especially into certain aspects of Islamic esotericism possible, despite the obvious external differences between the astrological attempt to predict future events and the Islamic emphasis upon the omnipotent character of the Divine Will.'

Astrology in China

Chinese astronomy differed from its Western counterpart in two important respects. First, it was an activity sponsored by the state rather than by individual priests and scholars. Second, the Chinese astronomers concentrated more on the stars that were near the north pole of the sky, the circumpolar stars, rather than on those parts of the sky through which the Sun, Moon and the planets moved. The most important Western authority on Chinese science is J. Needham of Cambridge University. He started his career as a biochemist but has spent a considerable amount of time on research into the history of science and civilization in China. His results are contained in the classic, seven-volume work *Science and Civilization in China*. 'I think one could really say that the celestial pole was the fundamental basis of Chinese astronomy. It was connected also with the microcosmic–macrocosmic type of thinking, because the pole corresponded to the emperor on Earth, around whom the vast system of the bureaucratic agrarian state revolved naturally and spontaneously.'[3]

The differences between Chinese and Western astronomy naturally led to differences in their astrology: 'Chinese astrologers . . . paid less attention than their Western counterparts to the planet that was in the ascendant at any time. What mattered to them was the particular constellation in or near which a planet or the Moon happened to stand.' A further contrast was that the Chinese sky was mapped out in constellations that were entirely different from those of the Middle East or Europe, and so quite naturally they used different constellations for their astrological predictions. 'It is likely, then, that what passed from Mesopotamia to China in about the first millennium BC was nothing more than the conviction of the possibility of a system of divination using the stars.'[4]

Mayan Astrology and Astronomy

The highlands of Guatemala, the western edges of Honduras and El Salvador, the eastern Chiapas and the whole of the Yucatan Peninsula formed the region occupied by the Maya. Mayan civilization was at its height from AD 200 to AD 900. Their calendar was really a very complex mixture of three concurrent ways of marking the passage of the days. The first consisted of 365 days, the second consisted of 360 days, and the third was a sacred almanac of 260 days. They made a careful study of certain periods connected with the planet Venus, and they could successfully predict eclipses, although they did not know which eclipses would be visible to them from their part of the world. In 1972 J. E. S. Thompson delivered a brilliant lecture, which I attended, on this later aspect of their work. He said that the 'means were astronomical; ends, astrological . . . we must try not to look at Maya astronomy through European eyes. The Maya astronomer–astrologer . . . completely ignored phenomena which seem important to us . . . presumably because those phenomena had no effect on mundane affairs.' Thompson concluded:

I believe that Maya calendrical and astronomical achievements were made independently of the Old World, except that giving animal names to constellations in the Maya 'zodiac' and in other parts of the heavens, as well as of some days in Middle American calendars, may have been a custom surviving from very simple systems of counting of hunter–gatherers brought by immigrants to the New World by way of the Bering Strait, perhaps as early as 10,000 BC.[5]

Astrology and History – A Brief Selection of Incidents

There are several ways in which astrology has influenced history. Over many centuries and in many cultures and societies, pharaohs, kings and other heads of state have made decisions on the basis of advice from their astrologers. These decisions would often influence national events, or the relationship between one country and another. This still holds true for some parts of the world. In the next few sections we look at a selection of astrologers and an example of the influence of astrology on the lives of ordinary people.

Two Ancient Astrologers

The Pharaoh of Egypt, Ramases II (*c.* 1300–1256 BC), had a great interest in celestial omens and used them to govern his kingdom. It has been claimed by some astrologers that he was responsible for the fixing of the cardinal astrological signs of Aries, Libra, Cancer and Capricorn, which are the signs associated with the equinoxes and the solstices. It is difficult to give undue weight to this claim, because much of the evidence on the history of astrology seems to indicate a much later date for the invention of the zodiac. Some astrologers have also claimed that he designed the temple at Abu Simbel so as to incorporate astrological principles.[6]

From 668 to 625 BC, King Assurbanipal reigned over Assyria. He had a great interest in astrology, and founded a large library in Nineveh, which was supposed to contain many important works on astrology dating back several centuries. He employed astrologers at his court, and made many decisions on the basis of the daily advice that they gave to him.

Omar Khayyám

Edward FitzGerald has immortalized this Persian poet for the Western world by his translation of *The Rubáiyát*. Omar Khayyám (AD *c.* 1050–1123) was not only a poet, he was also a mathematician, who wrote a book on algebra, and an astronomer, who prepared some improved astronomical tables. This latter task may well have been prompted by an interest in astrology. Reynold A. Nicholson, sometime Emeritus Professor of Arabic at Cambridge, tells us that 'while staying in the house of the Prime Minister . . . he [Khayyám] showed his skill in astrology by promising the king fair weather for a hunting expedition'.[7] Several references speak of Omar as an astrologer and make little mention of his interest in poetry, science and medicine. However, one of the commentators on this man, Nizami Aruzi, a professional poet who lived round about the twelfth century, was of the opinion that Omar was rather sceptical about astrological prediction. Nicholson says of Khayyám: 'Omar was a man of science in the first place, a poet occasionally, a freethinker by necessity, in some moods, perhaps, a mystic, but he played with Sufi-ism rather than believed in it. Thus do I read the salient features of his character using the only evidence available at present.'

Nostradamus

Nostradamus (1503–66) was venerated as an outstanding and extraordinary seer. Much of his fame rests on his book *Centuries*, first published in 1555. This contained a series of prophecies into which many successive generations have read the history of their own time. It is said to have forecast the French Revolution, many political events in England, and the Second World War. Catherine de Medici asked Nostradamus to cast the horoscopes of the royal children. He predicted, correctly, that Henri II would be killed in a tournament by a courtier. This made him extremely unpopular, although Catherine continued to seek his advice until his death.

John Dee

John Dee (1527–1608) had a brilliant career in the classics at Trinity College, Cambridge. He also showed an early interest in astrology, and at successive times was patronized by King Edward VI, Queen Mary and Queen Elizabeth. It has been claimed that Queen Elizabeth asked John Dee to cast a horoscope that could be used to set the most appropriate date for her coronation. There is some evidence that he might have been a secret agent of Elizabeth's, that in the pursuit of his duties he travelled widely in Europe, and that he often gave advice to the Queen based on his astrological predictions.

The Predicted Storms of 1186

Derek and Julia Parker, in their book *A History of Astrology*, tell of severe storms that were to occur in 1186. The astrologers of the day, in England and on the Continent, predicted that a conjunction of planets in Libra, during September, would give rise to very severe storms, since Libra was what astrologers call an air sign. As a result many people took precautions by strengthening their homes, and apparently many churches held special services to pray for deliverance from this natural disaster. People became more and more alarmed as September approached, some on the verge of panic. The Parkers conclude: 'As it happened, September was a rather mild and unexceptional month, and the astrologers were forced to admit that they were mistaken: the conjunction did not provoke storms at all – instead, it instigated the victories of Saladin in the Holy Land in the following year.'

Astrologers and the Second World War

A Swiss astrologer, Karl Krafft, supposedly predicted an attack on

Hitler's life, which took place in a beer-cellar in Munich. Krafft was later employed by Goebbels to find evidence in the prophecies of Nostradamus indicating that Nazi supremacy was in the natural order of events. Goebbels believed that such prophecies could be used as propaganda against the allies. Krafft eventually wrote a pamphlet based on the works of Nostradamus, in which he forecast the downfall of Britain.[8]

Another astrologer who played a part in the Second World War, this time on the Allied side, was Louis de Wohl from Berlin. He settled in Britain in 1935 and, when war was declared, persuaded the government in England that he could predict Hitler's strategy on the basis of what he believed astrologers would be telling the German government. On this basis he was alleged to have received an honorary commission in the British army for the rest of the war.

Much more recently the United Nations undertook a study into the international effects of astrology, which showed that at least a dozen nations made political decisions on the basis of astrological prediction. The report concluded that 'the influence of astrological forecasts extends to decisions of the most vital and far-reaching importance. It would seem that this is not the most responsible way to conduct national and international affairs'.[9] It appears, then, that old traditions die very hard.

Language, Literature and Art

The symbolism of astrology has evolved over a considerable period of time, and its influence has been even more widespread and enduring than the belief in astrology itself, permeating our language, literature and art.

We often talk about someone's star being in the ascendant, and the word 'influence' has had astrological connotations for several centuries. Adjectives like 'jovial', 'martial' and 'saturnine' all reflect the astrological qualities associated with particular planets. There are also many references to astrological symbols and beliefs in classical literature. In fact, some scholars believe that a proper appreciation of Greek and Latin literature requires an acquaintance with astronomy and astrology. Since much of Western culture has its roots in the classical world, it is not surprising that many English writers and poets also made extensive use of celestial symbols. For example, the works of Chaucer are full of astrological references. As with many other poets and writers, Chaucer's use of astrology does not imply, in most instances, a belief in astrological prediction; he uses the symbolism of astrology to make factual statements about time of day or year.

The highly pictorial and very powerful images of astrology have also influenced the art of many countries and cultures. The use of astrological symbolism, in the form of the signs of the zodiac, and astronomical symbolism, in the form of the constellation figures, goes back to ancient Egypt and Greece.

In many artistic representations of the signs of the zodiac, each sign was often linked to the agricultural tasks or terrestrial events that were taking place at the time of year when the Sun was in a particular sign. This motif came to be known as the signs of the zodiac and the labours of the month. The Christian Church made frequent use of this motif: for example, it is to be found in the Book of Hours, a prayer-book that the Duc de Berry commissioned from the Limbourg brothers. It is also to be seen in the exterior decorations of the Cathedral at Amiens in France. I found an example of it on the lead surround of a baptismal font at a church in Brookland, Kent. The Church did not support astrology, but this particular motif is really a symbolic way of saying that what people do at different times of the year depends on the cycle of the seasons, and this in turn depends on the apparent position of the Sun along the zodiac.

One of the great historians of astronomy, Otto Neugebauer, has this to say about astrological lore and symbolism:

To the historian of science the transmission of ideas is rightly one of his most important problems. Astrological lore furnishes us with one of the most convincing proofs for the transmission of Hellenistic astronomy to India ... And the history of art and philosophy of the Renaissance has gained immensely from the researches carried out by the Warburg Institute on the astrology of preceding periods.

In the following sections I will illustrate some of these points by discussing a few quotations from English literature, and a few examples of astronomy and astrology in art. Not all the quotations will be concerned directly with astrology. However, they all highlight the astronomical framework from which astrology eventually developed.

Stellar Time-keeping in Literature

The actual time of birth has always been important to astrological practice. This meant that accurate methods of time-keeping were required before one could cast a natal chart. One of the most reliable methods of finding time at night was to employ the stars, which can be used for time-keeping in much the same way as the Sun is during the day. As we will see in a later chapter, this method was discovered by the ancient Egyptians. The next two quotations illustrate the basic idea of the method, but they are based on much later developments of the ancient Egyptian star clock.

In the following passage from *Far from the Madding Crowd*, Gabriel Oak, the shepherd, is using his knowledge of the sky, and the stars and constellations visible at a given moment, to work out the time:

> The Dog-Star and Aldebaran, pointing to the restless Pleiades, were halfway up to the southern sky, and between them hung Orion, which gorgeous constellation never burnt more vividly than now, as it soared forth above the rim of the landscape. Castor and Pollux with their quiet shine were almost on the meridian: the barren and gloomy Square of Pegasus was creeping round to the north-west; far away through the plantation Vega sparkled like a lamp suspended amid the leafless trees, and Cassiopeia's chair stood daintily poised on the uppermost boughs. 'One o'clock,' said Gabriel.

Since, as we have already seen, the sky changes with time of night as well as with time of year, we can use this quotation to work out the time of year, which turns out to be near the end of November.

Shakespeare also makes use of this method in *Henry IV*. Here he uses the position of Charles's Wain with respect to a local landmark to estimate the time. Charles's Wain is also sometimes called the Plough, the Wagon or, in North America, the Big Dipper.

> *An't be not four by*
> *the day I'll be hang'd; Charles Wain is over*
> *the new chimney and yet our horse not pack'd.*

About 400 years ago this method was made more accurate by the invention of a device called a nocturnal. This was really the night-time equivalent of the sundial, and it helped people to tell time using the Great or Little Bears. The available evidence suggests that it was largely used by navigators and astrologers.

Solar Time-keeping in Literature

Although the sundial was the most accurate instrument for telling time during the day, it was by no means the only one, and many people in the days of Chaucer used the lengths of their shadows or the lengths of shadows cast by familiar objects. The following two quotations illustrate this point. The first is from 'The Parson's Prologue':

> *The story of the Manciple had ended.*
> *From the south line the sun had now descended*
> *So low, it stood – so far as I had sight –*
> *At less than twenty-nine degrees in height.*
> *Four o' the clock it was, to make a guess;*
> *Eleven foot long, or little more or less,*
> *My shadow was, as at that time and place,*
> *Measuring feet by taking in this case*
> *My height as six, divided in like pattern*
> *Proportionally; and the power of Saturn*
> *Began to rise with Libra just as we*
> *Approached a little thorpe*

The references to Saturn and Libra are clearly related to astrology.

The second quotation, which is from the Introduction to 'The Man of Law's Tale', shows that solar time-keeping is not as simple as it may seem at first sight:

> Our Host perceived the sun upon its arc
> Of artificial day (from dawn to dark)
> Quarter way up plus half an hour or more;
> And though not deeply versed in heavenly lore
> He knew quite well it was the eighteenth day
> Of April that is messenger to May,
> And was aware the shadow of every tree
> Was of the same extent and quantity
> As the erected body casting it.
>   So, by the shadow cast, he had the wit
> To judge that Phoebus, shining clear and bright,
> Had climbed some forty-five degrees in height;
> So for that day, and in these latitudes,
> It must be ten o'clock, our Host concludes.

Thus, to tell time by the Sun we must know three things: the height of the Sun above the horizon, in degrees, the date and the latitude of the place. In this case the Sun is 45 degrees above the horizon, because shadows are equal to the height of the objects that cast them, and the date is 18 April. Familiarity with the variations of the Sun in that particular latitude leads to the correct time. This quotation is also evidence of Chaucer's detailed knowledge of astronomy.

The Zodiac as a Calendar

As we saw in an earlier chapter, the position of the Sun against the zodiac constellations was, and still is, an important astrological concept. In personal horoscopes the particular sign in which the Sun is when a person is born is called the Sun-sign. There are many examples in literature in which the time of year is given by the position of the Sun along the zodiac. In many instances it is really used as a literary device, sometimes called the chronographia, and does not necessarily imply that the author supports astrological principles. Chaucer uses this device very often in his work.

> and the young sun
> His half-course in the sign of the Ram has run,

These lines from the 'Prologue' to the *Canterbury Tales* tell us that the Sun is in the constellation of the Ram, thus setting the 'Prologue' in April.

In 'Prosopopoia, or Mother Hubbard's Tale' Edmund Spenser describes the time of year with this method:

> It was the month, in which the righteous Maide,
> That for disdain of sinful worlds upbraide,
> Fled back to heaven, whence she was first conceived,
> Into her silver bowre the Sunne received,
> And the hot Syrian Dog on him awayting,
> After the chafed Lyons cruell bayting.

The 'hot Syrian Dog' is Sirius, the dog-star, and 'the chafed Lyon' is Leo the Lion. This means that the Sun must be somewhere between the two, and the time of year the month of August.

John Lydgate in 'The Temple of Glas' uses both the Sun and the Moon:

> Whan that Lucina with hir pale light
> Was Joyned last with Phebus in aquarie

In this quotation the suggestion is made that on a previous occasion the Sun and Moon were close together in the constellation of Aquarius; the reference is therefore to a time in late February.

A Famous Literary Conjunction

Conjunctions occur when two celestial objects are very close to each other in a particular part of the sky. They are considered to be important by astrologers. Chaucer makes use of this concept in his long narrative poem *Troilus and Criseyde*. Troilus was the warrior son of the King of Troy, and the beautiful young widow Criseyde was his beloved. In Book III of the poem, a severe rainstorm forces Troilus and Criseyde to spend the night in the same house, and this naturally has inevitable consequences. This freak weather coincides with a conjunction of Saturn and Jupiter, with the crescent Moon very close by, in the constellation of Cancer:

> *Bent was the moon in Cancer, silver-pale,*
> *And joined with Saturn and with Jupiter,*
> *And such a rain from heaven, such a gale*
> *Came smoking down that all the women there*
> *Were terrified, quite overcome with fear;*
> *Pandar made comment, laughing up his sleeve,*
> *'Fine time, your ladyship, to take your leave!'*

In the early 1920s Robert Root, a Chaucer scholar from Princeton University, considered the possibility that Chaucer had actually included in this poem an astronomical event that he had witnessed. If this was the case, then it would perhaps be possible to place a rough date on when Chaucer had written *Troilus and Criseyde*. Root enlisted the help of an astronomer, very well known for his work on the classification of stars, Henry Norris Russell, also of Princeton. Russell carried out the necessary calculations, and showed that conjunctions of Saturn and Jupiter, in Cancer, happened every 60 years for periods of about 200 years, and these periods were separated by longer periods of about 600 years when such conjunctions did not take place. He also showed that such a conjunction had taken place in May 1385, and the two planets had been very close to the crescent Moon on 12 May. This, then, suggests that Chaucer wrote the poem after this date.

The story of Troilus and Criseyde was retold by Kenneth Weitzenhoffer in the March 1985 issue of *Sky and Telescope*, because a very similar meeting of the Moon and the two planets had taken place on 25 November 1984. His brief letter recounting this story was followed by an interesting editorial note by Dennis di Cicco, who checked through the calculations using a small desk-top computer. Di Cicco was able to show that this particular grouping of objects had taken place in the constellation of Gemini. The apparent discrepancy between his calculations and Chaucer's description was explained by Owen Gingerich of Harvard University. Chaucer had based his description on his own observations, which he combined with the tables of planetary motion used by the astrologers of his day. These were called the Alphonsine Tables, named after the Spanish King Alfonso X who had encouraged the preparation of revised tables of planetary motion. When these tables were checked by Gingerich, it turned out that Chaucer's description was consistent with them.

Eclipses in Literature

From the time of Plutarch, eclipses have been used to great effect in literature. H. Rider Haggard in *King Solomon's Mines* and Mark Twain in *A Connecticut Yankee in King Arthur's Court* both include eclipses, as does Hardy in *The Return of the Native*:

> His eye travelled over the length and breadth of that distant country − over the Bay of Rainbows, the sombre Sea of Crises, the Ocean of Storms, the Lake of Dreams, the vast Walled Plains, the wondrous Ring mountains − till he felt himself to be voyaging bodily through its wild scenes, standing on its hollow hills, traversing its deserts, descending its vales and old sea bottoms, or mounting to the edges of its craters. While he watched the far-removed landscape, a tawny stain grew into being on the lower verge: the eclipse had begun. This marked a preconcerted moment: for the remote celestial phenomenon had been pressed into sublunary service as a lover's signal.

The landscape that Hardy describes is obviously that of the Moon, and all the features here can be found on a lunar map, so it is obviously an eclipse of the Moon. The character Clym Yeobright uses the occasion of the eclipse to time a meeting with his lover Eustacia Vye.

To astrologers, eclipses represent extremely close conjunctions or oppositions of the Sun and Moon, and these relative positions are considered to be very powerful by astrologers.

Some Specific References to Astrology in Chaucer

There are also a few specific references to astrology in Chaucer. One occurs at the start of 'The Miller's Tale':

> Some time ago there was a rich old codger
> Who lived in Oxford and who took a lodger.
> The fellow was a carpenter by trade,
> His lodger a poor student who had made
> Some studies in the arts, but all his fancy
> Turned to astrology and geomancy,
> And he could deal with certain propositions
> And make a forecast under some conditions
> About the likelihood of drought or showers
> For those who asked at favourable hours,
> Or put a question how their luck would fall
> In this or that, I can't describe them all.

In her tale, the Wife of Bath attributes aspects of her personality to her astrological chart:

> Venus gave me desire and lecherousness
> And Mars my hardihood, or so I guess,
> Born under Taurus and with Mars therein.
> Alas, alas, that ever love was sin!
> I ever followed natural inclination
> Under the power of my constellation
> And was unable to deny, in truth,
> My chamber of Venus to a likely youth.
> The mark of Mars is still upon my face
> And also in another privy place.

A still closer link between astronomy and astrology is to be found

48

in 'The Franklin's Tale'. The tidal effect of the Moon is very important to the whole story, but its inclusion draws attention to the fact that at this stage people did not always make a clear distinction between astronomy and astrology, and they did not understand the scientific reasons for the tidal influence and so attributed it to astrological causes. In this tale, Arveragus, a knight, is very happily married to Dorigen. However, he feels it necessary to go off to war in order to sustain his knightly honour. Dorigen is very worried that on his return Arveragus's ship will be sunk by the very treacherous rocks just off the coast at 'Penmarch Point, not far from Finisterre' where she lives. Aurelius meets Dorigen while she is out dancing with some friends who are trying to make her forget her sadness. Aurelius declares his love to her, and she, thinking of the safety of her husband, says:

> 'And yet, Aurelius, by the Lord above
> I might perhaps vouchsafe to be your love,
> Since I perceive you groan so piteously.
> Look; on the day the coasts of Brittany
> Are stone by stone cleared of these hateful rocks
> By you, so that no ship or vessel docks
> In danger, when, I say, you clear the coast
> So clean there's not a single stone to boast,
> I'll love you more than any man on earth;
> Accept my word in truth for all it's worth.'

In order to gain her love, Aurelius enlists the help of a sage:

> This subtle sage had pity on the man
> And night and day went forward with his plan
> Watching the hour to favour the conclusion
> Of his experiment, that by illusion
> Or apparition – call it jugglery,
> I lack the jargon of astrology –
> She and the world at large might think and say
> The rocks had all been spirited away
> From Brittany or sunk under the ground.

Basically the sage is using his knowledge that the height of the tide varies with time of day, time of lunar month and time of year.

> *And so at last the favouring hour was found*
> *To do his tricks and wretched exhibition*
> *Of that abominable superstition.*
> *His calculating tables were brought out*
> *Newly corrected (he made sure about*
> *The years in series and the single years*
> *To fix the points the planets in their spheres*
> *Were due to reach and so assessed their 'root'*
> *In longitude) and other things to suit,*
> *Such as his astrolabe, and argument*
> *From arc and angle, and was provident*
> *Of fit proportionals for the minor motion*
> *Of planets, and he studied with devotion,*
> *Measuring from the point where Alnath swam*
> *In the eighth sphere, to where the head of the* Ram
> *Stood in the ninth, in its eternal station*
> *(As we suppose), and made his calculation.*
> *And finding the first mansion of the moon,*
> *He calculated all the rest in tune*
> *With that. He worked proportionally, knowing*
> *How she would rise and whither she was going*
> *Relative to which planets and their place,*
> *Equal or not, upon the zodiac face.*
> *And thus according to his calculations*
> *He knew the moon in all her operations*
> *And all the relevant arithmetic*
> *For his illusion, for the wretched trick*
> *He meant to play, as in those heathen days*
> *People would do. There were no more delays*
> *And by his magic for a week or more*
> *It seemed the rocks were gone; he'd cleared the shore.*

It is impossible that the rocks would have been hidden by the high tide for a week or more, but it is possible that at the time of the highest spring tide of the year the rocks would have been covered, though only when the tide was in. This could have occurred on a few days on either side of the new or full Moon. According to Ken George, one of my colleagues at Polytechnic South West who is a specialist on tidal theory as well as the links between the languages of Brittany and Cornwall, the Bretons had worked out empirical tables of the tides many years before Newton worked out the theory of the tides in terms of the gravitational tug of the Sun and Moon on the waters of the oceans.

Astronomy and Astrology in Art: A Few Examples

Chauncey Wood, in his book *Chaucer and the Country of the Stars*, gives some examples of astronomical and astrological ideas that have been given artistic expression. However, he does point out that one should be extremely cautious about how these should be interpreted. Wood discusses the fifteenth-century humanist Agostino Chigi, who ordered his horoscope to be artistically represented in the vault of his Farnesina Palace. This seems to indicate that Chigi was a devotee of astrology. He is, however, buried in the vault of the Chapel Santa Maria del Popolo. Here the planets are depicted in a circle, with an angel over each, while God is shown above at the centre, with his arms raised up in a gesture of command. According to Wood, this motif, in which the planets are the instruments of the divine will, puts the horoscope of Chigi in an entirely different perspective: representations of astrology need not indicate a belief in astrology.

Wood also discusses a painting in the cupola of the old sacristy of San Lorenzo, in which the night sky of Florence is portrayed as it was on 9 July 1422. The painting depicts the heavens as they appeared on the day of the consecration of the main altar, and so the imagery is being used merely as an artistic device to express a date and time and not a belief in astrology.

The ceiling in the Painted Hall of the Royal Naval College at Greenwich has several different astronomical motifs. The archway leading from the lower hall to the upper is decorated with six signs of the zodiac possibly executed by Hawksmoor. The other zodiac signs are arranged around the perimeter of a large ellipse that dominates the ceiling of the lower hall. The rest of the ceiling is probably by Thornhill or one of his students. Here the reason for the astronomical imagery is obvious. The study of astronomy was important to navigation, which in turn played a great part in England's naval might, with which Greenwich was associated. In one corner we have human figures representing astronomy and geography, holding celestial and terrestrial globes. In another corner we have Archimedes consulting a globe, a figure depicting navigation with a fore-staff and Galileo with his telescope. In the third corner we have a sage looking at the drawings of Newton, and Copernicus is studying Pythagoras's system. In this corner we also have the great Danish astronomer Tycho Brahe. The effect of the Moon on the tides is depicted by Diana drawing up the rivers.

In the south-east corner we have the Revd John Flamsteed, the first Astronomer Royal at Greenwich, and his assistant, Weston. Flamsteed holds a sheet of paper depicting an eclipse of the Sun of 22 April 1715. The clock near by shows the time of the eclipse as being 9.02. When the ceiling was restored by Westby Percival-Prescott, Art Restorer of the National Maritime Museum, in 1960, he found that the time on the clock had been changed from 5.15 to 9.02. Since the main painting was completed in 1714, it has been suggested that when the painting was completed, the time of 5.15 referred to the predicted time of the eclipse. However, as a result of the poor tables that were then available, the eclipse was actually later than the predicted time, and so the time on the clock was subsequently changed.

Conclusion

In this chapter we saw that for a considerable part of recorded history, there has existed in various forms a belief that the cosmos does affect life on Earth. This belief has had an important cultural effect on history, language, literature, art and almost every other area of human thought. If we are to understand some of the roots of our present Western intellectual society, then it is necessary to understand something about the changing relationship between astronomy and astrology, as these subjects have evolved over

several centuries. It is also essential to try to understand the origins
of astrology, since its recorded history does not provide us with all
the important answers, and a belief in astrology did prove to be
important to the development of the exact sciences. These, then,
are some of the topics we explore in subsequent chapters. In
Chapter 12 I will argue that a belief in astrology also gave rise to
the Christian religion.

3

From Calendars to Horoscopes

Few statements are more deeply rooted in the public mind or more often repeated than the assertion that the origin of astronomy is to be found in astrology . . . all well-documented facts . . . show that calendaric problems directed the first steps of astronomy.

Otto Neugebauer

The Principles of Early Calendars

Sources for studying the history of astronomy are many and varied. They take the form of cave paintings, papyri, clay and stone tablets, and standing stones. They are to be found scattered across the globe, from the islands of Polynesia, right through the Far and Near East, across western Europe and early America. All the indications are that early cultures and civilizations were mostly concerned with calendar-making and time-keeping, and these show that systematic astronomy had an earlier origin distinct from astrology.

The chief reason for needing a calendar was the seasonal dependence on supplies of food. This applied equally well to the early hunter–gathering cultures as to the later and more developed agricultural civilizations. Today the calendar is very much part of our lives and it may be difficult to see why its construction should ever have presented a problem, so it is probably worth our while to take a few minutes to consider what knowledge is required before a calendar can be constructed.

The prime requirement is to know the number of days in a year. Today we know that the year is about 365.25 days long, but in ancient cultures this knowledge did not exist. It may seem that all that was necessary was to count the number of days that pass between, say, the first rains (or snows) of a particular seasonal cycle and the next. However, we are all familiar with the fact that such an event may not occur on exactly the same day each year, so this idea will not really work. The same goes for any other terrestrial phenomenon, for example, the first appearance of the cuckoo. This means that some date marker must be used that does repeat, very regularly, from one year to the next. In order to discover the length of the year the ancient calendar-makers turned to the sky, and by trial and error discovered the celestial phenomena that were the most reliable.

Many early communities made use of the Moon for this purpose. Most of us will have noticed that when the Moon is about 2–3 days old, only a thin crescent is lit up, and it is very low in the western sky, just after sunset. After 4–5 days the Moon reaches what we call the first quarter, when half of its face is lit up and it is seen fairly high up in the sky, just after sunset. The Moon will be full 7 days later, the whole of its face will be lit up, and it will be seen rising in the east just after sunset. This Moon will rise at about midnight 7 days after this, and the half of its face towards the eastern horizon will be lit up. This phase is known as the last quarter. After about 29½ days the Moon will once again be seen as a thin crescent in the western sky after sunset. This period is called the lunar month, and it was used as the basis of many ancient calendars.

It was soon realized that this calendar had one very serious problem. A simple calculation shows that 12 lunar months are equal to about 354 days. We now know that a year is a little more than 365 days long, so 12 lunar months are about 11 days short of the year. Although the early astronomers did not know the length of the year, their error would soon have been noticed, since they would have started each year 11 days earlier every year and so after 3 years they would have started the year earlier by more than 1 lunar month. It was as a result of such observations that a more precise length for the year was found.

The Egyptian Origins of the Gregorian Calendar

The Egyptians started with a lunar calendar, and then realized that the stars were more reliable, so they switched to a lunistellar calendar that was kept in place by the star called Sirius. They had noticed that there was a time of year when Sirius, because it was very bright, could be seen rising in the early morning just before sunrise. This happened just a few days before the Nile came down in flood, so Sirius was taken as a herald of the floods and a corrector of the calendar. Later in Egyptian history this calendar was replaced by one in which the year consisted of three seasons of four 30-day months each, with 5 additional 'days upon the year' or festivals, thus giving 365 days in all. Although the Egyptians also discovered the extra quarter of a day, they did nothing to incorporate this into their calendar. It was left to the Romans to correct this mistake.[1]

Julius Caesar had become acquainted with the Egyptian calendar as a result of his military campaigns to Egypt, and he was also aware that they had discovered that the year was 365.25 days long, so he decided to correct their calendar and introduce it into the Roman world. He decreed that the Julian calendar should consist of three 'common years' of 365 days each, and a fourth year of 366 days. Unfortunately, for 36 years his decree was misinterpreted, and every *third* year was made a leap year. Finally the error was realized by Augustus Caesar and he corrected the calendar. Just as Julius Caesar had named July in his own honour, so Augustus Caesar named August in his honour.

More recent observations have shown us that the year is 365.2422 days long. Thus even the Roman calendar was slightly inaccurate and by 1582 an error of ten days had accumulated. In that year Pope Gregory XIII decreed that the day following 4 October would be called 15 October to account for this. Henceforth, he said, leap years falling at the end of a century would not be counted as leap, unless the year was exactly divisible by four. This was how the Egyptian calendar gave rise to our own one, which we call the Gregorian calendar.

Differences between Protestants and Catholics, and division of the Eastern and Western Christian Churches, meant that the positive advantages of the Gregorian calendar were not accepted straight away in many countries. France, Italy, Luxembourg, Spain and Portugal adopted the new calendar in the same year that the papal bull was issued, which we have already seen was 1582. Belgium, the Netherlands and the Catholic states of Germany followed two years later. In Switzerland the changeover was started in 1583, but ended only in 1812. In the United Kingdom and its colonies the change was made rather late. In fact, it was made in 1752, when the difference between the two calendars amounted to 11 days so the day after 2 September 1752 became 14 September 1752. In many countries the changeover was accompanied by unrest, and in England the rioters against reform demanded 'Give us back our eleven days!' This was very well captured in an etching by Hogarth, *Four Prints of an Election*. However, the legislation authorizing the change had been so formulated that injustice and financial hardship were avoided.

Egyptian Shadow and Star Clocks

We all know that it is possible to tell time by the position of the Sun in the sky, and that a sundial is the instrument for doing this accurately. The Egyptians had also realized that the Sun was a time-keeper, and they invented the shadow clock to take advantage of this. Its shape resembled that of a modern bed with a headboard, but no footboard. In the morning the 'head' of this clock would be pointed towards the east, and the time would be marked by the position of the shadow of the headboard on the graduated base – the bed part. After midday the clock would be turned around, with the head towards the west. Using this clock, the Egyptians developed a system of daylight hours, which had 4 hours to the morning, 4 hours to the afternoon, 2 hours for dawn and 2 hours for dusk – giving a total of 12 daylight hours.

For the hours of the night they used a sequence of thirty-six stars more or less evenly spread across the middle part of the sky, the part called the celestial equator. On a particular night the first star that could be seen rising after dusk would mark the first hour of the night, and the second star in the sequence, called the deconal star, would mark the second hour of the night, and so on. About 10 days later the star that marked the first hour of the night would be rising about 40 minutes earlier, so it would not be seen in the dusk. The star that marked the second hour of the night 10 days earlier would now mark the first hour, and this was how one would progress through the year. During the equinoxes, when we have equal day and night, eighteen of the deconal stars would already be above the horizon at dusk, so only eighteen would rise in the course of the night. However, during the summer only twelve deconal stars could be seen rising at night, because the nights were shorter. The Egyptians decided to settle for 12 hours to the night for the whole year. Thus the Egyptians had 12 hours to the night and 12 hours to the day, giving a total of 24 hours. This then is the origin of our 24-hour day and night. It will, however, be apparent that the lengths of the hours varied from one season to the next. This was not uncommon in many time-keeping systems. Although equal hours were used in Greek theoretical astronomy, they became generally accepted only after the invention of mechanical time-keepers.[2]

Babylonian Theoretical Astronomy

Babylonian theoretical astronomy was largely motivated by the problems raised by the strict adherence to a lunar calendar. The techniques developed to deal with these problems were later applied to the predicting of eclipses, and the predicting of planetary motion (which was needed for astrological forecasting).

In the early Egyptian lunar calendar the month started with the morning when the old crescent of the waning moon could no longer be seen just before sunrise in the east. In the Babylonian lunar calendar they started their month on the day they first saw the thin crescent of the Moon in the west just after sunset, so their calendar was more in keeping with that of their neighbours than that of the Egyptians. The inconvenience of starting the month with the actual sighting of the thin crescent Moon is obvious, since it is so dependent on conditions in our atmosphere. It was for this reason that the Babylonians wanted to develop a theoretical astronomy, so that they could predict when *in principle* they should be able to see the crescent Moon, and they could then start the month on this day, without having to wait for the actual sighting. There were, however, several problems they had to overcome before they could achieve this.

We now know that as the Earth goes around the Sun we will see the Sun (assuming we could see the Sun and stars at the same time) against a different group of stars, or constellations, every month, so although the Sun does not move it does have an apparent motion against the background stars. The apparent pathway of the Sun against the stars is called the ecliptic because it is also the path along which eclipses occur. The Moon is going around our Earth, so it too has a pathway against the stars, which is different from that of the Sun. Twice in a lunar month the Moon crosses the Sun's path, and if the Sun is at this point when it crosses, then the Moon will blot out the light from the Sun and we have an eclipse. The speeds with which the Sun and Moon move against the stars are, of course, different; the Sun moves through about 1 degree per day, whereas the Moon moves through about 13 degrees per day. In addition to this the speeds of both bodies vary slightly as they appear to move against the background of stars. All this is very relevant to calculating when one should be able to see the crescent Moon.

First of all, the Moon must be a certain distance from the Sun in the sky for the crescent to be seen in the sunset glow. Also important is the angle which the line joining the Sun and Moon in the sky makes with the horizon. If this angle is very small, the Moon will be too close to the horizon to be seen. All this meant that the Babylonian astronomers had to make a careful study of the movements of both the Sun and the Moon; they had to invent a method for describing the positions of both bodies against the stars, which formed a natural map against which they moved. Just as the postman needs an address before he can deliver a letter to a given house, so astronomers have to define addresses for the Sun and Moon in the sky. This was normally done by giving the number of degrees that each body had moved into a given constellation.

To describe the motion of, say, the Moon, it was necessary to give the number of degrees by which it had moved into a given constellation on a number of different dates. In order to predict where the Moon would be at some time in the future, it was necessary to be able to predict these numbers for future dates. The Babylonians did this by noticing patterns in these sets of numbers, and then trying to reproduce these patterns using sequences of numbers, for example, 4, 8, 12, 16, 20, etc., to try to reproduce these observed sets. Their theoretical astronomy was purely arithmetical, and at no time did they seek to picture how the celestial objects were arranged in space. This numerical approach did, in fact, allow them to work out a predictable lunar calendar, and it also helped them to predict some eclipses. They were also aware that there were five other bodies that moved against the stellar background – the naked-eye planets – and when they started to use these bodies for astrological prediction they could use the arithmetical methods of prediction, developed to solve calendar problems, for predicting the movements of these planets.

The Origins of the Constellations

It is well known that the stars are grouped into a number of constellations. The origins of these constellations are most probably lost in pre-recorded history. However, some clues are to be found in the works of later Greek astronomers such as Hipparchus (190–120 BC) and Eudoxus (409–356 BC). Hipparchus was perhaps the greatest astronomer of the ancient world. He had an observatory on the island of Rhodes, in the south-eastern Aegean. Many of the instruments used for naked-eye astronomy for the next seventeen centuries were invented, and used extremely effectively, by him. Eudoxus started his studies in Greece, and then went to Egypt in search of the astronomical learning of the ancients. After his return, he wrote a book called *The Phaenomena* and produced a globe. The first clue concerning the origin of the constellations comes to us from the fact that Hipparchus criticizes the description of the sky given in this work, because the constellations described do not fit with those he viewed from the island of Rhodes, which was 31 degrees from the equator. Unfortunately neither Eudoxus's work nor his globe now exist in their original form. However Aratus (315–250 BC), a poet, was commissioned by the king of Macedonia, Antigonus Gonatus, to write a poem about the work of Eudoxus, and this poem has survived. It provides a very important clue on the constellation problem. It too is called 'The Phaenomena' and contains the following lines:

> So thought he good to make the stellar groups,
> That each by other lying orderly,
> They might display their forms. And thus the stars
> At once took names and rise familiar now.[3]

In 1965 this work was analysed by M. W. Ovenden, then of Glasgow University, in an attempt to discover the place and time the constellations were first put down in a systematic form.[4] In a postscript at the end of his paper, Ovenden made some comments that had a deep influence on the way in which I viewed the scientific enterprise:

> I cannot forbear to close without making a few comments of a general nature on research of this type. My main work is concerned with certain problems of modern astrophysics and astronomy – a far cry from the activities of the constellation-makers. Yet it well behoves a scientist to pause from time to time to consider the roots of his science, for we carry, deep in the recesses of our minds, preconceptions and attitudes that influence our own scientific attitudes, but which we inherited from times long past.

A. E. Roy was a colleague of Ovenden at the University of Glasgow, and he was asked by Ovenden to check his calculations. Before discussing the conclusions of these men on the origin of the constellations, it is necessary to explain some of the astronomical background to their work.

It is only from the equator that we can see all the constellations; from any other point in the northern hemisphere there are some stars near the south pole that we cannot see, and the reverse is true for points in the southern hemisphere. From a point in the northern hemisphere, there are some stars that never go below the horizon, and we call these the circumpolar stars. The circumpolar stars also change with time, because the Earth's axis is slowly making a cone in space. At the moment this axis points very nearly to Polaris, the North Star. When some of the pyramids were built 4,500 years ago, there was another star close to the point about which the sky seems to turn. This movement of the Earth's axis is called the precession, and it is rather like that of the axis of a child's top when it slows down. This means that from a description of the circumpolar stars, as well as the other stars in the rest of the sky, we can work out the position of the pole and its height above the horizon, and from this we can find the time and place to which the description applies. This is in outline the method used by Ovenden and Roy. Roy's analysis of 1980 gives a time of about 2000 BC plus or minus about 200 years, and a place about 36 degrees from the equator. So Eudoxus and Aratus were writing about the sky not as they saw it but as it existed about 1,600 years before they lived. They also did not check this description against the real sky that existed during their lifetime. Hipparchus did actually carry out these observations, and this was how he discovered the precession of the Earth's axis.[5]

The next question that Roy tried to answer was why the system of constellations was invented. He speculates it was invented for the purposes of navigation. Those constellations that are not circumpolar will always rise and set at points that make definite angles with the east and west. A set of constellations with the same angular distance from the celestial equator can be used to show compass directions throughout the night. This method of finding directions would have been of great benefit to navigation, especially in the absence of a fixed pole star, and long before the invention of the magnetic compass. At the conference on 'The Place of Astronomy in the Ancient World', D. Lewis, then of the School of Pacific Studies, Australian National University, Canberra, Australia, delivered a paper in which he showed that this method of navigation was still used by the inhabitants of the Caroline Islands in the Pacific, just north of Papua New Guinea.

A final question that Roy attempts to answer is who were the people that originated the constellations. He comes to the conclusion they were the Minoans who lived in Crete and the Cyclades more than 2,000 years ago.

Up until the beginning of this century the Minoan people

were a legend, the subject of marvellous Greek myths ... At the beginning of this century Sir Arthur Evans found the remains of the civilization of the Minoans. We now know that it was a superb civilization, the first great European civilization, based on the island of Crete that lies stretched north along the 26th parallel north. We also know that the Minoans were around during the second and third millennia BC.

This Minoan civilization was destroyed about 1450 BC by a volcanic explosion, but their astronomical ideas formed the basis of Eudoxus's work, which was described by Aratus.

Astrology in the Ancient World

Normally when we talk about astrology in the West, we have in mind horoscopic astrology, which links the personalities of individuals to the positions of the planets at their birth, and tries to determine their destinies in terms of the future movements of the planets. This type of astrology appeared fairly late in the ancient world, from about 500 BC to 200 BC. The earliest type of astrology was called judicial astrology, and it made use of celestial portents and omens in attempts to predict the future of kings, the royal household and the country. This type of forecasting can be compared to the weather forecasting used by weather wizards, who deduced the future pattern of the weather by combining present facts with past experience. A third type of astrology existed in Greece. This type of astrology was in reality an attempt at a generalized form of cosmic physics, or astronomical meteorology, in which terrestrial events were related to the position of the Sun along the zodiac, and the influence of the Moon and planets was also included in this work. The great astronomer–astrologer Ptolemy discusses this form of astrology in the first two volumes of his work on astrology, the *Tetrabiblos*.

A system of constellations, a reasonable calendar and astronomical methods of time-keeping were some of the necessary prerequisites for the development of horoscopic astrology. The apparent motion of the Sun, the Moon and planets against the background stars served to define a set of constellations that is called the zodiac. In order to cast a personal horoscope it was, and still is, necessary to know the positions of Sun, Moon and planets against the zodiac and the zodiac constellation that was rising at the time of birth. This meant knowing the positions of the planets even if they could not be seen in the sky during the night, because they rose with, just before or just after the Sun, or because of adverse weather conditions. This meant that one had to be able to predict the positions of the planets against the background zodiac stars. The development of theoretical or arithmetical astronomy by the Babylonians made this possible. However, although the Babylonian methods were reasonably accurate, what was required was a more detailed geometrical model that could explain how the heavenly bodies were arranged in space and a method for calculating future movements of the planets from such a model. These requirements were supplied by the Greeks.

Greek Cosmology and Astronomy

All cultures of which we have records have asked questions about the structure of the universe. A variety of methods were used to arrive at an answer. Some cultures based their view of the universe on mythology; others used religious principles or philosophical arguments. In ancient Greece they based their outlook on actual astronomical observations, and all those cultures that arose from the Hellenic culture have done so ever since. An overall theory of the structure of the universe is called a cosmology. In ancient Greek science, the subjects of astronomy, astrology and cosmology were distinct disciplines, but of necessity they were very closely related, so if we wish to understand something about their science, we must consider the relationship between these subjects.

The raw data for these disciplines were the movements of the planets and the stars. The word 'planet' comes from the Greek word *planetes*, which means wanderer, and it was used for several centuries to describe all those bodies that moved against the background of stars, so it included not only the five planets known to the Greeks (Mercury, Venus, Mars, Jupiter and Saturn), but also the Sun and Moon.

It was only after Copernicus's death that a distinction was made between the Sun and Moon on the one hand and the planets on the other hand. In this book I will use the word 'planet' in this later sense, except where it is specifically stated that we are using the Greek meaning. The Greeks were well aware from the astronomical work of their neighbours that the stars seemed to rise and set in the course of the night, but that they kept their relative positions with respect to each other, and so they could be conveniently grouped into the imaginary constellation figures. They were also aware that every star that rose in the east would rise slightly earlier every night (as I have already described) so from one night to the next the sky would gradually change until after a year the sky would be the same as far as the stars were concerned.

They knew that the Moon changed its position against the background stars during the lunar month, and that the Sun had a similar movement that repeated after 1 year. They also knew that the planets moved against the background stars, all with different speeds, and not always in the same direction. The planets Mercury and Venus never got very far from the Sun in the sky and were never seen at or near midnight. On the other hand, Mars, Jupiter and Saturn could be seen at midnight during certain times of the year. These were the basic facts that any geometrical picture of the universe had to explain.

Aristotle's Cosmos

One of the first Greek pictures of the universe was that of the philosopher Aristotle. He believed that the Earth was fixed in the centre of the universe, and that the stars were all fixed to one very large sphere, which I have already referred to as the celestial sphere, and that this sphere was concentric with the Earth (see illus. 6). This outer sphere was often called the sphere of the fixed stars, not because it was fixed, but because the stars were fixed with respect to each other, so they appeared as if they were fixed to this outer sphere. The sphere of the fixed stars was, in fact, supposed to spin around the Earth in slightly less than 1 day (or 23 hours, 56 minutes of our time). The space between the sphere of the fixed stars and the Earth was filled up with seven other crystalline spheres (they had to be clear so that the stars could be seen) and to each of these spheres was attached one of the planets, the Sun and the Moon. To the sphere in contact with the fixed stars was attached Saturn, Jupiter was attached to the next slightly smaller sphere, then Mars, then the Sun, then Venus, then Mercury, and finally the Moon.

The Earth, then, was in the centre. The motion of the outer spheres was transmitted downwards via friction between neighbouring spheres. Thus the sphere of Saturn moved least with respect to

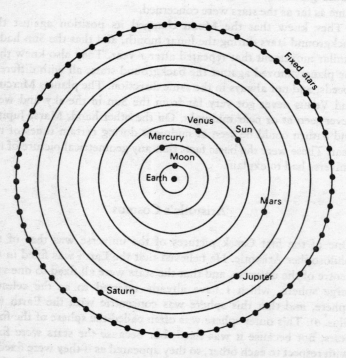

6 Aristotle's view of the universe.

the background stars, and the sphere of the Moon moved most, because the friction drive was least effective in this latter case, and the lunar sphere was in contact with a fixed Earth that further reduced the effectiveness of the drive. According to Aristotle, there was a prime mover, which was unmoved and the final cause of celestial movement, and this prime mover moved celestial objects in the same way people were moved by the Good. These heavenly objects were also the source of movement in the region below the Moon. God was the eternal, most good and unmoved mover.

Aristotle's cosmology also included two sets of physical laws, one for the region above the Moon – the superlunar region – and one for the region below the Moon – the sublunar region. In the superlunar region everything was perfect, motion had to be circular, there was no change (except cyclic change) and no corruption. It consisted of just one element: ether. In the sublunar region there was continual change, corruption, imperfection and motion in a straight line. Aristotle also thought that all things in the sublunar region were composed of four elements: earth, water, fire and air. These elements formed the basis of the astrological concept that the signs of the zodiac are divided into four groups that are to some extent typified by the quantities associated with these four elements.

Eudoxus and Ptolemy

This simple scheme of Aristotle could not explain the rather complex movements of the planets. In order to overcome the problems associated with these movements, Aristotle made use of a system of spheres invented by the astronomer Eudoxus, who had devised for each planet a set of spheres, nestling one within the other and pivoted about independent axes, rather like the gimbals of a ship's compass (see illus. 7). By giving each sphere an appropriate independent movement about its own axis, Eudoxus was able to simulate the movement of the planets. One great disadvantage of this scheme was that the planets were always on spheres that were concentric with the Earth, so they did not change their distances from Earth, yet it was known that the planets varied in brightness as they moved against the background stars.

Ptolemy was well aware of the problems of the scheme proposed by Aristotle and, because he wanted to make accurate planetary predictions for astrological purposes, he introduced various mathematical devices to overcome these problems. He suggested that each planet moved about its own small circle – called the epicycle – the centre of which orbited Earth in a circle called the deferent (see illus 8). He also introduced further technical refinements that are not relevant to this book.

Although the Aristotelian scheme may seem very far removed from our present knowledge of the solar system, it nevertheless lasted for over 1,000 years. It was important not only to astronomy and astrology but also to religious thought. Aristotle's cosmology

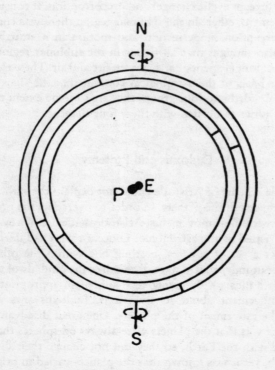

7 The spheres of Eudoxus.

was considered to represent physical reality, in spite of its limitations, while Ptolemy's refinements were considered to be merely mathematical devices useful for calculation, but not part of the pure and harmonious order represented by Aristotle's vision.

The Music of the Spheres

Although the mathematician Pythagoras did not himself develop the idea of the music of the spheres, the concept does have its origins in his work. He laid the basis of the idea of planetary ratios when he showed that intervals of the musical scale could be expressed as simple ratios. This was based on his experiments on the vibrating strings of musical instruments. Pythagoras applied these ratios to the supposed distances of the planets from Earth. He argued that since the ratios of the scales extended to the heavens, the whole sublunar sphere should echo to this heavenly music. This became known as the music of the spheres after Eudoxus formulated his own ideas on planetary motion.

After this initial work, several suggestions were put forward as to why this music was not heard in the sublunar region. Some thinkers claimed that we did not hear it because we were deafened by its perpetual sound, while others claimed that we heard it only in our sleep when our spirits were not so tightly bound to our

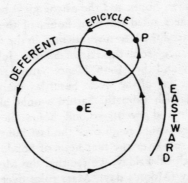

8 Ptolemy's mechanism for explaining planetary motion.

bodies. Pythagoras claimed that we did not hear it because our souls were out of harmony with the music of the superlunar regions.

As will be explained later in the book, my theory states that the Sun, Moon and planets play a complicated symphony on the magnetic field of Earth, and that different themes from this symphony are received by different developing foetuses because of genetic tuning. While the foetus is still in the womb, its normal sense organs are not yet fully effective, so it can pick up this music via its nervous system. After we are born, most of the information getting to our brain comes via our sensory receptors, and this information swamps the magnetic music under most circumstances. However, it is quite likely that we can respond in later life to those musical themes that are part of 'our tune' when they recur in the magnetic symphony of the solar system, especially in moments of reverie or when we are asleep. My theory does seem to indicate that the ancient philosophers wrought better than they knew. Why this might have been so will be explained later in the book.

Astrology, Astronomy and the Days of the Week

The naming of the days of the week was a rather complex mixture of astronomical and astrological ideas. It stems jointly from the ordering of the planets in decreasing distance from the Earth, the Egyptian day of 24 hours and the astrological belief that the Sun, Moon and planets ruled different hours of the day. The Greek astronomers placed the 'seven wanderers' in the following order of decreasing distance from the Earth: Saturn, Jupiter, Mars, Sun, Venus, Mercury and the Moon. Hence Saturn ruled over the first hour of the first day of the week, Saturday (Saturn's day), which was also the Jewish sabbath. Saturn would also rule over the eighth, fifteenth and twenty-second hours of Saturday, which means that Mars would reign over the last hour of Saturday and the Sun would rule over the first hour of Sunday. Following this sequence through till Friday, we see that the Moon rules the first hour of Monday (Moon's day), Mars rules over the first hour of Tuesday (Tyr's day, Tyr being the Teutonic equivalent of Mars),

Mercury over the first hour of Wednesday (Mercury's day – late Latin translation of the Old Norse Odin's day), Jupiter over the first hour of Thursday (late Latin Jupiter's day) and Venus over the first hour of Friday (Germanic translation of late Latin Venus's day, 'Veneris dies').

We thus see that many of our modern social conventions of time and the calendar have their origins in the ancient world.

Conclusion

In this chapter I have discussed the origins of astronomy and astrology, as well as some of the day-to-day practices, such as our calendar and time-keeping systems, which come from these subjects. I have also considered the relationship between ancient Greek cosmology, astronomy and astrology. Next we need to look at the most important twist in this history: the Copernican revolution.

4

From Astrology to the Mechanical Universe

*No man should hold it incredible that out of the astrologer's foolishness
and blasphemies some useful knowledge may come . . .*

Johann Kepler

Copernicus's decision to revive and refine a Greek idea of a Sun-
centred universe caused a revolution that had a profound effect on
all aspects of Western thought. In *The Copernican Revolution*,
Thomas S. Kuhn states:

> Initiated as a narrowly technical, highly mathematical re-
> vision of classical astronomy, the Copernican theory became
> one focus for the tremendous controversies in religion, in
> philosophy and in social theory which, during the two cen-
> turies following the discovery of America, set the tenor of the
> modern mind.[1]

It also had a very great effect on the relationship between astronomy
and astrology, and it was an important factor, though not the only
one, in the general decline of astrology.

We need to look at the work of those men at the centre of the
revolution, at its consequences, at its effect on astrology and at
the other factors that caused a decline in astrology and a change
in the direction of astronomy. We will also consider the attitude
of the astronomers of the revolution to astrology.

The Work of Copernicus

In the scheme proposed by Copernicus the Sun was at the centre of the solar system, and all the planets, including Earth, went around the Sun. The Copernican theory was able to explain the phenomena of day and night and the seasons in terms of an Earth spinning on its own axis once in 24 hours and going around the Sun in about 365.25 days. The apparent movement of the Sun against the background stars was easily explained in this theory. As the Earth went around the Sun, so, from the Earth, the Sun would seem to move against the background stars, assuming we could see the Sun and stars at the same time.

The Copernican theory was also able to explain more naturally the fact that the planets sometimes seem to move in one direction and sometimes in the opposite direction against the background stars. The planets Mercury and Venus, being closer to the Sun than Earth, will take less time to move once around the Sun, so sometimes they will overtake the Earth on the 'inside', and at other times they will be moving around 'the back' of the Sun as seen from Earth. This means that at these different times they will appear to move in different directions against the background stars. The outer planets – Mars, Jupiter and Saturn – move around the Sun further out than our Earth. At certain times Earth will overtake these planets on 'the inside', and at these times the outer planets will seem to move in the opposite direction to their normal motion.

Despite his boldness in moving the Earth from the centre of the universe, Copernicus was still very reluctant to dismiss most of the other ideas of Aristotle. He stuck rigidly to the Aristotelian concept of circular motion, and so to describe the detailed motion of the planets he had to resort to the use of epicycles and deferents, although this time the deferent had the Sun as centre, and the epicycles were much smaller than those of Ptolemy's scheme. He also did not want to give up a belief in Aristotle's laws of motion, and, since these were not consistent with a moving Earth, he had to produce highly artificial arguments in order to reconcile the two points of view. However, he had paved the way for an even more radical rethinking of the basic ideas of ancient science and astronomy.

The Contribution of Tycho Brahe

It was in 1572 that Tycho Brahe (1546–1601) made an impact on the world of astronomy when he discovered a nova, or new star. Such stars are not really new, but due to violent changes within them their brightness increases considerably over a few days, then after a longer period they seem to fade away. Quite often the original star that gave rise to the explosion was too faint to be seen with the naked eye, but the increase in brightness would have made it visible, so it is not surprising that to naked-eye astronomers it would have appeared as a new star. Brahe tried to estimate the distance to the nova by using a method called parallax. Before we look at the results of his estimate, it is necessary to describe, very briefly, the *method* of parallax.

Parallax is a consequence of the fact that light travels in straight lines, and it can be demonstrated very simply without any special instruments. With your arm stretched out, put your thumb upright, and then with your left eye closed and your right eye open note the position of your thumb with respect to the background. Now open your left eye and close your right eye. Your thumb will appear to have moved with respect to the background. This principle can be used to find the distances to celestial objects. If one had to photograph the Moon from two observatories almost on opposite sides of the Earth, at the same Greenwich Time, then the two photographs would show the Moon in slightly different positions against the background stars. This is also a result of parallax. It was this method that Brahe used to estimate the distance to the nova that he had discovered.

By combining his own observations with those of other observers in different countries, he was able to show that the nova that he discovered was much further away than the Moon. This was a serious blow to the Aristotelian point of view: Aristotle had taught that everything in the heavens was perfect, and yet here was a case of a new star flaring up, in a non-cyclic way, in the superlunar region.

He used this same line of reasoning to study the nature of comets. When a large comet appeared in the sky in 1577, Brahe studied it very carefully, and by combining his results with those of observers in other countries, he was also able to show that it existed in the superlunar sphere, and this was another blow to the world view of Aristotle. Until Edmund Halley discovered that some comets were periodic, no one had realized that there was anything cyclic about comets. This naturally was also the case in Aristotle's day, and, since he saw comets as erratic and irregular visitors to our skies, he placed them in our own atmosphere rather than in the superlunar sphere of perfection. By showing that the comet of 1577 was beyond the sphere of the Moon, Brahe had once again shown that Aristotle was wrong.

Despite the fact that he had found things wrong with Aristotle's ideas, Brahe still accepted many of the basic concepts of the Aristotelian universe. He still believed in a fixed Earth, so he invented his own modification to the scheme suggested by Copernicus. In his scheme the Earth was fixed, the Sun went around the Earth, and all the planets went around the Sun. Thus he was able to retain the merits of the Copernican scheme, while still having a fixed Earth.

The Planetary Laws of Johann Kepler

Central to the laws of planetary motion formulated by Kepler are the basic properties of the geometric figure called the ellipse. An ellipse is rather like a flattened circle. A line drawn from the centre of a circle to the circumference (such a line is called a radius) always has the same length, no matter in which direction it is drawn. With an ellipse, this length will depend on the direction in which it is drawn. Suppose we have an ellipse with its long axis (called its major axis) pointing in an east–west direction. A line from the centre of the ellipse to the east (or west) will have a maximum length, whereas a line drawn from the centre to the north (or south) will have a minimum length. At two points along the major axis, at equal distances from the centre, are the foci of the ellipse. These foci have an important property: if two lines are drawn from the same point on the curve of the ellipse to each of these foci, the sum of the lengths of these two lines will always be the same, no matter from which point on the curve these lines are drawn.

Kepler's First Law (see illus. 9) says that all the planets go around the Sun in elliptical orbits, with the Sun at one of the foci of each ellipse that is used to represent the orbit of a planet. His Second Law says that a line drawn from the Sun to a planet will sweep out equal areas in equal times as the planet goes around the Sun (see illus. 10). This means that a planet moves faster when it is closer to the Sun than when it is far from the Sun. The Third Law states that the time it takes a planet to complete one orbit is related to its distance from the Sun. So, those planets close to the Sun take a shorter time to complete one orbit than those far from the Sun. For example, it takes Mercury 88 Earth days to go once around the Sun, whereas it takes Uranus 84 Earth years to orbit the Sun once. The reason for this Third Law is not simply that the orbit is larger, but also because the planets further from the Sun are moving more slowly along their orbits.

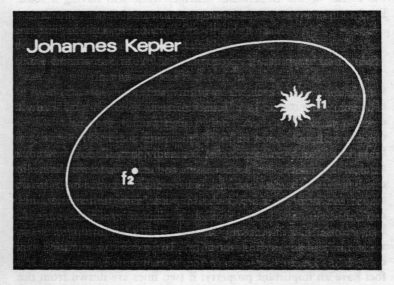

9 The properties of the ellipse. F_1 and F_2 are called the foci. The sum of the distances $F_1 P$ and $F_2 P$ is always constant, no matter where P is on the ellipse.

Even before Kepler formulated these laws, his physical intuition had led him to introduce forces emanating from the Sun and planets to provide a causal foundation for planetary motion. The first of Kepler's solar forces was the *anima motrix*. According to Kepler, this was a force that pushed the planets around their orbits by a system of rays, radiating out from the Sun. These rays, he believed, were restricted very closely to a plane in which most of the planets moved. He reasoned that the number of rays that impinged on a planet, and hence the corresponding force that drove the planet around the Sun, would decrease as the distance between the planet and the Sun increased. In his *anima motrix* Kepler very vaguely anticipated the interplanetary magnetic field, which, as we have already seen, is carried by the solar wind. The similarities are that they both originate from the Sun, that they are both nearly confined to the plane in which most of the planets

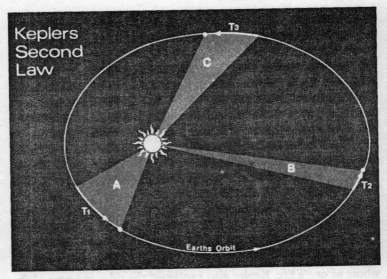

10 As a planet goes round the Sun, it sweeps out equal areas in equal times. This is Kepler's Second Law of Planetary Motion.

move, and the number impinging on a planet will decrease with the distance of the planet from the Sun. The differences are that the lines of force of the interplanetary magnetic field are curved, it consists of four sectors, with the field pointing in the same direction in alternate sectors, and whereas Kepler's *anima motrix* was supposed to influence the movement of the planets, the actual interplanetary magnetic field does not do so.

Kepler again anticipated some modern ideas with his intro-duction of magnetism. In this he was influenced by the publication in 1600 of *On the Magnet* by William Gilbert. Gilbert had re-cognized that the Earth itself was a magnet, and Kepler reasoned that not only the Earth but also the Sun and the other planets were all huge magnets. He further reasoned that the attractions and repulsions of their various poles determined the paths in which the planets moved. The Sun, Mercury, Jupiter and Saturn do have magnetic fields, so of the 'seven wanderers' known to Kepler, four have been shown to have magnetic fields, and the Moon also has some permanent magnetism.

Kepler's mathematical laws have survived for more than three centuries, but his physical ideas lasted no longer than he did. Some of his ideas on dynamics were already out of date when he proposed them. The Sun rotates too slowly to account for the observed periods of the planets. We also now know that the magnetic fields of the planets are not strong enough, and they are not orientated in the right direction, for them to do what Kepler was proposing.

Kepler's involvement with astrology will be discussed in more detail later in this chapter, but here I just want to draw attention to some of his thoughts on how astrology works, because they antici-pate in some way the concepts incorporated into my own theory. In his theory for astrological aspects, the geometrically formed human soul created the zodiac as a projection of itself. According to him, the heavenly bodies travelling along the zodiac produced an excite-ment within our souls whenever they formed angles corresponding to those of the regular polygons. He believed that the planetary configurations at birth remained impressed on the soul for the whole of one's life. Kepler also explained the tides in terms of the Moon's attraction.

The Telescopic Observations of Galileo Galilei

Galileo was convinced by the Copernican scheme and did much to promote its acceptance. His most important work in this connection was his use of telescopes to study the Sun, Moon, the planets and the stars. He then used his observations to support the Copernican scheme, and to demolish the other rival theories that stood in its way.

In 1609 Galileo heard that a device, consisting of two tubes with lenses at either end, had been invented in Holland, and that with this instrument it was possible to get closer views of distant objects. Within a few months of hearing this report, Galileo had made his own telescope, and with this he made a number of discoveries that undermined still further the universe of Aristotle and the Ptolemaic spheres, and also strengthened belief in the Copernican scheme.

Galileo discovered that the surface of the Moon was full of craters and mountains, and that it resembled, to some extent, the surface of the Earth. This provided still further evidence that Aristotle's idea of perfection in the heavens was wrong. The sphere of the Moon had been considered as part of the superlunar region, so it should have reflected the qualities associated with this part of the universe. He also discovered dark patches on the Sun, which we now call sunspots. Here was another example of imperfection in the heavens. Galileo also discovered that Jupiter had four moons, which he could see with his telescope, and that these moons circled the planet. Here was a very good example that there were bodies in the universe that circled around an object other than the Earth. The fact that Venus showed phases – similar to the phases of the Moon – was another of his important discoveries. This particular one showed quite clearly that Venus was going around the Sun. Aristotle had taught that the irregular and amorphous features of the Milky Way meant that it had to be part of our atmosphere, and he discussed it in his book on meteorology rather than in his work on astronomy. Galileo showed that the Milky Way consisted of a very large number of stars, and, since these stars showed no parallax, they must lie well beyond the outer planets. Thus by providing a new tool for astronomers, and using it with such great effect, Galileo was to give a tremendous boost to the reform of astronomy as a science.

The Universe of Isaac Newton

The work of Isaac Newton (1642–1727) was far more radical than that of any of his predecessors, because his laws were universal; that is, they could be applied to all large-scale phenomena everywhere in the universe. They were valid, unlike the laws of motion of Aristotle, in the sublunar and the superlunar region. They not only applied to planets, like Kepler's laws of motion, but they were, and still are, applicable to all physical phenomena larger than atoms and the collective groupings of atoms that we call molecules. This is an extremely important point, because at last it was possible to apply physical laws discovered in the laboratory to celestial situations. They also made it possible to discover new physical laws that could be useful to terrestrial science in an astronomical context, and Newton's own work on motion and gravity provides us with the first example. This point is important because it means that the whole universe can be used as a physical laboratory to complement terrestrial research into fundamental physics. It also means that laboratory physics can be used to decode celestial messages from the Sun, Moon, planets and stars. So what were Newton's three laws of motion?

The First Law: A body continues in a state of rest or uniform motion in a straight line unless it is acted on by a force that would tend to change that state of rest or uniform motion.

The Second Law: The rate at which a body changes its speed (if it is moving in a straight line) or the rate at which it changes direction (if it is moving at a constant speed) depends on the strength of the force exerted on it and on its mass.

The Third Law: If one body exerts a force on another body, the second body will exert a force on the first that is equal in strength but in the opposite direction.

Newton's law of gravitation states that every particle in the universe attracts every other particle, and that this force of attraction is proportional to the masses of both bodies, and it gets very much weaker as the distance between the bodies is increased.

The law of gravitation is not, in itself, sufficient to explain planetary motion; it has to be combined with the laws of motion. We have already seen that according to one of these laws, bodies tend to move in straight lines unless they have forces acting on them. We are all familiar with the consequences of this law when we drive around a corner in a car. The car (and our bodies) really wish to continue in a straight line, but the forces of the road on the wheels, and the wheels on the car, impel the car to change direction when we turn the steering wheel. A planet in the solar system, like any other body, has a tendency to travel in a straight line. However, the force of gravity acting between the planet and the Sun causes the planet to 'fall' towards the Sun, and we say it orbits the Sun. Similarly, the Moon and all artificial satellites are really 'falling' towards the Earth. However, orbiting bodies do not actually 'fall' and hit the surface of the body being orbited. This is because the body being orbited, i.e., the Sun or the Earth, is spherical and the surface is constantly curving away from the orbiting body.

Newton's laws of motion and his law of gravitation were thus able to explain the movements of the planets around the Sun, the movements of moons around the planets, and the tides. Their impact on astronomy was tremendous and they still continue to play a major role in many of our efforts to understand the structure and evolution of several parts of the universe.

Newton's work on celestial mechanics, and indeed some of the work of his predecessors, was very closely linked with the development of astronomy for the purposes of navigation – the branch of the subject known as nautical astronomy. Nautical astronomy also played a large part in the change of emphasis in other branches of astronomy, and it caused a further decline in the general interest in astrology.

The Haven-finding Art

In J. D. Bernal's monumental work, *Science in History*, he had this to say about the great voyages of discovery: 'These were the fruit of the first conscious application of astronomical and geographical science to the service of glory and profit.'[2]

The Portuguese had much to do with the new methods of navigation. They set courses until the appropriate latitude was found by observations of the stars, and then, sailing due east or west, they 'ran down' the latitude until it was hoped that landmarks for entry to a port could be sighted straight ahead. At first they found latitude by using the Pole Star, or North Star. This method worked reasonably well in the northern hemisphere, but as this star was not visible in the southern hemisphere, and as there was also no southern equivalent of this star, they had to develop methods for using the Sun. Since the Portuguese made frequent voyages across the equator, they had to undertake detailed observations of the Sun so that they could perfect this method. Although these methods could be used to find latitude – how far north or south you were from the equator – they could not be used to find longitude, i.e., how far east or west you were from some given reference point. It was the longitude problem that was to tax astronomical methods to the limit. In another part of his book, Bernal states that 'The motion of the stars now had a cash value and astronomy stood in no danger of being neglected, even after astrology had gone out of fashion.'

In 1667 Louis XIV of France set up the Paris Observatory. The main purpose of this institution was to improve our understanding of the shape of the Earth, and for the general improvement of maps and charts. This naturally meant that some method of finding longitude had to be worked out. Basically it is, in principle, easy to find longitude if you can find time by two independent astronomical methods. In the last chapter we saw that it was possible to find time using the positions of certain stars. However, another method of finding time had to be found in order to calculate longitude. Soon after making his discovery of the moons of Jupiter, Galileo noted that these moons constituted another clock in the sky, so they could be used to find longitude. Giovanni Cassini, the first director of the Paris Observatory, decided to develop this method. Once the latitude and longitude of Paris had been established, a survey of the whole of France was put in hand. Many coastal positions were fixed in relation to the position of Paris, allowing the whole coastline to be redrawn by 1681. It is rumoured that this redrawing did not please the king, since it turned out that France was smaller than it was shown to be on previous, less accurate maps. He accused the astronomers of depriving him of some of his kingdom.

Cassini's method of determining longitude could not be used at sea, because it required a telescope on a suitable mounting to observe the satellites of Jupiter, and this was impossible on board a ship. It is for this reason that other methods were sought. Sieur de St Pierre, a young Frenchman, suggested to King Charles II of England that the Moon moving against the background stars could serve as a clock for finding longitude. This method required an accurate knowledge of the positions of the fixed stars and the movement of the Moon against these stars, and to obtain this knowledge Charles II set up the Royal Observatory in Greenwich Park, and appointed the Revd John Flamsteed as 'our astronomical observator, forthwith to apply himself with the most exact care and diligence to the rectifying of the tables of motions of the heavens, and the places of the fixed stars, so as to find out the so-much desired longitude of places for perfecting the art of navigation'.

The method of using the position of the Moon against the background stars to find longitude became known as the lunar distance method, and it made greater demands on astronomy than any of its other previous social uses. John Flamsteed set about equipping the Royal Observatory with telescopes fitted with accurately engraved circles, so that he could measure the positions of the stars as precisely as possible. The improved observations made by Flamsteed were very useful to Newton, since he could use these data to test his theories in celestial mechanics with far greater accuracy than was possible with previous information. On the other hand, Newton's improved mathematical techniques and his theories on celestial motion provided the framework for calculating the position of the Moon, and it became possible to construct sets of tables for the Moon's motion. Armed with such a set of tables, called the nautical almanac, and a sextant, for measuring angles, a seaman could work out his latitude and longitude with respect to the Greenwich Observatory. Thus it was the demands of navigation – requiring greater accuracy of observations and of theories – that formed the bridge between the old type of naked-eye astronomy and the more scientific approach to the subject that is so character-istic of modern astronomy.

Astrology and the Astronomers

It is often claimed by some astrologers that all the astronomers discussed earlier in this chapter were themselves astrologers.[3] The historical evidence shows that although this was true in some cases, it is by no means generally true. We will briefly consider the evidence for each of the astronomers involved in the Copernican revolution.

Derek and Julia Parker claim that Copernicus was an astrologer. They claim that the fact that Copernicus had well-thumbed works on astrology in his library indicates that he had an interest in the subject. This could well be the case, but this interest could have been a result of an interest in the roots of his own studies, and this evidence in no way implies that he had a commitment to the subject. They call attention to the fact that a German astronomer, Rhaeticus, one of Copernicus's first converts to the new scheme, wrote an early report on Copernicus's work that had astrological undertones, but there is no evidence that he wrote it under 'the older man's direct supervision'. A more balanced account of the matter is to be found in *The Sleepwalkers* by Arthur Koestler,[4] in a section on '*Narratio Prima*: The First Account' (the name by which Rhaeticus's early report came to be known). 'In between, Rhaeticus inserted an astrological digression in which the rise and fall of the Roman and Muslim empires, and the Second Coming of Christ, are made directly dependent on changes in the eccentricity of the Earth's orbit.' Koestler also says that: 'Copernicus himself did not seem to have believed in astrology, but Rhaeticus did . . . and Schoener [the person to whom 'The First Account' was addressed] did . . . and since the digression . . . about the Second Coming was calculated to please them, Copernicus apparently raised no objec-tions.'

Also with regard to Copernicus, Thomas S. Kuhn writes in *The Copernican Revolution*: 'It may even be significant that Copernicus, the author of the theory that ultimately deprived the heavens of special power, belonged to the minority group of Renaissance astronomers who did not cast horoscopes.'

With Kepler, astrology was a different matter. He did actually practise astrology and he did cast horoscopes. In fact, he ended his career as the Court Astrologer to the Duke of Wallenstein. He practised astrology partly because he needed to earn his keep and partly because he had leanings towards mysticism, and astrology fitted in with his view that the movement of the heavenly bodies should have some effect on terrestrial events and human destiny. However, he was not entirely happy with astrology as it was in his day. At one stage he wrote that 'A mind accustomed to mathematical deduction, when confronted with the faulty foundations [of astrology] resists a long, long time, like an obstinate mule, until compelled by beating and curses to put its foot into that dirty puddle.'

The most sympathetic treatment of Kepler's ambiguous attitude to astrology is that given by Arthur Koestler in *The Sleepwalkers*: 'To a questing mind without an inkling of the processes by which heredity and environment shape a man's character, astrology ... was the obvious means of relating the individual to the universal whole ... by establishing an intimate sympathy and correspondence between microcosmos and macrocosmos.' Later in the same section Koestler says: 'In a word, astrological determinism, to a scientific mind like Kepler's, was the forerunner of biological and psychological determinism.' But I think that the last words should be left to Kepler himself: 'No man should hold it incredible that out of the astrologer's foolishness and blasphemies some useful knowledge may come.'

The factual evidence for this statement is provided by the development of planetary astronomy from Ptolemy to Copernicus, by the formulation of Kepler's own laws of planetary motion and, indeed, by the whole of the Copernican revolution and its aftermath. As Kuhn says: 'Astrology therefore provided the principal motive for wrestling with the problem of the planets.'

Koestler is much less sympathetic to Tycho Brahe. 'Like Kepler,

Brahe stood with one foot in the past and was devoted both to alchemy and astrology. Like Kepler, he became a court astrologer ... like Kepler, he did it with his tongue in his cheek ... Unlike Kepler's, however, his belief in astrology derived not from mysticism – which was completely alien to his domineering nature – but from stark superstition.' This assessment of Brahe is rather harsh, and not entirely justified, since he did produce a religious argument in defence of astrology.

Brahe's defence of astrology was mentioned by T. G. Cowling, one time Professor of Mathematics at the University of Leeds, in the Fifth Milne Lecture, 'Astrology, Religion and Science', delivered at the Oxford Mathematical Institute in November 1981:

> In 1574 he [Brahe] produced a defence of astrology in terms that Ptolemy would not have disowned. He argued that God would never have created the countless heavenly bodies without a purpose. The Sun was responsible for the four seasons, the Moon for tides, and the fixed stars were useful in navigation. The near approach of two planets had on occasion been attended by storms or pestilence; clearly, then, the use of the planets was for predictive purposes.

Cowling also investigated a story, often told by astrologers, about Newton's involvement with astrology. According to this story, Edmund Halley chastised Newton on one occasion for taking an interest in astrology. Newton is reported to have replied: 'Sir, I have studied the matter, you have not.' With the help of Newtonian scholars at Cambridge, Cowling tried to trace the origin of this story. It now turns out that the context of the remark had been misquoted. Apparently Halley had criticized Newton for his interest in the Christian religion and the Bible, and Newton's retort was in reply to this criticism.[5]

Galileo went to the other extreme in his dislike of astrology, and dismissed Kepler's theory that the tides were affected by the Moon as 'occult and astrological nonsense'. It was left to Newton to give scientific respectability to this idea of Kepler's.

In seeking approval for astrology from the astronomers of the Copernican revolution, astrologers show that they have not critically examined the evidence, and also misunderstood the history and nature of science. In the past many great scientists have had theories and ideas for which there was only limited scientific evidence in their day, but which were nevertheless part of the intellectual climate of their times. Kepler's and Brahe's belief in astrology should be seen in this light. Science makes progress not on the basis of beliefs of scientists, but by building on those aspects of this science that have, over the years, withstood the tests of observation and experiment. This is what I did when I constructed my theory for certain concepts of astrology.

Conclusion

The schism between astronomy and astrology that took place soon after the general acceptance of the Copernican view of the universe occurred for several reasons. First, there was the revolution itself. Copernicus placed the Sun at the centre of the universe, and realized that Earth was one of the orbiting planets, and this of course completely changed the unique position of Earth that was vital to Aristotle, Ptolemy and astrology. Newton's law of gravitation and the laws of motion showed that, although every particle in the universe attracts every other particle, gravitation is greatly weakened by distance. Therefore the Sun, Moon, planets and stars could not conceivably affect life on Earth in the direct ways astrologers seemed to believe they could.

The application of astronomy to the problems of navigation was another factor in the decline of astrology. Many astronomers in different countries found that royal powers were willing to fund their work, because improved navigational methods based on astronomy were useful for trade and defence. Certain other social innovations entailed a decrease in status for astrology. Improved communications meant, for example, that relatives or friends could contact each other without needing to ask astrologers for information on their well-being. Whereas a ship-owner might have relied on astrological prediction to plan safe journeys for his ships, the introduction of insurance companies changed his reliance on this type of information.

We have seen some of the complexities of the history of astronomy, but there are questions still to answer: so much of the origin of astrology is left unsolved by the documentary evidence. As I unveil my theory, it will be clear that my work overcomes many of these problems. So onwards, to the skirmishes of science and astrology..

5

Science and Astrology

As a pseudoscience, astrology is considered to be diametrically opposed to the findings and theories of modern Western science.

Encyclopaedia Britannica

So what of current attitudes to astrology? Let's look at them with particular reference to those that highlight the deep divisions between the scientific and astrological approaches.

Newspaper Astrology

Several newspapers, some scientists, many people and all astrologers have attitudes to astrology. These attitudes vary a great deal, not only from one group to the next but also within each group. There is even a great deal of argument among astrologers themselves about the techniques used in practice, and there is even more disagreement about whether their subject has a scientific basis or whether it is an ancient form of divination that has nothing to do with science. Most astrologers, however, would agree with the statement made by Lyall Watson in his book *Supernature*:

> For a start, we can disregard the popular newspaper version of astrology altogether. Glib, all-embracing predictions, in which everyone born under Pisces will have a good day for making new plans ... have nothing to do with astrology. They are held in well-deserved contempt by both astrologers and their critics.[1]

89

According to their attitudes to astrology, newspapers can be divided into three main groups. The first group consists of those who support, by commissioning daily horoscopes, the type of astrology condemned in Lyall Watson's statement. The second group consists of those that, for the most part, ignore astrology, or occasionally carry uncritical reports of scientific tests that claim to disprove all of astrology. By far the smallest group is made up of those papers that are willing to discuss seriously the possibility that some evidence does exist for some parts of astrology, and that there may well be a scientific basis for these branches of the subject. The editors of these papers challenge the attitudes of orthodox science, which say there is no way in which astrology can work, and they also respect the intellectual ability of their readership by exposing them to challenging ideas.

Why does the first group continue to carry daily horoscopes that do not have the support of anyone seriously interested in the subject, including astrologers themselves? One reason is that the world view presented by astrology, in which life is an integral part of the cosmic whole, is much more comfortable and humane than the world view of modern science and astronomy, in which life occurs almost by accident in a largely hostile universe. Another reason is that the astrology based on the position of the Sun along the zodiac, the so-called Sun-sign astrology of the newspapers, is the easiest and most straightforward way of presenting horoscopes in daily or weekly form, even if they are virtually useless.

Science and Astrology

Science plays an important part in our lives. The medical and biological sciences produce important research results that are vital to our understanding and conquering of diseases, and for improving our health. Our lives are full of technological equipment, from home computers to satellite television, that is based on scientific principles. Scientific evidence is an important part of our legal system, and many a case has been won or lost on the basis of evidence given by pathologists or forensic scientists. It is not surprising, then, that for many people science represents some sort of truth about the world we inhabit. Is this really the case, and are scientists really honest, dispassionate, unbiased searchers after truth? The facts of the matter are that scientists are not unbiased and dispassionate, and their belief in a particular theory can cause them to be intellectually dishonest on some occasions. This is nowhere more apparent than in the attitude of most scientists to astrology.

Scientific Arguments against Astrology

The most detailed collection of arguments against astrology to date is *The Gemini Syndrome* by Culver and Ianna, which was mentioned in Chapter 1. In this book they calculate the gravitational tug of the Sun, Moon, planets, the hospital building, the mother and the doctor on the child at birth, using Newton's law of gravitation. These calculations show that the tug of the Sun is almost one million times stronger than that of Mars, while the tug of the Moon is about 5,000 times that of Mars. They also show that the tug of the hospital building is about 500 times that of Mars, whereas the tug of mother and doctor on the child is 20 and 6 times that of Mars respectively. Jupiter and Venus are the only two planets that have comparable tugs to these two people.

They do a similar calculation for the tidal forces of all these bodies on the child at birth. Tidal effects are also due to gravitational tugs, but they depend on these tugs in a more complicated way. They are really a measure of how the force of gravity changes from one place to the next. Thus in the case of the tidal effects of the Moon on the oceans, it measures how the gravitational tug varies from one side of Earth to the other. Their calculations show that the tidal effect of the Moon, which, because of its closeness to Earth, is greater than that of the Sun, is more than a million times less than that of the mother and doctor.

They also produce a table showing that the energy from the Sun, mainly in the form of heat and light, is stronger than that of a 200-watt bulb 2 metres from the child by a factor of about 1,000, but the bulb, on the other hand, is stronger than the radiation from any of the planets or even the full Moon. Thus they argue that local effects in most cases will swamp the weak celestial effects, with the exception, sometimes, of the Sun and Moon. They conclude from this that there is no way in which the planets can play a part. This is very typical of the general type of argument used by scientists. What they have done is to propose a rather naïve single-link theory, and, having shown that this cannot work, reached the conclusion that all other theories must of necessity be excluded. This is in spite of the fact that they are aware of other ways in which the Sun, Moon and planets do affect parts of our physical environment, and these parts can, in turn, affect life on Earth. In other words, they have refused to think of other possibilities and more complex theories, which is what many scientists do when faced with similar problems, which do not involve astrology.

An article germane to the views held by science appeared in the very prestigious scientific journal *Nature*, described by *The Times* as the heavy-weight of world scientific journals. In 1985 it carried a seven-page article on a scientific test carried out by a physicist, Shawn Carlson, at the University of California. This physicist concludes that 'Their [astrologers'] predicted connection between the positions of the planets and other astronomical objects at the time of birth and the personalities of test subjects did not exist. The experiment clearly refutes the astrological hypothesis.'[2]

The theory that I have constructed leads me to conclude that astrology, as practised by most astrologers, is a highly embroidered version of some basic scientific principles, and what Carlson tested was the embroidery, not the principles. To dismiss astrology on this basis would be the same as dismissing the historical facts and basic teachings of Christianity on the basis of the highly embroidered doctrines of the various Christian Churches.

The editors of *Nature* supplied a booklist with Carlson's article, under the heading 'Scientists wishing to familiarize themselves with astrology as astrologers practise it may find the following works useful'. The booklist is very dated and some of the books do not do what the editors claim they do. Three of the books, two of which are by the French psychologist Michel Gauquelin, are highly critical of conventional astrology, and readers would be hard-pressed to find out about current astrological practices from these works. It is as if the editors picked out these books at random from a booklist on astrology, with no idea of their contents. One of the books, *Recent Advances in Natal Astrology*, by Dean and Mather, says that 'much of astrology's apparent validity arose out of the gullibility of practitioners and clients alike'. On the other hand, they add: 'Not all is fallacious. Enough remains that cannot be explained by gullibility or coincidence to justify further study.' Eysenck and Nias had reached similar conclusions, as did Gauquelin, several years ago. The article made no mention of the work of these three scientists.

The orthodox scientific view, I repeat, is that astrology just cannot work.[3] We must not forget that. A variety of reasons are put forward to back this point of view. It is pointed out that the gravitational pull of the doctor, or midwife, on the child at birth is greater than that of the Sun, Moon or any of the planets. It is shown that the lights in the delivery room are stronger than the radiation we receive from the planets. In other words, scientists set up a very simple theory, then they shoot down their own theory, and from this they conclude that no scientific theory can be constructed to explain any part of astrology. This is the view passed on from one generation of scientists to the next. As a trained physicist and astronomer, this is the view I picked up from my tutors, lecturers and colleagues. This is the view I held until about 1986. It is this view that has caused astrologers, although many do not admit it, to propose other methods by which astrology could, perhaps, work.

How Astrology Works – by Astrologers

Undiscovered Forces

Julia Parker, sometime President of the British Faculty of Astrological Studies, wrote *A History of Astrology* with her husband Derek. In their book they discuss the attitude of N. Oresme, a theological student from Paris who later became the Bishop of Lisieux, to astrology. It makes stimulating reading:

One point he [Oresme] makes very clearly is one that would

appeal to most modern astrologers: he disclaims that the planets or stars could have any occult effect on man. If there is an influence, he says, it must be material – the result of light and heat, he thought. Modern astrologers would mostly say, rather, that any planetary effect is the result of some very real but so far unfathomed force (similar in nature to that of gravity), but would agree with Oresme that whatever the force is, it is certainly not occult.

Most physicists and astronomers do not at the moment see the necessity of introducing a new force. At the moment we know of four different forces: the force of gravitation, the electromagnetic force (which consists of electricity and magnetism), and two nuclear forces. A great deal of current interest in theoretical physics is centred on unifying all these forces into one superforce, and in recent months a great deal of progress has been made in this direction. Although a group of physicists have claimed to have discovered a fifth force, the experiments on which they based their conclusions will have to be replicated before scientists will wish to change the current state of affairs. A great deal of the astronomical, physical, chemical and biological worlds (including biological behaviour) can be understood in terms of these forces. This means that the hope of finding a new force that can explain astrological effects is rather remote at the moment.

However, in many ways, this is the most palatable of the many different attitudes of astrologers to their subject. It at least tries to see astrology in scientific terms, even if it does require a modification or extension of the current world view. I met Julia and Derek Parker at the Urania Trust conference that I mentioned at the start of the book. Both the Parkers said they enjoyed the talk I had given, because they had always felt that some physical mechanism could be used to explain astrological effects. This is indeed in keeping with the statements they have made in their books on the subject.

An Alternative Reality

Some astrologers have tried to see astrology as an alternative

94

reality to the reality of science. They argue that modern physics makes use of two separate levels of reality: quantum reality, in which strict determinism is not always observed, and classical or Newtonian reality, which is strictly deterministic. These arguments are quite often produced by astrologers who have not studied, or not understood, the nature of quantum physics. The whole universe obeys quantum laws, but on the large scale the non-determinism of quantum physics approximates to determinism to a very high degree of accuracy. In other words, Newton's laws of motion are incorporated in the laws of quantum mechanics. They also point out that quantum mechanics allows the instantaneous interaction between two subatomic particles separated by a large distance – a result called Bell's Theorem – and argue that if this can happen between two subatomic particles, why can it not happen between a planet and a person? In support of this, they point out that some planetary effects in astrology are almost instantaneous. More often than not, these suggestions show that the astrologers have misunderstood the physics of the situation. Quantum mechanics tells us that we cannot know both the speed and position of a subatomic particle at the same time. This result is called Heisenberg's Uncertainty Principle.

A staunch supporter of the alternative reality approach is Dennis Elwell. Many of his views are contained in his book *The Cosmic Loom: The New Science of Astrology*.[4] Elwell's mistake, I think, was to desert his alternative reality approach, and to seek a justification for astrology in terms of the most recent results from the frontiers of theoretical physics. When he starts talking about science, he shows that he has misunderstood the methodology, the nature, history and content of science. In his discussion of the astrological links between the planets and metals, he says: 'Modern science looks on these ascriptions as entirely fanciful, although it can be shown that atomic numbers (which the ancients knew nothing about) and other properties of metals form sequences which are directly related to the orbital periods of the planets, a somewhat remarkable "coincidence".' There is absolutely no sense in which this is true, no matter how one juggles the numbers. The orbital periods of the planets do not follow any simple sequences of numbers. At one time it was thought that the distances of the planets from the Sun followed a simple numerical sequence, a result known as Bode's Law. It is only approximately true for some of the planets, and even if it were exactly true, it would not have given a simple sequence for orbital periods, because of the way these periods are related to distances from the Sun. When the ancients made this connection, there were seven planets and seven metals. We now know of over eighty metals and nine planets. The periodic table of elements, as drawn up by the Russian chemist Dmitri Ivanovich Mendeleev (1834–1907), could be used by him to deduce correctly the properties of some elements that had not yet been discovered in his day. We have also seen that Newton's law of gravity was used by Adams and Leverrier to find the planet Neptune from the abnormal behaviour of Uranus. Thus scientifically formulated laws can be used to make precise predictions. Astrology failed to give any hint of other planets or of undiscovered elements.

In his book Elwell talks of Bell's Theorem:

And what is Bell's Theorem saying? It says that not only in the subatomic realm but at the macroscopic level – the level of puppy dogs and London omnibuses – there are no 'separate parts', because what we deem parts are, in fact, associated. By their mathematically demonstrable connectedness Bell proved that events in the world at large must be behaving very differently from our common-sense view of them.

Unfortunately, Bell's Theorem presents astrology with more new problems, rather than solving the old ones. It does tell us that everything is connected to everything else, instantaneously. It also shows that this interaction is not weakened by distance, and it does not involve the sizes of the interacting parts. This means that all the one hundred thousand million stars that form the Milky Way, most of which we do not see, play just as important a part as the planets and stars, which we do. It also means that all the other galaxies in the universe are involved, which is just as important, even if we cannot see them with the unaided eye. This means that in order to predict what is happening at the local level, we must know about what is happening in the far reaches of our universe. Bell's work does not help us to understand why only the objects close to us, and which we can see, should play a part in astrological prediction.

Astrology without a Cause

A third suggestion proposes that astrology works without a cause – that is, acausally. A scientist who supports this approach to astrology is Michael Shallis, an astrophysicist from Oxford University. In his book *On Time* he says: 'Astrology is an acausal system, even though it contains the continuity of the causally connected motions of the planets. To search for its origins and power by looking at those causal parts, is of course a mistake and an ignorant mistake.' Further along he says: 'Whereas many critics of astrology attack it on the grounds that there can be no sensible causal connection between a person on Earth and the actual planets, the truth of the situation lies in the acausal correspondence between an apparently random moment in time, the time of any event, and the exact but relative positions of the planets at that time. There is no causal connection.' He claims that 'astrology works because each planet, each angular interrelationship or aspect between the planets, each zodiac sign, each house and even each degree of the zodiac, all have special qualities or essences, that, once known, can be interpreted'.[5]

Shallis's view that astrology is acausal does not take account of a great deal concerning the history of astrology and the history of science. When astrology first started, it embraced all aspects of human destiny and terrestrial events. It was used to predict the weather, and terrestrial disasters such as earthquakes. With the progress of science, our knowledge of the workings of atmosphere and Earth has improved, and we can, at least in principle, forecast weather with some accuracy, and a day may well come when we can do the same for earthquakes. The search for causal connections has been the mainspring of science, and if scientists in the past had accepted the viewpoint that Shallis supports, then not much progress would have been made. Fortunately for us, they did not.

Carl Jung was one of the first people to develop the idea of an acausal connecting principle. After drawing attention to the possible link between the sunspot cycle, the mortality curve and the effects of the planets on the solar cycle, he says, with reference to acausal astrology: 'One would therefore do well not to regard the results of astrological observations as synchronistic phenomena, but to take them as possibly causal in origin. For, wherever a cause is even remotely thinkable, synchronicity becomes an exceedingly doubtful proposition.'[6]

Astrologers and the Scientific Method

Those astrologers who say that the scientific method can do nothing for astrology are denying the possibility that it can be used to correct and improve astrology. Fortunately, some of the great astrologers of this century were, and are, aware that not all is well with astrology, and have taken steps, and are taking further steps, that involve research to improve the age-old practices.

The late John Addey is considered by many to be one of the greatest astrologers of this century. In 1976 he published a book entitled *Harmonics in Astrology*, in which he set out the theory on which he had been working for several years. This theory puts forward the principle that 'all astrology is based on the harmonics of cosmic periods'. Many astrologers all over the world saw this work as the most far-reaching contribution to the techniques of astrology for centuries, and he was honoured by astrological bodies in the East and the West. Despite his great knowledge of, and contributions to, astrology, he was quite aware that the subject was in some difficulty, and he had the intellectual integrity to say so: 'No doubt some will say that astrology is perfectly all right as it stands and needs no radical re-examination, yet the truth is that no science or body of knowledge can be effectively applied unless and until its constituent elements can be clearly distinguished and defined, and this state of affairs does not yet pertain in the field of astrology.'[7]

He also criticizes those students of astrology who dismiss the study of natural cycles (cosmic, geophysical and biological) as being of no relevance to astrology: 'This is a misunderstanding of the nature of astrology. Astrology always and everywhere deals directly with nature – nature and its operations through the cryptic order, upon matter; nature in mankind; nature in the individual man; nature in the "natural" world.'

Conclusion

The many modern attitudes to astrology differ considerably, not only from one group to the next but also within the groups themselves. We have looked at some scientific arguments against astrology, and how these arguments have been countered by astrologers. The scientific theory proposed and developed in this book provides scientific criteria for judging the relative merits of these conflicting points of view. And we must start with a closer look at the Earth itself.

6

Cosmic Earth

I . . . believe that there is one philosophical problem in which all thinking men are interested. It is the problem of cosmology: the problem of understanding the world – including ourselves, and our knowledge, as part of the world. All science is cosmology, I believe, and for me the interest of philosophy, no less than of science, lies solely in the contributions which it has made to it.

Karl Popper

Considerable evidence exists to show that a wide range of living organisms have biological behaviour patterns that are linked to geophysical cycles. These cycles are themselves linked to extra-terrestrial factors. There is thus a possible mechanism for linking cosmic phenomena and biological behaviour that would relate to astrological beliefs.

Biological Clocks

Many plants and animals roughly follow 24-hour rhythms; these are normally termed circadian, from the Latin words *circa*, meaning about, and *dies*, meaning day. Just as many industrial plants work a shift system to maximize the available resources, so many animals work on different 'shifts' in order to maximize the use of habitable niches of the environment. Among those that work the day shift are many birds, butterflies, honeybees and lizards. Bats, owls, moths, mice and cockroaches are just a few examples of those that work the night shift. Green plants use sunlight during the day in the process of photosynthesis and during the night are involved in the processes of assimilation and growth. Many plants follow daily sleep rhythms, raising their leaves by day and drooping them at night. This discovery was first made by the French astronomer Jean Jacques d'Artois de Mairan on bean seedlings in 1729. Since then, many other discoveries relating to plant rhythms have been made. Some plants synchronize the opening of their blossoms to the activity rhythms of the animals that pollinate them.

The plants and animals of the seashore often follow cycles that are synchronized to the ebb and flow of the tides. In an earlier chapter we saw that there are two high tides (and two low tides) per day, and that the interval between two high tides is about 12 hours, 25 minutes. Barnacles, clams, snails and oysters are active when submerged by the incoming tide, whereas the fiddler crab and many shorebirds feed on the living organisms that are exposed by the ebb tide. Some of the animals of the intertidal zone have two sets of rhythms: one following the tide and one following the solar day. For example, the fiddler crab has an activity rhythm synchronized to the times of the local tides, and a daily rhythm of skin-colour change. Since the lunar day is 24 hours, 50 minutes, it means that the two rhythms of the fiddler crab will synchronize at two tides during a lunar month and these two tides will be separated by about a fortnight.[1]

Lunar Annual Changes and Solar Annual Changes

We are all aware of annual changes in plant and animal life. The keen gardener must understand and use these annual changes if he is to make a success of his gardening. We also know that migratory birds appear and disappear at specific times of the year, and that some animals hibernate in the winter. Indeed, it was this realization that led early cultures to an interest in calendar-making and astronomy. Perhaps less well known are the cycles followed by some animals in which use is made of either combined daily and annual changes, or combined tidal and annual changes.

An example of a combined daily annual rhythm is shown by migratory birds. Many migratory birds rapidly increase their weight before they start their long flights, as they build up the large deposits of fat used as food reserves en route. These fat deposits are laid down in spring, within about 10 days, and there is another period of migratory fattening in the late summer, but the rate of gain is slower than in the spring. Experiments have shown that the start of these periods is controlled by the changing of the day length that accompanies the seasons. These experiments took the form of exposing the birds to light for periods that varied in a similar way to that of the annual changes in day length. Another activity of migratory birds that is controlled by changes in day length is the nocturnal restlessness – known as the *Zugunruhe* – that they display shortly before they set off on their migratory flights.

The palolo sea worms of the South Pacific provide an excellent example of a tidal annual cycle. These worms are about 18 inches long and normally live in dim caverns of the South Pacific. The main sex cycle of these worms occurs once a year, during the last quarter of the Moon in November, which corresponds to spring in the south. The annual aspect of the swarming is mentioned by Basil Thomson in *The Confessions of Lady Asanath*, who describes the effect of this behaviour on the inhabitants of the islands of the region in these terms: 'The time of the annual swarming is a great occasion for the natives, as the palolo is regarded as a delicacy . . . Cakes of the gelatinous mass are fried, and taste just like oysters.' Further details of the rising of the palolo are noted by William Burrows, who was a commissioner on one of the islands in the 1940s. He writes that there were normally two risings: a small one in October and a larger one in November. He also records that: 'The main rising always occurs at dawn and, literally, the worm comes up with the sun. It is, also, always at the time of high water.' The swarming of the palolo thus represents a fairly complex type of cycle. It occurs during a specific month of the year (November), at the last quarter of the Moon, and at dawn and high tide.

A still more spectacular example in precision timing of a lunar annual rhythm is provided by the reproductive cycle of a deep-sea creature of the biological family known as echinoderms, which lives just off the coast of Japan. This creature liberates its sex cells just once a year in October at about 3 o'clock in the afternoon, on the day of one of the quarters of the Moon. In the years that follow the time of the first release, the time of the lunar month at which the sex cells are released changes from one year to the next, but it always alternates between first and last quarters of the Moon. Hence it alternates first–last–first, getting earlier in October each year, until about the first of the month, whereupon it jumps abruptly to near the end of the month to start the same cycle again. The result is an 18-year cycle, called the Saros cycle, which is linked to the motion of the Moon.

This Saros cycle, which is really 18 years and 11.3 days long, is the period after which the relative positions of the Earth, Sun and Moon repeat themselves. The Moon does not have the same apparent pathway against the background stars as that of the Sun. However, twice in a lunar month the Moon crosses the apparent pathway of the Sun, and the points at which it crosses are called the lunar nodes. These nodes change their positions against the background stars with the Saros cycle. An eclipse of the Sun occurs when the Sun and Moon are very near to one of these nodes at the same point in time, and an eclipse of the Moon occurs when the Sun is near the one node and the Moon near the other node at the same time. This means that eclipses also follow the Saros cycle of the little sea creature just off the coast of Japan. This is not to say eclipses directly cause the strange behaviour of this little echinoderm. The same sequence of events that is responsible for the eclipses also causes changes in the behaviour of the tides, and the deep-sea creature is responding to these changes. Some astrologers claim that the astrological effect of an eclipse can actually precede the eclipse itself. I would argue that what they are witnessing in these cases is something similar to the behaviour of this creature. This same argument can be applied to another claim made by some astrologers concerning the winter solstice.

In the *Cosmic Loom*, Elwell says: 'The possibility of anticipating something which has not yet happened in the sky is found elsewhere in astrology; for example, the planetary line-up at the winter solstice, which takes place just before Christmas every year, seems relevant for many months ahead, but here too it can make itself felt some weeks prematurely.' We have already seen that some birds that fly south for the winter start to fatten up months in advance, and they exhibit a pre-flight pattern of behaviour long before they actually leave for the south. We also saw that there is scientific evidence to show that this behaviour is triggered by changes in day length. The birds are flying south to avoid the rigours of the northern winter, which are naturally a consequence of the winter solstice. However, the actual trigger for the flight is part of a larger pattern of physical changes associated with the seasons, and there is no reason to evoke bird-brain astrology to explain this behaviour!

The Nature of the Biological Clock

The general subject of biological clocks raises the question of whether the clocks are direct responses to the environment or whether they are of internal origin. Most experiments show that many of the rhythms discussed above will persist even after the organism is shielded from the external stimulus to which it is apparently synchronized, but if the organism is removed from its own environment for a long period of time the various parts that exhibit rhythms become desynchronized. The results of these experiments suggest that most organisms possess fairly stable internal timers, which do not always correspond exactly with associated astronomical cycles, but these internal timers occasionally have to be adjusted by external geophysical periods. This is rather like resetting one's own clock and watch using the radio time-pips. It seems very likely, then, that the processes of evolution gave selective advantages to those individuals that had internal timers with periods very close to those of the physical environment of our Earth.

The possibility that the magnetic field of the Earth could play some role in the periodic behaviour of animals was demonstrated by Brown, a biologist who strongly supports the importance of geophysical factors in the timing of biological rhythms.

The first studies, with mudsnails, dealt with their responses to altered directions of weak experimental horizontal magnetic fields. Not only were these animals responsive to fields very close in strength to the Earth's own field, but their responsiveness to these fields gradually altered with time of day, and with phase of moon, or to the relationships between times of day and times of tides. These last were quite what one might expect if the magnetic fields were, indeed, affecting daily and tidal rhythms of the organisms.[2]

An important general rule concerning the role of light in animal rhythms (to which there are a few exceptions) was discovered by a German physician, Jurgen Aschoff, and it is usually called Aschoff's Rule. He discovered it by subjecting many different animals to conditions of constant light and constant darkness, and noting the effects of these conditions on their activity cycles. This rule states that as light intensity is increased, the activity of nocturnal animals will increase, while that of day-active animals will decrease. Aschoff also did very important work on rhythms of human beings.

Animal Navigators

Very closely allied to biological clocks are the methods of navigation used by animal navigators. Several different investigations have shown that those birds that migrate during the day can employ the Sun as a navigational aid. This implies that they are using their internal clocks to adjust the direction in which they are flying, with respect to the Sun. If they are flying south, then in the early morning they must have the Sun on their left, at midday they must have it directly ahead of them, and in the afternoon it must be on their right. This hypothesis has been tested using the following experiment. Some birds were placed in artificial daylight conditions, in which the times of sunrise and sunset were changed by a specific number of hours. This had the effect of resetting their internal clocks by the same number of hours. When released under the real sky, the birds flew in the wrong direction by the number of degrees the Sun would have moved in that time. These experiments provided strong support for this theory.

Bees also use the Sun as a compass, but instead of using the actual direction of the Sun, they use the polarization of the sky that is associated with the direction of the Sun. The sky near the zenith, on a clear day, is polarized at right angles to the direction of the Sun, and this polarization can be detected by the complex eyes of bees. Since the polarization of the sky depends on the direction of the Sun with respect to the compass directions, it means that the bees must be finding direction by using their ability to detect polarization in conjunction with their internal biological clocks. This important discovery was made by Karl von Frisch, the world authority on the social life of bees.

Birds that migrate at night seem to use the stars as a navigational aid. There have been several different investigations that support this idea. The first comes directly from observations in the field. Birds released under clear skies tend to fly in definite compass directions, whereas birds released under overcast skies fly in random directions. In another experiment one group of birds was fitted with contact lenses that allowed them to see objects under normal conditions of daylight but that fogged out starlight, while a second control group were not fitted with these lenses. When released under the night sky, the birds in the first group took longer to find their way home than those of the second group. In a variation of this experiment the birds were divided into three groups. The first group were fitted with contact lenses and had small magnets tied to their feet; the second group were fitted with contact lenses only; while the last group had neither contact lenses nor magnets. The birds of the first group never returned home, while those in the second group took longer to reach home than those of the last group. This seems to indicate that birds can navigate either by the stars or by the magnetic field of the Earth, although they seem to use the stars for preference. Further experiments under the simulated night sky of a planetarium seem to confirm this. Normally when birds are placed in cylindrical cages, under a real clear sky, just before they start their migratory flights, they tend to hop in the direction in which they will eventually fly. Under the artificial sky of the planetarium they tend to do the same thing. Does this mean that they can actually identify constellations and hence find the Pole Star? No. The planetarium experiment was repeated, with the sky moving about a different 'Pole Star'. The birds then took their directional cue from this new 'Pole Star'. This suggests that the birds might be using the movements of the sky rather than recognizable patterns of stars.

Human Rhythms

'It is well known even to the layman that each day the body temperature reaches a highest value towards the evening and a low point in the morning.' Since this phenomenon was described by Gierse in 1842, numerous clinical and physiological studies have shown that there is apparently no organ and no function of the body that does not exhibit a similar daily rhythmicity.

This is such a wide-ranging subject that we will restrict ourselves to a brief mention of a few typical examples. Experiments by Jores and Frees showed that there existed a daily cycle in the tolerance of humans to pain, at least as far as the skin and teeth are concerned. Between the hours of 8 p.m. and 8 a.m. the teeth are much less sensitive to painful stimulus than they are at other times of the day. The sensitivity to pain reaches a maximum at about 6 p.m. There also exists a daily rhythm in the metabolism of alcohol in the body. Between 2 p.m. and midnight, alcohol is burned up more quickly than during the other hours of the day.

An important set of results on human rhythms was obtained from a series of experiments carried out by potholers, who spent periods in isolation, in caves, ranging from 8 to 25 weeks. These potholers, under these conditions of isolation, developed sleep–wakefulness rhythms that were all longer than 24 hours, with the average being 24 hours, 42 minutes. In order to repeat and extend this type of work under more controlled laboratory conditions, an isolation facility was specially built at the Max Planck Institute for Physiology of Behaviour near Munich. Using this facility, called the *Tier Bunker* (*Tier* being the German for animal), Aschoff made a number of interesting discoveries. He investigated several different human rhythms, including body temperature, sleep–wakefulness cycles, total urine volume and the excretory products calcium and potassium. Aschoff found that all these parameters and functions followed rhythmic cycles, but their periods were not necessarily related to each other, nor were they related to the solar day. Another investigation, by N. Kleitman and T. Engelmann, on the sleep rhythms of infants, showed that after 3–6 weeks their sleep–wakefulness rhythms were still rather erratic. However, after 23–6 weeks there existed a definite period of sleep between 8 p.m. and 8 a.m.

There also exist daily rhythms in the ability of people to perform simple tasks. For example, the ability to estimate an interval of 60 seconds varied with the time of day. Between 7 a.m. and 1 p.m. there was a tendency to underestimate the interval, whereas there was a tendency to overestimate it between 1 p.m. and 8 p.m. This was further borne out by an investigation of interval estimation on patients displaying non-normal temperature variations. The estimation ability decreases as the body temperature rises above the normal value. Other abilities that are related to body temperature are card-dealing and sorting speeds, and the speed and accuracy with which people can carry out simple calculations.

M. J. F. Blake made a comparison of the daily temperature variation of two groups of people: one consisting of introverts and one of extroverts. The results from the two groups show that the body temperature of introverts rose earlier in the morning, reached a maximum sooner, and fell earlier at night than that of the extroverts. Here we have an indication that some human rhythms may be related to personality traits.

Links Due to Gravitation

The seasons are the result of two things. First, the axis of Earth, as we have already seen, points in the same direction with respect to the distant stars over long periods of time; and second, our Earth is also going around the Sun. We have seen that it is the force of gravitation, combined with the laws of motion, that keeps the Earth on its path. The Earth, however, is not an exact sphere but slightly flattened at the poles, so it has a slight bulge towards the equator. The Moon and Sun both tug, via the force of gravitation, on this bulge. The Moon tries to get the bulge into the plane of its orbit around the Earth, and the Sun tries to get this bulge into the plane of the Earth's orbit around the Sun. These forces have two effects on our Earth. They cause both the precession and a slight nodding of the earth's axis. The precessional motion has a period of about 26,000 years and the nodding, called the notation of the axis, a period of about 18 years. These movements of the axis have known long-term effects on our climate.

If the Earth was the only planet going around the Sun, then its elliptical path would be fixed in space with respect to the distant stars. This, however, is not the case. Because there are other planets going round the Sun, they also tug, via gravitation, on our Earth, so the long axis of the Earth orbit gradually moves around the Sun, and how elliptical the orbit is also changes as a result of the influence of the other planets. Jupiter and Saturn are the main contributors to this effect, the other planets playing smaller roles. This behaviour of the Earth's axis also has an effect on long-term climate.

The Moon and Sun both tug, via the force of gravitation, on the waters of the Earth, but this tug varies over its surface, giving rise to the tides. If the Sun and Moon tug in the same direction, then we have bigger tides than normal – the spring tides. If they tug at right angles to each other, then we have smaller tides than normal – the neap tides. These bodies cause tides not only in the ocean but also in the atmosphere.

Radiation Links

The Sun radiates large amounts of different types of radiation. We are all familiar with the light and heat that we receive from the Sun. The amount we receive at any one time is modulated by the spinning of the Earth on its axis, and by the movement of our Earth around the Sun. But we are also receiving other types of radiation. The heat we receive is really called infrared radiation, and some of it is absorbed by the atmosphere, so if astronomers want to study the infrared radiation given off by other celestial objects, they have to use special telescopes and special detectors on board satellites.

White light really consists of all the colours of the rainbow. Although our eyes cannot see infrared radiation, it is just beyond the red end of the rainbow. At the other end of the rainbow we have another type of radiation that we cannot see: ultraviolet. The sun is also a very strong source of ultraviolet radiation. Once again other astronomical bodies give off this type of radiation, and in order to study the universe using ultraviolet radiation we have to use special detectors on board satellites. Astronomers have also used X-ray detectors on board satellites to study this type of radiation given off by the Sun. Radio astronomers discovered several decades ago that the Sun is also a strong source of radio waves. Fortunately for us the atmosphere of Earth filters out much of this radiation, especially those types that can be harmful to us. The radiation does have a variety of effects on the upper atmosphere of Earth, however, so it affects our environment in a variety of ways.

Particle Links

There are a variety of particles that come to Earth from space. They come in a variety of sizes. Some of them are called meteorites, and the smaller ones are called micro-meteorites. When they strike the surface of Earth, they are travelling so fast that they are heated by friction with the atmosphere, and as they burn up they leave trails of hot glowing gases that we call meteors – sometimes erroneously called shooting stars. The very big meteors can survive the heat treatment in the upper atmosphere, and they then strike the Earth as meteorites. Astronomers are still debating whether meteors and micro-meteors can affect our atmosphere sufficiently to play a part in our weather, but the consensus at the moment is that they cannot make a very great contribution.

There are also subatomic particles coming to us from all directions in space but from the Sun in particular. The American astrophysicist E. N. Parker, from the University of Chicago, is a specialist on magnetic fields in astronomy. In 1958 he did some calculations showing that the physical conditions of the extended atmosphere of the Sun – the solar corona – were such that it would flow away from the Sun in a continuous stream, which he called the solar wind. The presence of this 'wind' has been confirmed on many occasions by satellites and space probes, and these devices have revealed many of the interesting properties of this stream of subatomic particles. The solar wind impinges on the extended magnetic field of Earth, as we will see in a later chapter, and it gives rise to a large variety of effects, called solar-terrestrial relationships, which now form an important branch of the subject of geophysics.

There are other subatomic particles coming to Earth from space. Many of these have their origin in violent activity, such as the explosion of massive stars within our own Milky Way galaxy. They are contained within our galaxy by vast magnetic fields that thread their way between the stars. The shape of these vast fields has been a special study of mine for the past 20 years. Using observations made with optical and radio telescopes, we have been able to piece together the jigsaw puzzle of how these fields are arranged in space, and we now know that they play a part in guiding subatomic particles, generated in our galaxy, towards the Earth. There is evidence that still more violent activity, on the scale of whole galaxies, also generates very energetic subatomic particles. These sweep across the vast distances that separate galaxies, and some of them reach the Earth. All this means that we cannot separate ourselves from the rest of the universe. There are a wide variety of forces, fields and particles that link our Earth to the rest of the universe. Science has been aware of this for a very long time.

Science and Cosmic Belief

Although most modern scientists reject astrology, the idea that the large-scale universe can affect local and terrestrial events has, over the years, surfaced in a number of different forms. I believe that this is, to some extent, an intellectual response to the growing feeling that the technical universe of modern science is rather remote from our day-to-day existence.

In the last century an Austrian physicist and philosopher, Ernst Mach, proposed a principle that came to be known as Mach's Principle. Mach is best known for his work on fluid dynamics and supersonic flow, and the speed of a supersonic aircraft, given in terms of the speed of sound, bears his name in the form of its Mach number. Mach's Principle says that the mass of a body is generated by forces originating in all the matter of the universe, including all the distant matter. This means that the resistance offered by a particle to changes in its position or movement is the result of the effects of the whole universe on the particle. In other words, the universe exerts a form of social pressure on the particle to maintain the status quo, and it is this pressure that we call the mass of a particle.

Albert Einstein was one of the many people attracted to this idea, and he tried hard, though without success, to incorporate it into one of his theories – the General Theory of Relativity – which is our best theory of gravity to date. Some time later Dennis Sciama, an English cosmologist then working at Cambridge, was able to give a scientific basis to it. He achieved this not in general relativity but by modifying Newton's law of gravitation. He argued that just as moving electric charges generate magnetic fields, so moving masses have a gravitational equivalent to the magnetic field. He was then able to show that the mass of a body was due to the influence of the more distant fast-moving galaxies of the universe. In other words, the distant matter of the universe was influencing the behaviour of particles on our Earth.[3] It is not surprising, then, that Nigel Calder, in his book *The Violent Universe*, refers to Mach's Principle as modern astrology.[4]

Fred Hoyle, formerly of Cambridge University, was also interested in Mach's Principle. Hoyle's work spans every aspect of astronomy. He has worked on problems concerning the structure of stars, the Sun, the Milky Way, other galaxies and the universe. He has also done important work on the possible astronomical significance of Stonehenge. Early in the 1960s Hoyle and his close collaborator, Jayant Narliker, formulated a new theory of gravity that was similar in many ways to Einstein's General Theory of Relativity. An important feature of this theory of Hoyle and Narliker is that it incorporates Mach's Principle in a very natural way.

Scientists have also tried to explain the direction of time in terms of the large-scale structure of the universe. In the mathematics describing the interactions between charged particles, it does not really matter if one uses negative time or positive time. In other words, according to most theories time could either go backwards or forwards. It is, however, a matter of common experience that time does *not* go backwards. This experience has been captured very well in *The Rubáiyát of Omar Khayyám*, translated by FitzGerald:

The Moving Finger writes; and, having writ,
Moves on: nor all thy Piety nor Wit
Shall lure it back to cancel half a Line,
Nor all thy Tears wash out a Word of it.

Some astronomers and physicists, including Hoyle and Narliker, have explained this paradox by showing that the direction of time's arrow depends critically on the large-scale structure of the universe. Hence the common observation that we cannot reverse time is telling us something about the structure of the universe.[5]

More recently some astronomers have tried to construct theories that make use of an idea called the Anthropic Principle. There are a few different versions of this, but we will define only the first two, using the definitions given in *The Anthropic Cosmological Principle* by John Barrow, from the University of Sussex, and Frank Tipler, from Tulane University, New Orleans.[6]

They first of all define the Weak Anthropic Principle as 'The observed values of all physical constants and cosmological quantities are not equally probable but they take on values restricted by the requirement that there exist sites where carbon-based life can evolve and by the requirement that the universe be old enough for it to have already done so.' They define the Strong Anthropic Principle as follows: 'The universe must have those properties which allow life to develop within it at some stage in its history.' In other words, our very existence and ability to observe the universe is a consequence of its large- and small-scale structure, as well as how these two levels are related.

Comets

Fred Hoyle and another close collaborator, Chandra Wickramasinghe, have over the last few years put forward the theory that microscopic forms of life are being formed all the time in the vast spaces between the stars, and that the dust grains in interstellar space, which block out the light from the distant parts of our Milky Way, are really these viruses. Some of these life forms came to our Earth many millions of years ago, and evolved into the present life forms that inhabit this planet. Some of the viruses spawned in interstellar space are still coming to Earth in the tails of comets, and in the past they brought epidemics and death on a large scale. This, they argue, gives scientific justification to the idea that comets were the bringers of death and disaster.[7]

Comets have also been invoked to explain other natural disasters such as the extinction of the dinosaurs. One theory concerning the origin of comets says they are formed in the vast clouds of interstellar dust that are known to exist in interstellar space. Such a cloud, called the Oort Cloud, is supposed to surround our solar system, and a relatively close encounter between this cloud and another star of the Milky Way would send large numbers of comets into our solar system. This would lead to an increase in the number of meteors striking the Earth, which would in turn increase the amount of dust in the atmosphere. This dust would reduce the amount of sunlight reaching the surface of Earth, thus leading to the death of some types of plants. Those animals that depend for their existence on this type of plant would then die off as a result.

Conclusion

Evidence has been presented showing that extraterrestrial factors have effects on Earth life that are unusual and unexpected. When, however, the complexity of the cosmic forces acting on the Earth is taken into account, it is surely possible that further relationships, not yet recognized, might well exist. In subsequent chapters I will show that this is indeed the case.

7

The Magnetic Music of the Spheres

The Moon feeds oysters, fills sea urchins, puts flesh on shell fish and on beasts.

Lucilius

My first real breakthrough in my full scientific theory for astrology came in the summer of 1985. I had a vague suspicion that the Moon, being so close to the Earth and having a much more noticeable effect on life in the sea, held the key to any theory of astrological effects. Many other people had had the same inkling, but it needed to be taken a great deal further if it were to form the basis of a scientifically proven argument. I believed that the Moon was somehow influencing the fluid parts of the Earth's interior, and by doing so it was altering the magnetic field of Earth, which Gauquelin had already shown was involved with astrological effects; but I needed much more information.

A brief study of the available literature at Exeter University revealed that my initial idea was wrong. Any magnetic changes occurring in the interior of the Earth would take at least several months to diffuse outwards and could not give rise to variation of a few hours' duration. Further study, however, focused my attention on the lunar daily magnetic variation. If such a variation was operating on a two-way switch, tuned to the Moon, for people with a 'lunar' type personality, then we could explain Gauquelin's results relating to the Moon. So for me the Moon provided the major clue, just as it provided Newton with the clue to gravitation 300 years ago. I will now expand on my theory, with particular reference to the Moon.

The Magnetism of the Earth

According to J. Needham in *Science and Civilization in China*, knowledge of the attractive properties of lodestone was to be found in the East and West by the middle of the first millennium BC. However, he produces very convincing arguments to show that the direction-finding properties of lodestone were discovered by the Chinese: the first text from China that describes the magnetic compass dates from AD 1080. He also argues that this device was connected with their methods of divination.

Chinese divination made use of a variety of different techniques; these included their own approach to astrology, and the methods of geomancy, which depended on the influences of the Earth. The belief inherent in Chinese geomancy was that the houses of the living and the tombs of the dead had to be properly aligned if living people wished to enjoy wealth and happiness, and to avoid evil influences. The shape of the land and the direction of streams, winds and waters were all important to the geomantic diviners. They developed the geomantic compass (see illus. 11) to help them in their craft. Needham says that this compass was a development of the diviner's board, which consisted of a spoon carefully carved out of lodestone and able to rotate freely on the smooth surface of the board (see illus. 12). The mariner's compass, used for navigation, was a development of this device. Geomancy required a knowledge of the compass directions at different places on the surface of the Earth, and how these directions varied with time. Needham has described geomancy as the true precursor of geomagnetism (the study of the Earth's own field), much as astrology was the stimulus to astronomy, and alchemy to chemistry.

In the twelfth century, knowledge of the compass reached Europe. We know this because Alexander Neckham, an English monk, refers to the compass in a work of that period. Later, by making use of compass directions collected from the worldwide navigation of his day, William Gilbert, physician to Queen Elizabeth I, formulated a theory of the Earth's magnetic field. He shows that the magnetic field of a magnetized sphere is very similar to that of the Earth. In other words, he demonstrated that the Earth

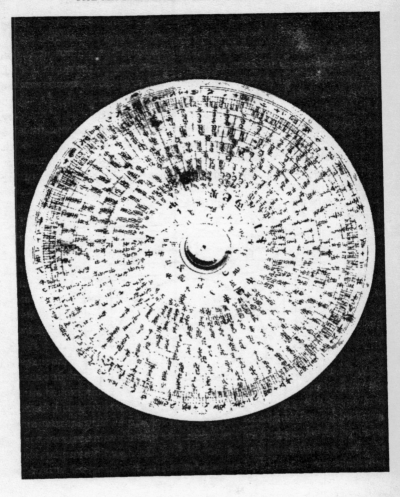

11 The geomancer's compass.

behaves as if it has a bar magnet situated close to its centre and almost aligned with its rotation axis.

Modern work on the magnetic field of Earth is based largely on data collected from magnetic observatories around the world. Some of these observatories were initially set up because of the importance of the compass to the mariner. This work seems to show that the major part of the Earth's field can be described by imagining an ordinary bar magnet situated about 400 km from the Earth's centre, with its axis inclined by 11.5 to the north–south axis. The modern theory of the Earth's magnetic field holds that the field is generated by electric currents flowing in the molten part

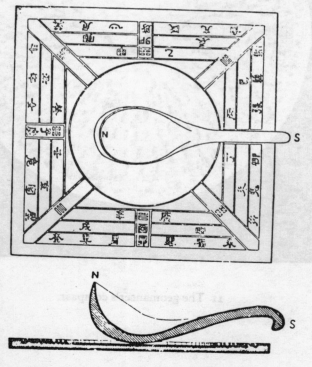

12 The diviner's board with lodestone spoon.

of the Earth's core, so the Earth is really like an electromagnet similar to that found in an electric motor.

Over the last two decades the use of magnetic measuring instruments on board Earth satellites has greatly increased our knowledge of Earth's magnetic field far above the surface. Those satellite measurements have revealed that the field is contained within a region called the magnetosphere, which is compressed on the sunward side and drawn out into a long tail on the opposite side. The Sun emits a continuous stream of very fast-moving particles known as the solar wind. These particles consist of bits of atoms, called protons and electrons, and larger pieces called ions. Since these particles carry electrical charges, some of them are deflected by the magnetic field of Earth, and, as they stream past it, they make a bow wave very similar to that of a ship as it passes through the water. Somewhere behind the Earth the various strands of the solar wind join up again, thus enclosing the Earth's field within a pear-shaped region called the magnetosphere (see illus. 13). Also trapped in the magnetosphere are two regions of charged particles called the Van Allen radiation belts. The entire magnetosphere is about 20–30 times the size of Earth.[1]

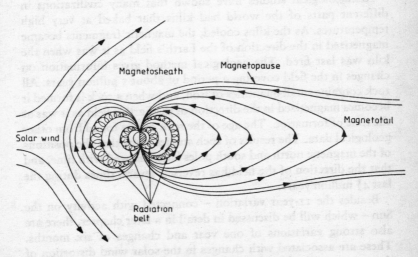

13 **The magnetosphere of Earth.**

Changes in the Earth's Magnetic Field

The changes in the magnetic field of Earth occur on a large variety of time scales, from those lasting hundreds of thousands of years right down to those lasting a few seconds. In other words, the magnetic field of Earth 'broadcasts' on a very wide band of frequencies. One can claim that there is a greater range of variations in the direction and strength of the field than in any other quantity connected with our Earth. Many different techniques have been used to investigate these changes.

The very long period changes are investigated by using the fact that many substances contain small amounts of magnetic materials. When these substances are melted, the magnetic fragments become like little compass needles and orientate themselves in the magnetic field of Earth. When these substances are cooled and solidify, these little compasses become 'locked into' the direction of the field as it was when solidification took place. This basic method can be used in conjunction with archaeological or geological data to give information on changes in the field long before the period for which recorded observations exist.

Archaeological studies have shown that many civilizations in different parts of the world had kilns that baked at very high temperatures. As the kilns cooled, the magnetic fragments became magnetized in the direction of the Earth's field as it was when the kiln was last fired. The geological method gives information on changes in the field covering a period of about 5 million years. All rock contains small quantities of iron, and when a rock is formed it becomes magnetized in the direction of the Earth's field as it was at the time of formation. The age of the rock can be found from other geological data. The results of such studies show that the positions of the magnetic north and south poles have changed with time, and that the direction of the field has reversed several times during the last $4\frac{1}{2}$ million years.

Besides the 11-year variation – connected with activity on the Sun – which will be discussed in detail in a later chapter, there are also strong variations of one year and changes of six months. These are associated with changes in the solar wind distortion of the magnetosphere that results from the motion of the Earth around the Sun. Variations consisting of 27 days and 13.5 days are partly due to the spinning of the Sun on its own axis and partly due to the motion of the Moon around the Earth. There are also variations of 1 day and 12 hours that are associated with the spinning of the Earth on its axis. These are not the only variations, although they are stronger than the others. The gaps between these are filled up with a host of other weaker variations, many of which have not yet been investigated and are only partially understood. One variation of particular interest to this chapter is that associated with the rising and setting of the Moon. In fact, this change in the field provides the major key to understanding the links between the extraterrestrial universe and personality.

The variation connected with the Moon is called the lunar daily magnetic variation. As the Moon rises, a very sensitive compass needle will be deviated to the east of north; as it reaches its highest point in the sky, the needle will be deviated towards the west; as the Moon sets, it will be deviated towards the east, and about 6 hours later it will be deviated towards the west again. The amount of deviation at each stage is not quite the same, and it also depends on the phase of the Moon. As has already been noted, the direction and variations of the field can influence biological organisms, but in order to understand the theory presented in this book, it is necessary to discuss the nature of these influences in more detail.

The Biological Effects of Magnetic Fields

Over the last few decades a great deal of work has been done in the field of magnetobiology – the general study of magnetic fields, natural and artificial, on biological organisms. Much of this was prompted by the start of the space age about 25 years ago. Some of the early designers of spacecraft suggested that the creation of strong magnetic fields around the spacecraft would protect the astronauts from the harmful effects of the fast-moving particles that bombard the craft and that originate mainly from the Sun. This initiated research into the effects such fields would have on humans. Other research was undertaken because flights to the Moon would mean that astronauts would be separated from the

Earth's field, and this could affect their biological behaviour. These experiments and many others gave very interesting results.

One series of experiments was concerned with the study of the effect of reversals of the Earth's field on microscopic forms of life. By studying fossilized remains of such organisms, it became apparent that certain species that had existed for millions of years became extinct over relatively short periods of time. Some of the scientists working in this field showed that these extinctions seem to be closely linked with reversals of the Earth's field, and as a result they suggested that these organisms actually used the field for some purpose.

In 1975 R. P. Blakemore, a biologist working in America, discovered that certain bacteria were influenced by the Earth's field in that under a microscope they would be observed to swarm consistently towards the north. This discovery was confirmed by experiments with simple bar magnets. Further experiments showed that the bacteria were moving towards the north because they wanted to move downwards – the Earth's field not only points north but also dips downward in the northern hemisphere. The same bacteria swim towards the south in the southern hemisphere, once again because they want to move downwards towards the sediment and away from the surface of the water where the concentration of oxygen, which is toxic to them, is higher. When the bacteria were studied under the electron microscope, they were seen to contain a string of 'beads', each bead consisting of a magnetic substance known as magnetite. Thus these bacteria do use the Earth's field for a purpose. If similar microscopic organisms used the field for a similar purpose in the past, then the reversal of the field would have led them to the higher, toxic levels of oxygen in the water and thus to extinction.[2]

Evidence has also been growing over the past few decades that shows birds and other animals are able to use the Earth's field as a navigational aid, although most birds are able, when skies are clear, to use either the Sun or the stars for the same purpose. Robin Baker from Manchester University has tested the ability of humans to find north using the Earth's field, and he was able to show that, on average, most people were able to do this to some extent, but some people were better at it than others. It has also been suggested on numerous occasions that human dowsers are able to find underground water because the flow of such water courses can cause fluctuations in the magnetic field of Earth. The results of some scientific experiments suggest that dowsers may well be using the magnetism of the Earth and its changes to discover water sources.

Magnetism and the Central Nervous System

Some Russian scientists have employed the well-known biological technique of conditioned reflexes to investigate the effects of magnetic fields on the central nervous systems of various animals. This technique can be illustrated by the following example of using sound or light to condition food-seeking reflexes. If a light was switched on or a bell sounded whenever a group of animals was fed, then at a later stage the animals would show food-seeking behaviour when the light (or the sound) was switched on but no food was given. The Russian biologist Y. A. Kholodov showed that magnetic fields stronger than that of Earth could be used to condition food-seeking reflexes in fish, by exposing them to a magnetic impulse, instead of light or sound, whenever food was given.

In another series of experiments Kholodov subjected pregnant rats to artificial magnetic fields similar in strength to that of Earth, but this time they were pulsating rapidly, to simulate the behaviour of the Earth's field during a geomagnetic storm. The offspring of such rats were less active than normal offspring, and they committed more errors in the laboratory mazes in which they were placed. When Kholodov subjected the pregnant rats to fields a hundred times stronger than that of Earth, they produced distinctly fewer foetuses than normal; there was an increase in the number of still births; and some of the offspring were born with 'ruptures of the spinal column'. In another series of experiments Kholodov showed that the brains of vertebrates, which had been surgically separated from the sense organs and other parts of the nervous system, responded more positively to magnetic fields. From this he concluded that the sense organs prevent the brain from fully reacting to the magnetic field. Other experiments on humans have shown that our reaction times, our ability to adapt to seeing in the dark, and our ability to distinguish a very rapidly fluctuating light source from a continuous one were all affected if we were shielded from the geomagnetic field. There seems little doubt that magnetic fields can influence the central nervous systems of animals and humans.[3]

An Austrian scientist, K. Birzele, collected yet another set of evidence that is important to my theory. From investigations on the state of the magnetic field within 1–2 days of birth, Birzele found that the similarity between personality characteristics of the child and one of its parents was linked to the similarity of geomagnetic activity close to the birth of the child and the particular parent. These results indicate that geomagnetic activity can enhance the genetic inheritance of certain personality characteristics. These particular results are also, to some extent, embodied in the work of Michel Gauquelin.

Gauquelin's Work on the Lunar Personality

Gauquelin showed that there was no link between the position of the Moon in the sky at birth and the professions taken up by ordinary people. However, after collecting a great deal of data on eminent writers, he was able to show that such writers tended to be born either when the Moon was rising or when it had reached its highest point in the sky. Although these were the peak times for the birth of outstanding authors, two smaller peaks also occur when the Moon is setting, or when it is at its highest point on the opposite side of the Earth. Later investigations showed that outstanding politicians also tended to be born with the Moon in these positions. By studying published biographies of these two groups, Gauquelin was able to identify some of the personality characteristics associated with the 'lunar personality'. In his book *The Truth about Astrology* he lists some of these characteristics: amiable, disorganized, dreamy, easy-going, fashionable, friendly, generous, good company, good-hearted, helpful, imaginative, impressionable, impulsive, merry, nonchalant, popular, sociable, spontaneous, superficial and tolerant.[4]

The Moon and the Tides

The tides have been known for centuries. Their association with the positions and phases of the Moon must have been known for almost as long. But it was not until Newton had formulated his laws of motion and the law of gravitation that it became possible to understand the causes of the tides in physical terms. According to Newton, every particle in the universe attracts every other particle, and the force of attraction is related to the masses of the two particles and the distance between them. Since the Earth is very massive and we are close to the Earth, we feel the attraction of Earth much more than we feel the attraction of the Sun, Moon, planets or stars, although such attractions do, in fact, exist. The particles of water in the sea are being attracted not only by the Earth but also by the Moon and Sun. Although the Sun is much more massive than the Moon, the Moon is much closer to us than the Sun, so its force of attraction is about twice that of the Sun.

The water on the Earth immediately below the Moon is closer to the Moon than any of the other water, so it feels the attraction of the Moon more than the rest, and as a result there is a slight piling up of the sea at the point just below the Moon. But there is also a bulge of water on the side of Earth furthest from the Moon: how does *this* arise? It comes about because the Moon does not really go around only the Earth; rather, both bodies go around their common centre of mass. In other words, if one could make a mobile of the Earth–Moon system, because the Earth is more massive than the Moon, the point at which the two would be balanced would be about 1,000 miles below the surface of the Earth, on the line joining the two bodies. This point is called the barycentre, and the Earth and Moon really go around it. As the Earth moves around this centre, the waters on the far side of Earth (from the Moon) have a tendency to be flung off into space, and this gives rise to the second bulge. Between these two bulges are two shallows of water. When we pass through a bulge, we say the tide has come in; when we pass through a shallow, we say the tide has gone out. At first sight this would seem to show that the two high tides should be separated by 12 hours. But, during the interval between passing under the first bulge and passing under the second bulge, the Moon has moved, so this interval becomes 12 hours, 24 minutes.

Although the tide-rising force of the Sun is less than that of the Moon, it does nevertheless contribute to the overall performance of the tides. Just as there are two bulges associated with the Moon, so there are two associated with the Sun: one just below the Sun and one on the other side of Earth from the Sun. When the bulges of the Sun coincide with the bulges of the Moon, as they do at new and full Moon, then there are higher tides than normal – the spring tides. When the bulges due to the Sun are at right angles to those of the Moon, as they are at first and last quarters of the Moon, then we have lower tides than normal – the neap tides (see illus. 14).

The Sun and Moon also give rise to tides in the atmosphere, including the upper atmosphere, and the electric currents in the upper atmosphere generated by these tides give rise to the lunar daily magnetic variation mentioned earlier. On average, over a lunar month the north-pointing field is deviated to the east as the Moon rises, to the west when the Moon reaches its highest point in the sky, to the east again when it sets, and to the west when it reaches its highest point on the other side of the Earth. It is this variation that triggers the birth of people with a lunar type of personality, according to my theory. How this happens is explained in the next section.

Understanding the Birth Trigger

The body normally reacts to outside stimulus in response to the information it receives via its sense organs. These consist of highly specialized groups of cells that are capable of receiving specific kinds of information. The receptors in our eyes, ears, noses, mouths and beneath our skin detect light, sound, smell, taste and touch respectively. These sense organs produce a message about the stimulus in the form of nerve impulses, which travel along the nerves from the sense organs to the rest of the nervous system. The neuron is the fundamental building block of the nervous system. It consists of a cell body that contains a nucleus, or control centre, an axon along which nerve impulses are conducted away from the cell

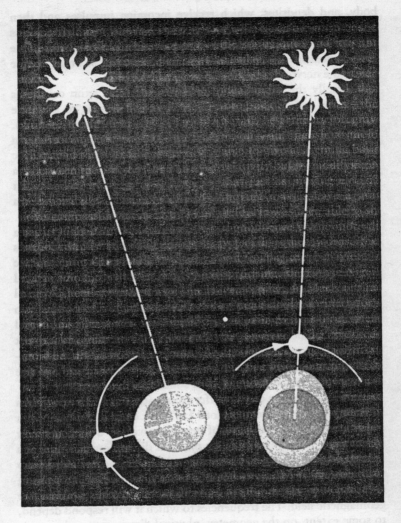

14 The spring tides (right) and neap tides (left).

body, and dendrites, which receive incoming impulses and then pass these towards the body of the cell. Motor neurons pass information from the central nervous system to the muscles, while sensory neurons transmit information from our sense organs to the rest of the nervous system.

Normally the passage of an impulse along an axon originates within the main body of the cell, but it is possible to start the propagation of an impulse at any point along the axon's length. This can be done by applying an electrical stimulus – via an electrode – to any point of the axon. Since a changing magnetic field generates an associated electrical field, it can also act as a stimulus to the axons of the nervous system. The Russian scientist V. A. Chigirinskii demonstrated this for a single nerve cell of a gastropod mollusc.

'Neurons . . . are the basic timers of our bodies. They also play a central role in storing and processing information in our brains. As timers, neurons drive higher-level biological clocks in much the same manner as an alternating electric current (such as is supplied to our homes) drives an electric clock.' Because of the electrical properties of neurons, it is not surprising that the attempts to understand their behaviour are based on analogies with electrical circuits. One such circuit is very similar to the type of tuning circuit found in radio receivers. I propose that the influence of the fluctuating magnetic field of Earth on the whole nervous system can be described in terms of its effect on a similar electrical circuit.[5]

The basic neurons do not differ from each other, so where does heredity come into the situation? Let's use a radio receiver as an analogy. The station capable of being received by a given receiver depends, to some extent, on the physical dimensions, proportions and geometry of the aerial, but more so on the frequencies to which the receiving circuit is tuned. The nervous system, including the brain, constitutes a receiving system for fluctuations of the geomagnetic field. The frequencies to which it will respond depend, to some extent, on the geometry, physical dimensions and proportions of the body in which it is embedded, and this can be genetically inherited, but more so on the way the system is internally wired up, and this is linked to the personality of the individual, which is also to some extent genetically inherited.

With regard to the role of the neurons as timers, I believe that the geomagnetic field can actually synchronize the electrical activity of the loops of nerve cells within the nervous system. It is this synchronization that co-ordinates the various biological activities that cause the baby to push and be pushed out into the world.

In order to clarify this, I want to use the analogy of the magnetic mine that was used at sea in the Second World War. This mine was detonated by a device triggered by the magnetic field of a passing ship. In such a mine there would be, in addition to the magnetic trigger, a timing device that would 'arm' the bomb some time after it was laid. Thus mines could be placed safely without being triggered by the magnetic field of the ship laying the mines. If we consider birth as an explosion, the biological energy of baby and mother as the explosive, and the other biological processes in baby and mother (including the breaking of the water) as the timer that arms the bomb, then the nervous system is the magnetic aerial and trigger that detonates the explosion. This trigger is 'tuned', in the case of those who have inherited basic 'lunar' characteristics, to the lunar daily magnetic variation. This theory is then able to explain Gauquelin's observations concerning the position of the Moon at the birth of eminent writers and politicians.

Conclusion

In this chapter I have outlined my theory in general terms, and have discussed some of the evidence on which it is based. I have also shown the consequences of the theory for the specific case of the Moon. An outstanding feature of the theory is that it is able to reconcile the science of genetics with some of the basic concepts of astrology. This has been a major problem facing astrology, as was already noted by John Addey:

Of all the astrological problems which beckon us from the future there is one which must excite the thoughtful astrologer more than any other . . . This is the question of how astrology and genetics are to be related and, specifically perhaps, how the genetic code is expressed astrologically . . . It therefore follows – and we must be quite clear about this, it does inevitably follow – that the astrological code, by which the horoscope is interpreted, must be in agreement with the genetic code by which natural traits are transmitted from one generation to the next.

In the next chapter I will extend this theory to the planets.

8

The Magnetic Midwifery of the Planets

The fault, dear Brutus, is not in our stars,
But in ourselves, that we are underlings.

Shakespeare, *Julius Caesar*

In this chapter I discuss Gauquelin's work on the links between the planets and the personalities of individuals. I will also extend the theory outlined in the previous chapter, and illustrated for the case of the Moon, to those planets for which Gauquelin found positive evidence. The result is my extended theory, which overcomes the previous objections that have been put forward as arguments against astrology.

More about Michel Gauquelin

I have already touched upon the work of Gauquelin in connection with the Moon and personality, but since his research is so important to any serious scientific theory of astrology, we need to know more about the man himself.

Gauquelin was born in 1928, in Paris. He took an interest in astrology as a child, and as a teenager read as many books on astrology as he could get hold of. Later, at the Sorbonne, he studied psychology and statistics, and completed his studies by taking a doctorate in psychology. Although I had corresponded with Gauquelin since 1985, I first met him at a conference in London in February 1986, and then again at another research conference in London in November of the same year. The over-whelming impression I have of the man is that he is utterly sincere and modest; that he has a great deal of integrity and intellectual honesty; and that he is extremely rigorous in his scientific approach to astrology. I am not alone in this. Eysenck and Nias of London University have this to say about him: 'Gauquelin represents a rare combination, possessing both a detailed knowledge of astrology and a genuine scientific outlook based on a formal academic training. He certainly does not see himself as an astrologer, and indeed he is very critical of astrology as a whole, having learned from his own research that much of it is untrue.'

His initial research was an investigation of the consequences of Sun-sign astrology. This is the type of astrology with which most people are familiar from the horoscopes in daily newspapers, and maintains that one's personality is largely dependent on the time of year at which one is born. Since this is related to the position of the Sun along the zodiac – the apparent pathway of the Sun through the sky – as seen from Earth, it has become known as Sun-sign astrology. The zodiac constellation in which the Sun would have been seen at the time of year covering your birthday in the ancient world is called your Sun-sign. Gauquelin tested the assertion, made by astrologers, that 'professional soldiers are seldom born under Cancer, but often under Scorpio or Aries'. Using the rigorous statistical methods in which he was trained, he found that there was no evidence for this and other claims involving Sun-signs.

Gauquelin and the Planets

Most of Gauquelin's important results are discussed in his books, of which *The Truth about Astrology* is the most recent. The first positive result obtained by Gauquelin was that relating to the births of 576 members of the French Academy of Medicine. These doctors had obtained academic distinction as a result of their research work. Gauquelin selected them from medical directories, and to avoid bias he used objective criteria for this selection process. Theoretically these people could have been born at any time in the course of a day, yet these medical men tended to be born when Mars or Saturn had just risen, or had just passed their highest point in the sky. To check his results Gauquelin used another group of people chosen at random from the electoral register and covering the same period of births as the doctors. This second group did not show the same pattern as the doctors: their birth times were evenly spread through the day. In a further experiment Gauquelin used a different set of 508 doctors, and came up with the same result as before.

Exhaustive studies by Gauquelin of many different groups of people who had obtained success in their various professions led him to the following conclusions. Saturn, in the positions previously mentioned, was associated with much higher than average frequencies of births of scientists and physicians; but the frequencies of births under Saturn were low for actors, journalists, writers and painters. Few scientists and physicians were born under Jupiter, but a more than average number of actors, playwrights, politicians, military leaders, top executives and journalists were born under the planet. For Mars the high-frequency groups were physicians, military leaders, sports champions and top executives, whereas the low-frequency groups were painters, musicians and writers.

Having investigated the Moon, Gauquelin went on to assess the character traits connected with each planet, and came up with the following results. The 'Jupiter personality' possessed the following traits: ambitious, authoritarian, conceited, gay, harsh, humorous, independent, ironical, lively, mocking, prodigal, proud, show-off, social climber, spendthrift, talkative, warm, well-off, witty and worldly. The 'Saturn personality' had the following characteristics: cold, concentrated, conscientious, discreet, introverted, methodical, meticulous, modest, observant, precise, reserved, sad, simple, sombre, stiff, taciturn, thoughtful, timid, uncommunicative and wise. Mars people were characterized by the following: active, ardent, belligerent, brave, combative, daring, dynamic, energetic, fearless, fighter, lively, offensive, reckless, spontaneous, strong-willed, stormy, tireless, tough, valiant and full of vitality. Affable, agreeable, ambiguous, attractive, beloved, benevolent, charming, considerate, courteous, elegant, flattering, gallant, gracious, juvenile, kind, obliging, pleasant, poetic, polite and seductive were the characteristics that could be used to describe the Venus personality.

By combining his results for eminent individuals from all professions and born under any of the four planets discussed above, or the Moon, Gauquelin was able to demonstrate that such people were most frequently born when one of the celestial objects had either just risen or had passed its highest point in the sky. Although these two peaks of birth times were the major ones, there were two smaller ones just after one of these bodies had set, or was overhead on the other side of Earth. This means that the peaks of birth times showed a remarkable similarity to the results that one would obtain if each of the planets gave rise to magnetic tides in the Earth's field that were similar to that of the Moon. How this can happen will be shown later in this chapter.

Gauquelin's Planetary Heredity

The idea that people tend to be born when the state of the solar system, as seen from Earth, is the same as when their parents were born, has run through astrology for almost 2,000 years, starting with Ptolemy, the great Greco-Egyptian astronomer–astrologer. Kepler provides further support for this belief: 'There is one perfectly clear argument beyond all exception in favour of the authenticity of astrology. This is the common horoscopic connection between parents and children.'

Gauquelin decided to investigate this hypothesis. He was able to show, using statistical methods, that parents and their children showed little or no tendency to be born at the same time of year. Some of his further investigations revealed a very significant result: if one or other parent was born when a given planet was just rising, or near the highest point in the sky, then there was a significant tendency for their children also to be born under these conditions of that particular planet. This tendency was increased if both parents were born with the same planet in one of these positions. This increase was in keeping with the known laws of genetics. The effect was most marked for the Moon, Venus and Mars, followed by Jupiter and Saturn, but it was absent for the Sun, Mercury and the other planets. This particular result applies to all people investigated, and, unlike some of his other work, the sample included both eminent and ordinary people. Gauquelin's conclusions, based on these results, are founded upon objectively measurable quantities, such as times of births and planetary positions, and not subjective criteria, such as what constitutes eminence in a profession. Because of these factors, this aspect of Gauquelin's work is treated as very important to the theory developed in this book.

In a later replication of this experiment, Gauquelin divided his sample into two categories, according to whether the births were induced or not. The results of this replication showed that the planetary effect applied only to natural births. This strongly suggests that the planets are actually, in some way, influencing the natural timing of birth, making it more likely that a person of a certain type will be born at one particular time rather than another. These results, together with his earlier work, suggest that for people with different genetic constitutions, different planets will act as the trigger of the moment of birth, and that these genetically inherited characteristics can also play a part in determining success in different walks of life.

In another repeat of this experiment Gauquelin again divided his sample of natural births into two groups, but this time the one group was born on days when storm conditions prevailed in the magnetosphere of Earth, and the other group was born on geomagnetically quiet days. He was able to show that the planetary heredity effect was enhanced when the magnetic field of Earth was highly disturbed, but although still present on magnetically quiet days, it was much less evident at such times. This enhancement differs quite a lot from one body to the next, and here I want to quote from John Addey's book *Harmonics in Astrology*: 'It was interesting . . . while the planet-geomagnetism relation was apparent from Mars, Jupiter and Saturn, it came through most clearly for Venus, but scarcely existed for the Moon.' My theory is able to explain why this should be the case.

These particular results of Gauquelin's are the most important of all his findings, as far as my theory is concerned. This is because they are based on objectively measurable quantities, like planetary positions and birth times, but they also indicate quite clearly that a physical agency is involved, and that this agency is the magnetic field of the Earth. However, although this is the starting point of my theory, the theory itself, as will be seen in subsequent chapters, shows that Gauquelin's findings support more of the basic ideas and concepts of astrology than he thought they did, and the theory is also able to explain other parts of astrology not immediately evident from Gauquelin's results.

Replication of Planetary Effects by Gauquelin and Others

Gauquelin's first investigations were all restricted to data collected from France. Since it was just possible that the data reflected a peculiarity of the French, he decided to extend his studies to include Germany, Italy, Holland and Belgium. The same pattern emerged from an analysis of these results.

In Belgium the Committee for the Scientific Investigations of Alleged Paranormal Phenomena decided to see whether Gauquelin's results could be replicated. This Committee, called the Committee Para for short, consisted of a team of thirty astronomers, demographers, statisticians and other scientists. They decided to test Gauquelin's work on the links between the planet Mars and sports champions. Using a new group of 535 sports champions from France and Belgium, they came up with the same result as Gauquelin. They decided not to publish the results, but issued the following statement instead: 'The Committee Para cannot accept the conclusions of the research of M. Gauquelin based on hypotheses in which the committee has found inexactitudes.'

A rather similar set of circumstances occurred when an American group tried to replicate these results. This group is called the US Committee for the Scientific Investigations of Claims of the Paranormal. They ran into difficulties when most states refused to provide the necessary information on account of the privacy laws of America. Their first sample consisted only of 128 sports champions, and so to increase their sample they included some sports people who were not in the international class. They viewed their resulting negative conclusions as an indication of a flaw in Gauquelin's work. Nobody has yet tried to replicate Gauquelin's results on planetary heredity outside of France.

In many of his experiments Gauquelin was joined by his first wife, Françoise Gauquelin, and their joint work has been thoroughly investigated by the two eminent British psychologists, Eysenck and Nias, who came to the conclusion that: 'The work of the Gauquelins, to go no further, stands up to a careful degree of scrutiny, and compares favourably with the best that has been done in psychology, psychiatry, sociology or any of the other social sciences.'

Naturally Gauquelin has had his detractors, and it is worth mentioning some of their criticisms. The American astronomers Culver and Ianna write: 'Basically, the Gauquelins' analysis has been criticized on a number of counts . . . The claim is made that if these factors are properly introduced, the Gauquelins' odds against random distribution drop considerably from the value of roughly 10^{-6} [one in a million] quoted in their early work on the subject.' They quote the claim but then they merely sit on the fence, and they make no critical assessment of it. Eysenck and Nias also draw attention to this: 'Note that in this rather vague statement Culver and Ianna do not even say that they agree with these criticisms; they simply quote them as claims but do not attempt to evaluate their accuracy.'

This concern about the application of probability and statistics to the problems of astrology implies that the physical sciences are above such problems, and that all physical theories are not plagued by errors and uncertainties. This is far from the truth. Edwin Hubble, the great American astronomer who discovered the expansion of the universe, wrote:

> From our home on Earth we look out into the distances and strive to imagine the sort of world into which we are born. Today we have reached far out into space. Our immediate neighbourhood we know rather intimately. But with increasing distance our knowledge fades . . . until the last dim horizon we search among ghostly errors of observations for landmarks that are scarcely more substantial.[1]

The same is true for the frontiers of much of our knowledge. The reason why most scientists can live with these uncertainties is that there are well-constructed theories that can explain many of the results. They reject astrology, not only because of what they believe to be a lack of evidence, but more because a realistic scientific theory about how it works has never been constructed in a rigorous form that can be tested by the normal methods of science. My own work now provides us with such a theory.

Planetary Magnetism and Astrology

We will now consider the possibility that planetary effects could be due directly to the magnetism of the planets. Mercury has a magnetic field, detected by instruments on board spacecraft, but it is much weaker than that of Earth, and since it is closer to the Sun than Earth this field is considerably compressed by the solar wind. The presence of this field causes a 'wake' (rather like a ship passing through water) in the solar wind on the far side of the Sun (see illus. 15). Although the Earth can on occasion pass through this

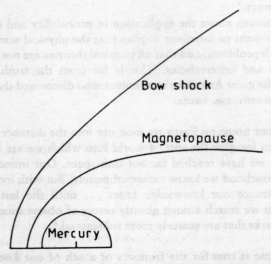

15 The magnetic field and magnetosphere of Mercury. The field is similar to that of Earth, except that it is a great deal weaker.

wake, its dimensions and magnetic strength are so small in the neighbourhood of Earth that no measurable effect has been detected.

Venus does not have a magnetic field but the solar wind causes currents to flow in the conducting parts of its atmosphere so it too has a 'wake' in the solar wind, but no convincing effect has been measured near the Earth (see illus. 16).

The presence of a magnetic field on Mars is still being debated. Measurements made by the American space probes show extremely weak fields, which they interpreted as due to currents in the Martian atmosphere caused by the solar wind. Russian measurements were interpreted, by the Russians, as evidence for a very weak large-scale field (see illus. 17). Even if it did have a field, it would not affect the Earth, because Earth is closer to the Sun than Mars, so we would never pass through its 'wake', which would have always pointed away from the Sun. The planets Jupiter,

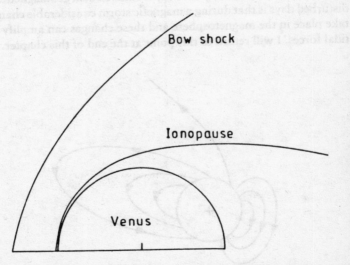

16 Although Venus does not have a field of internal origin, the solar wind does cause currents to flow in its extended atmosphere and it results in a 'wake', or bow shock, in the solar wind (coming from the left).

Saturn and Uranus also have magnetic fields, but since these planets are all further from the Sun than Earth, we do not pass through their magnetic 'wakes' caused by the solar wind interacting with their magnetospheres.

The Magnetic Tides of the Planets

The magnetic field of the Earth vibrates with a wide range of natural frequencies. According to my theory, some of these frequencies are almost exactly the same as those associated with the weak tidal forces of the planets, and these tidal forces, though weak, are able to make the natural frequencies keep in step with them or, to use the normal language of science, the natural frequencies become phase-locked to the tidal frequencies. In other words, some of the natural frequencies are tuned to some of the planets. The reason why Gauquelin's planetary heredity is enhanced on geomagnetically disturbed days is that during a magnetic storm considerable changes take place in the magnetosphere and these changes can amplify the tidal forces. I will return to this point at the end of this chapter.

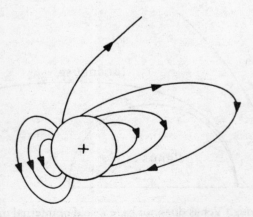

17 A Russian view of the magnetic field of Mars. Measurements made by American space probes have been interpreted rather differently.

The detractors of my theory point out that the tidal effect of the Moon on the magnetic field of Earth is very much stronger than that of the other planets, so the other planets could not possibly have the effect discovered by Gauquelin. Let's look at oceanic tides as a refutation. The calculation used to show the weakness of planetary tides is based on a particular theory of tidal effects: the so-called equilibrium theory of the tides. This assumes that the whole Earth is uniformly covered by water and that there are no land masses or atmosphere with which the water can interact.

When applied to the oceans, it tells us that the tidal range, the average difference between high and low tides, can be 4–5 feet. Yet in many bays and estuaries the tidal range can be four or five times greater than this theory predicts. In the Port of Bristol the range is about 15–20 feet. In the Bay of Fundy in Canada the range is over 50 feet, and there the Sun and Moon move 100 billion tons of water in and out twice a day. This is in spite of the fact that their gravitational attraction on the waters of the Earth is a million times weaker than the gravitational tug of the Earth itself. The reason for these high tides is that the shape of the bay and the, way the bay shallows as it goes inland amplify the weak tidal forces of the Sun and Moon. Scientists call this tidal resonance, and it occurs because the natural frequency associated with the movement of the water in the bay is very nearly equal to the tidal frequency associated with the Moon. Resonance can occur in many different situations in nature, whenever the fluctuations of an external force are in tune with the natural vibrations of a system.

Another well-known example of resonance is the shattering of wine glasses by the voice of an opera singer. A further example was provided by the destruction of a suspension bridge in America by severe winds. In this case the gusting of the wind was in tune with the natural frequency of the bridge.

How can one apply this to the magnetic field of Earth? This field extends far into space in all directions. In the direction of the Sun it extends to about five times the diameter of the Earth, and in the opposite direction it extends to about twenty-five times this diameter. The sheer size of the magnetosphere also serves to amplify the weak tidal forces of the planets, even if we use equilibrium tidal theory. Since the magnetosphere, on a magnetically quiet day, is at least ten times the size of Earth, the tidal range of a particular planet is ten thousand times greater in the outer parts of the magnetosphere than it is near the surface of Earth. Trapped in this extended magnetic field are a number of charged particles that form what is known as a plasma. The magnetic field forms a series of bays, estuaries and canals that can amplify the tidal forces of the planets on the plasma. The situation is further improved by the fact that the magnetic field itself can be pictured as a series of elastic bands, stretching into space, that have their own natural frequencies, and some of these are in tune with the tidal pull of some of the planets.

The interaction between magnetic bays and plasmas has been investigated in terrestrial laboratories, and these experiments show that it is very easy to start vibrations in magnetic fields. This research was initiated because scientists have been trying to generate energy on Earth, using the same processes by which the Sun generates energy deep in its interior. But for the process to work it is necessary to contain gases that have temperatures of several millions of degrees Celsius. Since these temperatures are so high, any container would just melt, so a method had to be found to keep the gases from the walls of the container. This can be done by using coils of wire, through which large currents of electricity are passing, to create a magnetic 'bottle' within the container. It was soon found that the magnetic fields have vibrations of their own, so these 'bottles' behave like elastic containers, and as soon as the gases touched the container a great deal of heat was lost and the nuclear process necessary to generate the energy would not start. Similar vibrations are to be found wherever magnetic fields contain plasmas, or collections of charged particles – whether this happens in the magnetosphere, the Sun or in the laboratory.

But there is another factor affecting the real tides, one that is overlooked by the simple equilibrium theory of the tides: the interaction between the sea and meteorological conditions. The height of the sea at a particular port can differ from that predicted on the basis of any theory, if the coming in of the spring tides coincides with severe weather conditions, such as very strong gusts of wind. Similarly, according to my theory, the influence of planetary tides on the magnetosphere can be considerably enhanced by magnetic storms. These storms are rather violent disruptions of the relatively quiet extended magnetic field of Earth. During these disruptions the dimensions of the field can change considerably, and there are measurable changes in the strength of the field at the Earth's surface. Most of these storms have their origins on the Sun, and they become much more frequent as the cycle of sunspots builds up to a maximum, which it does roughly every eleven years.

The solar wind, which we have already discussed, distorts the magnetosphere, rather as an ordinary wind would distort a windsock at an airfield. It is the gusting of the solar wind that gives rise to the magnetic storms of the extended magnetic field of Earth. According to my researches, the sunspots' cycle is linked to the positions and motions of the planets as seen from the Sun, and this part of the theory provides a further link with some ancient concepts in astrology. These matters will be discussed in the next chapter.

Harmonics in Astrology

Before discussing the work of the late John Addey and his collaborators on harmonics in astrology, it is necessary to explain what we mean by harmonics. In order to do so, it is also necessary to explain something about the movements of the Moon and planets as seen from the Earth. As the Earth spins on its own axis, the Sun, Moon, planets and stars will seem to move from the eastern part of the sky to the western part of the sky. Since our Earth and the other planets are all going around the Sun, the planets will seem to move slightly against the background stars, as seen from Earth. This means that each planet will rise at a slightly different time every night, and we can define a 'planetary day' for each planet. This 'day' will differ from one planet to the next, because the speed with which a planet moves against the background stars is a combination of our own speed around the Sun, and the speed of the planet around the Sun, which is different for each planet. The Moon is going around the Earth, and so we can also define a lunar day, which is roughly about 25 hours of our ordinary Sun time.

The idea of harmonics is best illustrated by using the tides of ocean and then expanding this to discuss the lunar tides in the magnetosphere. Since there are *two* high tides and *two* low tides per lunar day, we can say that the most important component of the lunar tide is the *second* harmonic – the number of the harmonic being equal to the number of peaks, or troughs, in the wave that we can use to represent the lunar tide. In fact, very careful studies of the tides reveal that this is not the only harmonic present in the tides. Theory, borne out by measurements, shows us that the two high tides and the two low tides are not exactly equal, and that this results from the presence of the first harmonic in the tidal pull of the Moon. In other words, the tidal pull of the Moon on the waters of the ocean can be represented by two separate waves, one with one maximum and one minimum per lunar day (the first harmonic) and one with two maxima (and two minima) per lunar day (the second harmonic). The situation can be further complicated by the interaction between the waters of the ocean and the geometry of the coastline. These complications can introduce further harmonics into the actual tides.

The lunar tides in the magnetosphere are even more complicated, and also have higher-order harmonics. This is because they result from the effect of the tidal pull of the Moon on the upper atmosphere, the effect of this on barometric pressure, the movements of the atmosphere that result from these pressure changes and the electric currents generated by the movements. This means that the effect of the Moon on the magnetic field of Earth can be described not in terms of a single note but in terms of a set of notes, or 'chord', with each note corresponding to a different harmonic. It should be noted that harmonics always have whole numbers, that is, one cannot have one and a half harmonics. According to my theory, the tidal pull of the planets on the magnetosphere generates similar sets of harmonics as a result of tuning of, and amplification by, the geometry of the magnetic field.

John Addey, widely held by many astrologers to be the greatest British astrologer of the twentieth century, is the recognized founder of harmonic astrology. Using the data collected by Gauquelin, he shows that certain types of personality are associated not with a particular harmonic of the Moon or one of the planets but with a set of harmonics. To illustrate his theory, Addey points out that there are two distinct types of sportsmen: one corresponding to the third harmonic of Mars and the other corresponding to the fourth harmonic of Mars. Some of Addey's work was described by one of his collaborators, Peter Roberts of the City University, London, at a conference held in London in November 1986. Extending the work of Addey, Roberts demonstrates that the harmonics associated with particular planetary types are linked to the actual positions of the planets in the sky at the time of birth. From this he concludes that: 'Even without resolving the influence question it is a matter of importance to have established that astrology conforms with one well-founded physics principle – that no causative link or information transfer can take place faster than the velocity of light.'

In a paper based on the talk he gave in London, Roberts tries to dismiss my theory with the following statement: 'Because of this snag [the weakness of the gravitational forces that give rise to the tides], tidal effects depending on resonance have been invoked but such explanations founder on the requirement of close time precision (certainly to a few minutes) and the requirement to explain harmonics below and beyond the fourth.' Neither of these arguments is valid.

The first (the requirement of close time precision) arises from a misunderstanding of my theory. He also seems unaware of some work on gravitation carried out by four Princeton specialists on relativity (Lightman, Press, Price and Teukolsky)[2] in 1975. These physicists show that the angle between the direction in which one sees an extraterrestrial object and the maximum of gravitational tug of that object is the same for all such objects, and at most it is about 1/180th of a degree, which would give a difference in time of about 1.3 seconds. The message that a particular planet is tidally distorting the outer parts of the magnetosphere then has to travel down to ground level, and the appropriate calculations on the magnetosphere show that this will not exceed 2 minutes, so the first objection put forward by Roberts is not valid. In fact, his own calculations provide convincing support for my theory.

I now deal with Roberts's second objection (the requirement to explain harmonics below and beyond the fourth). The first thing that we have to clarify is that there is a distinction between the forces acting on a system and the response of that system to those forces. If a time-varying force, with a given period, acts on a simple system, and the period of the force is equal to the natural period of the system, then we have resonance, and there is a steady build-up of the amplitude of disturbance of the system. For a wide variety of systems, the increase in amplitude gives rise to what scientists call non-linear effects. In many cases this means the system vibrates not with one frequency but with a number of different frequencies that are multiples of the original forcing frequency. So we now have a host of other frequencies that will distort the simplicity of the original 'tone'. This can lead to the type of distortion that one associates with a tidal bore, with distortion of speech by a public address system, and with the richness of tone of musical instruments. If there are two frequencies in the forcing, then the situation is still more complicated. We now not only get multiples of the two frequencies but also combinations of the old and new ones. A celestial object such as the Moon normally has two forcing terms, one with a period equal to the lunar day and one with a period of half the lunar day (called the semi-diurnal lunar tide). When this acts on the waters along the coastline, it gives rise to a range of frequencies that are multiples and combinations of the two original frequencies. Because of the many frequencies in the tides, it is convenient when undertaking tidal prediction to analyse a long-period run of tidal observations, look for the basic harmonics present, and then do predictions by projecting all this forward into the future. This gives more reliable predictions than just using tidal theory, which maintains that only the first and second harmonics are important. It is also known that the lunar daily magnetic variation and the solar daily magnetic variation have several harmonics, because the response of the magnetosphere to the movements of these bodies is non-linear. If, as I claim in my theory, the planetary tides also need to be considered, because they are near resonance, then it is very likely that we have to deal with the basic harmonics as well as multiples and combinations of these.

Further along in his paper Roberts has this to say: 'I suggest that these recent findings point away from beams and tides affecting the cells of the embryo. Instead they hint at a relationship of awareness. We are aware of the planetary patterns, so knowingly or unknowingly we act accordingly.' Roberts's suggestions on how astrology works make no effort to explain why the planetary-personality relationship is enhanced on magnetically disturbed days. This finding is also a part of Gauquelin's research, so Roberts is being selective in which of Gauquelin's findings he uses to support his ideas.

The Magnetic Midwife Planets

I propose that just as the tides of the Moon in the upper atmosphere of Earth cause the measured lunar daily magnetic variation, so the tides of the planets in the magnetosphere, amplified by magnetic bays and estuaries, cause some of the variations of the magnetic field that have already been detected but not yet studied in any great detail. I also propose that these variations, linked to the planetary tides, have the same form as that of the Moon. In other words, particular lines of force of the geomagnetic field that are 'in tune' with a particular planet will be deviated to the east as the planet rises, towards the west as the planet reaches its highest point in the sky, to the east again as it sets, and finally to the west when the planet is on the far side of Earth. Such a variation, acting on the nervous system of individuals with the inherited characteristics associated with that particular planet, will synchronize the exact moment of birth to coincide with an easterly or westerly deviation of the associated lines of magnetic force. This, then, explains the Gauquelin planetary heredity effect. The link between the positions of the planets at birth and eminence, also found by Gauquelin, leads me to the further proposal that people who attain eminence in a given profession have their nervous systems more highly tuned to the magnetic variations connected to a particular planet.

It has been pointed out that Gauquelin's planetary eminence link, although it is evident in his analysis and statistically significant, does not show up very strongly, even when he uses fairly large samples of people. The same is also true for planetary heredity. I believe there are three possible causes that can explain this weakness. The first involves a spread in the frequencies to which nervous systems are 'tuned'. As far as planetary heredity is concerned, people with similar, but not the same, personalities are likely to have a small spread about the central frequency associated with that particular set of character traits. This would lead to some weakening of the effect in an analysis based on a large group of people. With regard to the planetary eminence effect, the spread is likely to be smaller – eminent people being more highly 'tuned' – but in the analysis of a large sample even this spread could lead to weakening of the effect.

The planetary heredity effect is also affected by the fact that for different places on the surface of Earth there are slight differences between the rising of a planet and the maximum deviation (either east or west) of particular lines of force. This effect has actually been observed for the case of the Moon. The reason for these time differences is the varying geometry of the Earth's magnetic field at different places on the Earth. A similar situation arises in the tides of the sea along a coastline, where the time differences between the Moon reaching its highest point in the sky and the high tide will depend on the geometry of the coastline at a particular point. The geometry of the magnetic coastline is undergoing continual changes due to what are called the secular variations of the geomagnetic field. These are of internal origin and occur over periods of one year in length or longer. Any faster changes of internal origin are prevented from leaking out because of the electrical properties of the Earth's crust. This means that over the period that elapses between the births of parent and child, there could have been changes in the phase shifts in the lunar and planetary magnetic tides and the positions of the Moon and planets in the sky. There could have been additional phase shifts if the child and parents were not born in the same place.

Two other causes of weakening could be artificially produced changes in the magnetic environment, for example, reinforced concrete in hospital buildings and 'magnetic pollution' produced by electrical equipment. This second cause is likely to be slight because in the case of the magnetic field of Earth we are dealing with large-scale 'open' lines of force, whereas in electrical equipment the lines of force are largely enclosed within the equipment, and there is little leakage of the magnetic field outside. In this last case, it is the very low frequencies associated with the movements of the Moon and planets that are of interest, whereas electrical equipment produces much higher frequency interference to which our nervous systems would not be 'tuned'.

I now turn to the effect of geomagnetically disturbed days on planetary heredity. We have already seen that during a geomagnetic storm considerable changes take place in the magnetosphere, and that these changes enhance the effects of the planetary tides on the magnetosphere. It does seem strange at first sight that the increase in the lunar daily magnetic variation due to increases in geomagnetic and solar activity has actually been observed and measured, yet the planetary-geomagnetism relationship discovered by Gauquelin hardly exists for the Moon. We also still need to explain why the planetary-geomagnetism relationship comes through more strongly for Venus than it does for Mars, Jupiter and Saturn. In dealing with this matter it is convenient to discuss at the same time another criticism made against astrology.

It has been argued that the distances of the planets from our Earth vary a great deal, and the distance between the Earth and any one planet will vary, since they are orbiting the Sun at different distances and speeds. Why then should the astrological effects of the planets on the Earth be the same? With regard to the first objection, Gauquelin's work has shown that the astrological effects of the planets on the Earth do differ. The effects of Mars, Venus and the Moon are similar, the effects of Saturn and Jupiter are weaker, and the planets Mercury, Uranus, Neptune and Pluto play no part in the Gauquelin effect. The second part of the criticism needs a more sophisticated explanation, in which I will use the analogy of the car radio.

As we drive along in our cars, with the radio on, we do not experience, for the most part, large variations in the loudness of the station to which we are tuned, even though we are varying our distance from the transmitter. The reason for this is the fine tuning of our receivers and amplification by the electronics and electrical energy of our car radios. However, if we get too far from the transmitter, fading does become apparent, and we have to turn up the volume, which in effect amounts to increasing the power of the amplifier by supplying more electrical energy to it. This analogy can be used to understand the planetary-geomagnetism relationship.

This can be explained by the fact that before a central nervous system can respond to a particular planetary magnetic tide, this tide must not only be of the right frequency but must also be above a certain threshold value; that is, it must have a certain minimum strength. However, if it has this minimum strength, further increases do not affect the response of the nervous system. The Moon goes around the Earth in an elliptical orbit, so at certain times it is closer to the Earth than at other times. At closest approach to Earth its tidal pull is one and a half times greater than when it is furthest from the Earth. When Venus is between the Earth and the Sun, then it is closer to us than when it is on the far side of the Sun, and its tidal force is about two hundred times greater. The tidal force of Mars is about a hundred times greater when it is on the same side of the Sun as Earth than when it is on the far side of the Sun. For Jupiter the difference between tidal force at closest approach to Earth and furthest approach is only a factor of three, whereas for Saturn it is two. Thus we see that the tidal variation is least for the Moon and greatest for Venus. This means that the tidal variation of the Moon does not require the added amplification of a magnetically disturbed day, whereas for Venus it is probably essential when Venus is furthest from Earth. This is exactly what Gauquelin found with regard to the effect of magnetically disturbed days on planetary heredity.

Conclusion

In this chapter we have seen that it is possible to extend the theory, developed for the Moon in Chapter 7, to include the planets. This has been possible because the weak tidal forces of the planets on the magnetosphere can be amplified by the geometry of the magnetic field. Further enhancement of these planetary magnetic tides occurs because of geomagnetic storms, which in turn are more frequent when solar activity is at a maximum. In the next chapter we will see how the movements of all the planets, including Earth, around the Sun affect the activity cycle of the Sun.

There are a few interesting philosophical points that can be made about the results described in this chapter. The 'tuning' of the nervous system aerial is determined by the genetically inherited personality of the individual, and this tuning also determines the actual time of birth. This means that although the cosmos cannot alter our inherited characteristics, by causing the actual moment of birth, the state of the solar system at that time is, in fact, *labelling* these character traits, and also telling us something of the magnetic music to which we were exposed in the womb. Thus how we interact with the magnetic music is determined by our genes. The quotation from *Julius Caesar*, which I used at the start of this chapter, is therefore an appropriate one. The influence of the planets is not, however, restricted to terrestrial magnetic fields. In the next chapter the theory is applied to important aspects of the behaviour of the Sun.

9

The Tides of the Sun

There is a tide in the affairs of men,
Which, taken at the flood, leads on to fortune.

Shakespeare, *Julius Caesar*

Sunspots are the result of violent magnetic storms on the Sun. The number of spots on the Sun reaches a maximum roughly every 11 years. My theory for this cycle explains how planetary positions as seen from the Sun control this cycle, thus providing yet another link with astrology.

The words 'square', 'conjunction' and 'opposition' are used to describe the angles between any two planets as seen from the Earth. If two planets are in the same part of the sky, they are in conjunction; if in opposite parts of the sky, they are in opposition. Square occurs when they are at right angles to each other. These angles are called aspects by astrologers. My theory helps us to understand why different angular configurations of the planets should have different effects on solar activity, and how this information is transmitted to earth via the solar wind. In this chapter I will discuss this part of my theory and show how it links up with the concepts of astrology. So I will start with an outline, and this will be followed by a discussion of the astronomy that underlies the theory. The chapter will end with a more detailed look at the consequences of my ideas for astrologers and a description of some of the consequences of solar activity on our Earth.

Planetary Effects on the Sun

Since the 1940s there has been increased evidence that the occurrence of particularly violent events on the Sun is somehow associated with particular planetary configurations as seen from the Sun. Much of this started with the work of a radio engineer, John Nelson, who was at the time employed by the Radio Corporation of America. He was given the task of trying to find a way of forecasting the occurrence of severe increases in solar activity, since it was known that such increases could disrupt radio communications. Nelson discovered that when Venus, Earth, Mars, Jupiter and Saturn were almost in a straight line with the Sun, or when they made 90 degree angles with each other, as seen from the Sun, conditions were likely to be particularly bad for radio reception. These are some of the aspects called powerful by astrologers. Conditions were good when the angles between these planets, as seen from the Sun, were 30, 60, 120 or 150 degrees. In this respect his work differs from the claims made by astrologers, at least to some extent. They claim that 30 and 150 are slight, 60 is fairly strong and 120 is powerful.

Nelson's work was reanalysed by the scientist and astrologer Geoffrey Dean, who was able to show that Nelson's work did not achieve what had been claimed for it, and in particular that the relationship between solar activity and radio reception on the Earth was not as clearly established as many people believed. Dean's work, which was published in *Correlation*, the journal devoted to scientific investigations into astrology, has been thoroughly discussed by Eysenck and Nias in their book *Astrology: Science or Superstition?* Nelson's work has also been criticized by the astronomers Culver and Ianna in *The Gemini Syndrome*. Despite the fact that most of Nelson's work has been discredited, it did give rise to some more substantial investigations on the links between planetary configurations and solar activity.

Paul José, working for the US Air Force, was able to find a link between the maximum of solar activity and the movement of the Sun about the common centre of mass of the solar system. The work of Nelson and José was carried further by J. B. Blizard and H. P. Sleeper, both of whom undertook projects on solar activity prediction on behalf of NASA. NASA was interested in such predictions, because it was known that severe activity on the Sun could damage sensitive communication satellites, so they wanted to avoid such activity when launching these devices.[1]

Blizard's work, undertaken in 1969, is particularly important to my theory. She shows that when the planets are in conjunction or opposition, as seen from the Sun, then there are very violent magnetic storms on the Sun. The fact that some violent events on the Sun are associated with square positions of the planets as seen from the Sun puzzled Blizard. She concludes that no physical explanation for this is reasonable. My theory provides such an explanation. She also concludes that two different links between the Sun and the planets are involved, because all the planets seemed to play some part, not just those with the strongest gravitational or tidal tug on the Sun. My theory also explains why this should be the case.[2]

Just as the Moon and Sun raise tides in the oceans, so, Blizard suggests, the planets can raise tides in the gases of the Sun. Normally, two arguments are put forward against this idea. First it is pointed out that tidal effects of the planets on the Sun are weaker than the gravity of the Sun itself. Although the tidal pull due to the gravitational attraction of the Sun and Moon on the waters of Earth is also much weaker than the Earth's own gravity, the tide can still shift (as we have already seen) 100 billion tons of water out of Canada's Bay of Fundy twice a day, because the shape and dimensions of the bay amplify the weak tidal forces.

Another objection is that the very big (spring) tides occur when the Sun and Moon are in conjunction or opposition, at new and full Moon, whereas the smaller (neap) tides occur when the Sun and Moon are square, at first or last quarter. It is just possible, so some scientists argue, to understand the effect of planetary conjunctions and oppositions on solar activity, but it is impossible to understand squares in tidal terms, since they correspond to neap tide positions. This overlooks important work done by George Airy, Astronomer Royal at Greenwich, in 1845.[3]

Airy worked out a rigorous mathematical theory, which shows that it is possible to build a water canal around the Earth, parallel to the equator, in which spring tides would occur at first and last quarter, rather than at full and new Moon. This corresponds to square positions for the Sun and Moon, as seen from Earth. Such a canal would also greatly amplify the rather weak tides associated with an open ocean. The dimensions of such a canal would have to be carefully worked out. If a rock was dropped in such a canal, the wave set up would travel along the canal at one specific speed. This is called the speed of a free wave – and its value depends on the dimensions of the canal. If the dimensions were properly chosen, such that the speed of this wave was faster than the speed with which the point immediately below the Moon travelled across the Earth, but slower than the speed with which the point immediately below the Sun travelled across the Earth, then spring tides would occur at first and last quarter.

How does this apply to the Sun? Surely the idea of canals on the Sun is as fanciful as the now debunked canals on Mars? It is known from observations on sunspots that magnetic canals parallel to the Sun's equator exist on the Sun in the build-up to maximum sunspot activity. Such canals can greatly amplify the weak tidal forces of the planets on the Sun, because they are able to channel the very hot gases of the Sun parallel to the solar equator. The present theory for solar gravity also tells us that the strength of this field increases towards solar maximum – when the number of sunspots on the Sun reaches a maximum. This strength will affect the speed with which a magnetic wave will travel along a magnetic canal. The speeds with which planets travel with respect to the material on the spinning surface of the Sun vary from one planet to the next. This means that as the speed in a magnetic canal increases, the 'tidal' waves will be tuned to each planet in turn, starting with Mercury. It also means that if the tuning lies between the tidal frequencies associated with two planets, a square of these planets will give rise to larger tides on the Sun. At other times conjunctions and oppositions will have the same effect. Thus my theory of tides in magnetic canals on the Sun supports the astrological contention that cosmic influences should be powerful at the time of conjunctions, oppositions and squares; it also agrees with the astrological claim that 30 and 150 degree configurations should be slight, but it disagrees with what astrologers say with regard to 60 and 120 degree configurations. I would say that they should be slight, but astrologers would claim that 60 degrees is fairly strong and 120 is powerful.

More about the Sun

The Sun is a fairly ordinary star, as far as stars go. It is, however, the star about which the planets of the solar system move, and it is the ultimate source of heat, light and energy for life on Earth. Since it is the dominant extraterrestrial object, it is not surprising that many people in different parts of the world should have worshipped it as a god, and that it has been a major part of the serious study of astronomy for thousands of years. The points on the horizon at which the Sun sets and rises at different times of the year were the basis for the first social use of astronomy, calendar-making, in many ancient cultures. The varying lengths of the shadows cast by the Sun were one of the earliest methods of time-keeping. The Sun was also used by Eratosthenes, Keeper of the library at Alexandria, to measure the size of the Earth in about 240 BC. In more recent times, over the last 400–500 years, the Sun has proved to be an invaluable aid to navigation.

The study of the detailed physical nature of the Sun had to await the invention of the telescope and a special device, a spectroscope, which could be used to analyse in detail the nature of its light. These developments revealed the intimate details of sunspot behaviour and the chemical composition of the Sun's atmosphere. Progress made by terrestrial scientists in our understanding of the structure of the atom and its nucleus helped us to obtain a better picture of the surface of the Sun and what lay beneath it. According to modern theories on the Sun, its interior consists of three regions: the core, the radiative zone and the convective zone. In the core, energy is generated by nuclear reactions very similar to those occurring in the explosion of a hydrogen bomb, but here they occur in a controlled way. Surrounding this core there is the thick shell of the radiative zone, in which the energy generated in the interior gets out by the process of radiation – the same process by which we receive heat from an electric radiator. Around this zone there is a thinner shell called the convective zone. In it the energy is transported outwards by the process of convection, the process by which the heat applied to the base of a saucepan of soup actually heats all the soup. The hot soup will rise to the surface, the cooler soup will sink down, and a pattern of convective cells can be seen in the soup on the surface. Detailed photographs of the Sun's surface reveal that very similar convective cells exist near the surface of the Sun. It is these convective motions that generate the magnetic field of the Sun in the very hot solar gases.

Sunspots

Sunspots were first seen with the aid of telescopes in about 1610, and ever since have been of intense interest to astronomers. Although they appear as dark regions on the visible disc of the Sun, this is entirely a contrast effect. The region of the sunspot is cooler than the surrounding areas of the Sun, so it emits less light and as a result it looks darker. Taken on their own, most spots are as bright as the full Moon. More often than not sunspots occur in pairs or more complex groups and whereas the smaller spots, known as pores, last only a few hours, the larger ones last for several days. Observations on the longer-lasting spots show that the Sun is rotating, but not as a solid body. The rotation rate near the poles is about 37 days, whereas it is about 26 days in the equatorial region.

The number of sunspots also varies and reaches a maximum roughly every 11 years, but the period between successive maxima can be as short as 7 or as long as 17 years. Each cycle begins with the formation of spots midway between the poles and the equator of the Sun, or about 40–50 degrees from the solar equator. Subsequently, spots form in regions closer to the equator until most of the visible surface – called the photosphere – is covered. After maximum coverage it is the high-latitude spots that disappear first, and the last to fade completely are those close to the equator.

Other Signs of Solar Activity

Photosphere faculae are bright areas that usually eventually engulf a sunspot group, but are normally noticeable before the appearance of the sunspots, and often last longer than the spots themselves. They are the first signs of solar activity and when they are near the limb (the edge) of the Sun they appear brighter than the photosphere. A flare is a sudden local increase in the surface brightness of the Sun, occurring in a region active with faculae and sunspots. The effect is produced by the sudden release of tremendous amounts of energy in the upper atmosphere of the Sun, and is the culmination of the activity that has been building up in the sunspot region. Solar prominences are another visible consequence of solar activity. When seen near the limb of the Sun, they appear as luminous arch-like structures with continual internal gas motions. Sunspot promi-nences, also sometimes called active prominences, are those that appear over a group of sunspots.

Solar-terrestrial Relationships

The Royal Observatory at Greenwich was established to provide astronomical data for ships' navigators. Since the position and motion of the Sun are important to navigation, it would have been natural for the detailed study of the physical nature of the Sun to develop out of the other work of the observatory. At Greenwich the reasons for setting up a Solar Department came from a rather different direction. In 1843 a German astronomer called H. S. Schwabe discovered the roughly 11-year period of the sunspot cycle, and in 1852 a British scientist, E. Sabine, found that the sunspot cycle was related to variations of the magnetic compass needle, which led to the establishing of a Solar Department at Greenwich. It was argued that as the main purpose of the Obser-vatory was to serve the interests of mariners, and as Greenwich had a magnetic observatory for this purpose, it was necessary to investigate the links between events on the Sun and the terrestrial magnetic field.

The Magnetic Field of the Sun

A Dutchman, P. Zeeman, made an important discovery that enabled astronomers to investigate the magnetic field of astro-nomical objects. All atoms of a given chemical element, when heated, give off a set of colours that are characteristic of the element. This makes it possible to find out the chemical composition of the Sun's atmosphere. Zeeman showed that when these atoms are placed in a magnetic field, there are slight changes in the colours they emit. This effect is called the Zeeman Effect, and these changes can be used to measure the magnetic fields of our Sun and of other stars.

The Zeeman Effect was first used to measure the strength of the magnetic fields in sunspots by the astronomer George Ellery Hale, who was at that time working at Mount Wilson Observatory. He was able to show that when sunspots occurred in pairs, the magnetic field emerged from below the Sun's surface at one spot and entered the surface again at the other spot. Moreover, during one 11-year sunspot maximum the spots in the two hemispheres had different east–west polarities from each other, but during the next cycle the polarities in each hemisphere would be reversed. Later work showed that the Sun has fields of opposite polarity at its poles, and in this respect it resembles the Earth's field. However, this polarity changes at the start of a new sunspot cycle. Magnetic fields are also found in prominences seen against the disc, and quite often these occur between the magnetic areas of opposite polarity that are associated with sunspot pairs.

Magnetic Fields and Solar Activity

From the observations described so far, it is obvious that the magnetic fields of the Sun are very closely related to solar activity. Before going on to describe the theory that can account for some of the features of this relationship, it is necessary to make a slight digression into the interaction between hot gases and magnetic fields. In the Sun the temperature is so high that most of the atoms are stripped of some of the electrons that are part of their outer cloaks. This means that these atoms have an electric charge, and as a result they become threaded on to the magnetic lines of force beneath the surface of the Sun, rather like beads on a string. When the atoms are moved about by the internal motions of the Sun, the magnetic lines of force are carried with them. These lines, as we have already seen, are rather like elastic bands, in that they have a tension along their lengths, and if plucked they will vibrate like a violin string. If a bundle of such lines, all pointing in the same direction, exists beneath the surface of the Sun, they have the additional property that they will tend to repel each other, and hence a magnetic bubble will form.

Suppose there is a single strand of a magnetic force line stretching from the north to the south pole of the Sun, immediately below the surface. Because the equator of the Sun is rotating faster than the poles, this line will soon be distorted, and after a few rotations it will be wound up, so that it comes in at the north pole, forms an open loop in the northern hemisphere, crosses the equator, and then forms another loop (pointing in the opposite direction) in the southern hemisphere, before emerging from near the south pole. Because the line is stretched it will have more energy stored in it, just as energy is stored in an elastic band. In reality there will be several strands of magnetic field lines stretched taut below the surface of the Sun, and since these lines are in the same direction they will repel each other, thereby creating a magnetic bubble in which the density of the gas is less than the surroundings. As a result this elongated bubble will rise and eventually break through the visible surface of the Sun. The momentum of the bubble will take it high above the surface, and, as the ends of the lines are still embedded in the surface of the Sun, there will be a magnetic tube of force forming an arch above the surface. This is a loop prominence (see illus. 18), and the two points at which the lines actually cross the surface will be cooler than the surroundings. It is these regions that we see as a sunspot pair.

More Recent Theories on Solar Activity

Unfortunately, the above theory is unable to explain all of the more recent findings on the solar cycle. In 1979 Karen Harvey and Sara Martin discovered that a little-known type of solar feature, known as ephemeral regions, forms before the first spots of a new cycle. These regions form close to the poles; they have magnetic fields with opposite east–west polarity to that of the cycle just ending; and they tend to drift towards the equator as the solar cycle progresses. This discovery led Harvey and Martin to suggest that two overlapping solar cycles with different polarities existed at the same time. Appearing even earlier and close to the poles are bright patches of emission coming from atoms of iron in the extended atmosphere of the Sun. Robert Howard and Barry La-Bonte detected, in 1980, currents in the solar atmosphere, which first appear close to the poles and drift towards the equator in step with the 22-year magnetic cycle.

An alternative theory, which can account for these observations, was put forward by Peter Wilson and Herschel Snodgrass at a conference held in Pasadena in January 1987. They suggest that near the poles at the start of each cycle, the convection currents are in the form of large doughnuts, with the rotation axis of the Sun passing through the centre of the doughnuts. These doughnut-

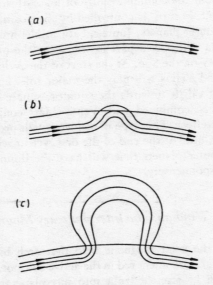

18   (a) A bundle of lines of force just beneath the Sun's surface.
(b) The appearance of a kink in the bundle. (c) The kink eventually emerges to form a loop prominence. The points at which it crosses the surface form a sunspot pair.

shaped rolls or eddies carry the hot gases from the solar interior. As the gas rises towards the surface, it loses heat, rolls over and descends again. These rolls cause the currents which Howard and LaBonte detected in the atmosphere. As the gas is deposited near the poles, the rolls will tend to move towards the equator. At the start of the next 18–22-year cycle, another roll will start near each pole, but it will rotate in the opposite direction. The magnetic field of the Sun will be strengthened, as it is squeezed between two adjacent doughnut-shaped eddies, and as a result magnetic canals will be formed between the eddies. As the eddies drift towards the equator, so will the magnetic canals. This is very much in keeping with the theory that I first proposed in December 1985, and described at a meeting in London in November 1986.

My theory says that the change in the direction of the eddies near the poles, at the start of the cycle, is triggered by the movement of the Sun about the common centre of mass of the solar system. This movement, in turn, is controlled by the positions and movements of the outer planets, Jupiter, Saturn, Neptune and Uranus. All the planets will play a part in triggering the onset of violent sunspot activity on the Sun. At the start of the cycle, conjunctions of Mercury and Venus will play the major role. Later on, as the magnetic canals drift towards the equator, square configurations of these planets, combined with Venus–Mars conjunctions, will have the same effect. This type of sequence will progress through all the planets, until at the end of the one cycle it will be conjunctions of the outer planets that will have the dominant effect in triggering sunspot activity.

The Solar Wind and the Interplanetary Magnetic Field

The loops of the solar magnetic field that arch high above the visible surface are still anchored in the active sunspot regions of the Sun. They will be stretched out into interplanetary space by a stream of very energetic fragments of atoms, called the solar wind (see illus. 19). While these loops are pulled out radially, the Sun rotates about its axis, leading to the winding up of the stretched-out lines of force. As a result these lines, which form the interplanetary field, have a spiral structure in the plane of the Earth's orbit around the Sun. This is called the garden hose effect, because the lines of the magnetic field, like the water jet of a rotating garden hose, form a curved spiral, but the solar wind particles, like the droplets of water, always move in a radial direction. Besides having a spiral form, the interplanetary field is divided into four sections, with the field pointing in different directions in adjacent sectors (see illus. 20).

Aurorae and Magnetospheric Substorms

The Northern Lights, or aurora borealis, have for centuries evoked awe and wonder in people living in high northern latitudes. It is not surprising, then, that descriptions of these phenomena are to be found in the poetry, literature and folklore of many northern countries, and that they form an important part of the culture of

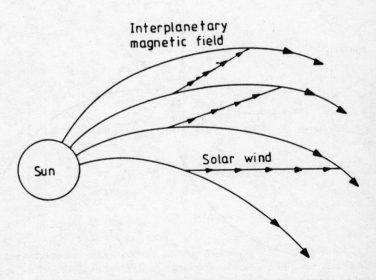

19 The solar wind and the interplanetary magnetic field.

the Scandinavian countries in particular. The Southern Lights, or aurora australis, were first reported by Captain Cook in 1773. Generally the Northern and Southern Lights are called the aurorae polares, and it has long been known that they are associated with changes in the Earth's magnetic field. The aurorae can best be described as moving curtains of light, mostly greenish-blue, though red aurorae are also seen on occasions. The extensive use of all-sky cameras, fast jet planes and, more recently, satellite observations has helped geophysicists to determine the area in which most of the aurorae occur. This region is called the auroral oval, and it is really

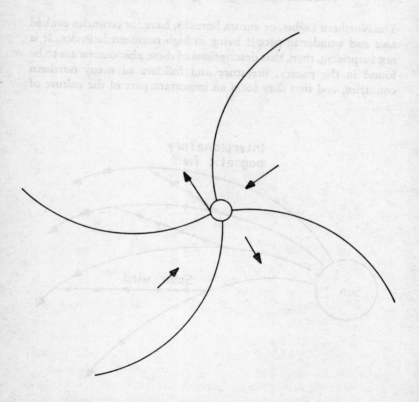

20 Sector boundaries of the interplanetary magnetic field.

the intersection of the outer Van Allen radiation belt, mentioned in Chapter 7, with the Earth's atmosphere. The auroral light is emitted by atoms and molecules of different gases in the upper atmosphere that have been excited by collisions with the energetic particles present in the belt.

The interaction of the solar wind with the magnetic field of Earth distorts the magnetosphere and consequently also distorts the auroral oval. This distortion accounts for the fact that the auroral oval is seen at higher altitudes on the dayside and at lower latitudes on the nightside of Earth. With increasing solar activity the auroral oval becomes wider and its lower boundary moves noticeably closer to the equator. The occurrence of aurorae and the width of the auroral oval are related to events on the Sun via phenomena known as magnetospheric substorms. A substorm is the process whereby some of the increase of energy in the solar wind and changes in the interplanetary field are fed into an aurora. The substorms are part of long-lasting and more extensive changes in the magnetosphere and consequent variations in the field strength at ground level. This is called a magnetic storm. The sudden storm commencement is marked by a sudden increase in the strength of the field at ground level. This increase is retained for a few hours, after which there is a gradual decrease to a strength below that experienced during the magnetically quiet times. The decrease is the main phase of the storm and it lasts for 1 or 2 days. Thereafter there is a gradual recovery to normal strength. One or more substorms occur during the main phase.

The Jupiter Effect Revisited

John Gribbin tried to make use of some of the above ideas to construct a theory linking earthquakes to the movements and positions of the planets. With Stephen Plagemann he wrote *The Jupiter Effect*, in which they developed this theory. According to them, the positions and motions of the planets control the sunspot cycle, although they do not specify in detail (as I have done) exactly how this happens. At sunspot maximum, according to Gribbin and Plagemann, the solar wind would slow down the spinning of the Earth by a very small amount, and this slowing down would be rather like putting the brakes on the Earth. This would, in turn, trigger earthquakes in those regions prone to such events. They speculated that 'the San Andreas Fault [on which Los Angeles is built] . . . might be triggered in this way in the late 1970s or early 1980s, shortly after the next period of maximum solar activity'. Later on they narrowed down this prediction to 1982. The failure of their prediction was taken as a failure of every link in the theory, so I think it necessary to discuss how my theory differs from theirs.

Their prediction of a sunspot maximum was based on work by K. D. Wood of the University of Colorado, who used the equilibrium theory of the tides to work out the tidal influences of the planets on the Sun. My theory involves resonant amplification of the weak tidal forces of the planets on the Sun by the solar magnetic canals. So the objections levelled against Wood's theory are not valid with respect to mine. Plagemann and Gribbin used a tenuous link between solar activity and the slowing down of the spin rate of Earth, whereas I make use of the much more direct link between solar activity and the magnetic field of Earth, which is backed by much more convincing evidence. Their theory makes use of the even more tenuous link between changes in the spin rate of Earth and earthquake activity: my theory makes use of a much more direct connection between changes in the magnetic field of Earth, their associated electric fields and their consequent effects on the central nervous system. This also rests on more substantial evidence. Gribbin and Plagemann do, however, deserve the credit for highlighting some very important work that the scientific establishment would like to see ignored.

This point is made very well by them in the following account from their book. At one stage of his career, when Plagemann was working for NASA, he was approached by a colleague. 'You know,' he said, 'I'm really glad to see that stuff in print. I've been working on predicting solar flares for years, and I've a file of evidence which shows a definite relationship with Jupiter–Saturn alignments. But I daren't put that in my report – it's more than my job is worth.' Further along Gribbin says: 'Steve [Plagemann] is now farming in Ireland, while his anonymous colleague still has a desk job in NASA.'[4]

In this story one can see shades of the inquisition that condemned Galileo. In terms of knowledge, understanding and information, science has come a long way, but there has been little corresponding improvement in the tolerance of new ideas.

Activity Cycles in Stars and Extraterrestrial Life

Since the Sun is a star of average size with a magnetic field, it might be expected that most similar stars would have magnetic fields. The great distances to other stars compared with the distance to our own Sun present a major difficulty in the investigation of stellar magnetic fields. As we have already seen, the magnetic fields associated with sunspot pairs have different polarities in each member of the pair; the magnetic fields near the poles are also of different polarities; and the general magnetic field varies in polarity from one region to another. Because of the closeness of the Sun it is possible, even with moderate-sized telescopes, to study the different parts of the visible surface separately. This cannot be done with other stars, where it is possible to study only the combined light of each star, and the effects of different polarities will tend to cancel each other out, so no net effect is measurable from the Earth in most cases.

It has been known for some time that the type of light associated with the element calcium is stronger in those regions of the Sun where the magnetic field is strong, such as sunspots. On the basis of these observations, astronomers at Mount Wilson Observatory began a search for fluctuations in the calcium light of a number of nearby Sun-like stars. Over a period of 16 years they detected such variations in a number of stars. From this they concluded that some ninety-one stars similar to our Sun undergo cycles like the sunspot cycle, but with different periods of activity. The proportion of stars they studied that turned out to be magnetic led these astronomers to argue that about half of the stars similar to the Sun may have magnetic fields.

Since this work at Mount Wilson, there have been several other investigations into stellar magnetic activity using different 'activity indicators'. From studies of our Sun it has long been known that solar magnetic activity is associated with X-ray and ultraviolet emissions from the corona, which is the extended atmosphere of the Sun. By analogy it would be expected that Sun-like stars, for which it is difficult to measure magnetic fields directly, would nevertheless exhibit the associated X-ray and ultraviolet output. The International Ultraviolet Explorer and the Einstein Observatory satellites have been used to study different types of stars to search for these effects, and the results have been spectacular, leading astronomers to believe that magnetic activity in certain types of stars is fairly widespread.

Since, according to my theory for solar activity, the movements of the planets around the Sun actually control the sunspot cycle and trigger violent events on the Sun, it leads me to conclude that all those stars that have similar activity cycles must also have planetary systems. Estimates based on these results are in keeping with the estimates for planetary systems based on other observations. These estimates imply that planetary systems are not uncommon in our Milky Way galaxy, and this means that there may well be other planets in the galaxy that support intelligent forms of life. Our own ability to send spacecraft to other parts of the solar system rests very much on our advanced technology, and on knowing Newton's laws of motion and his law of gravity. Much of this technology and all of celestial mechanics makes extensive use of Newton's laws. These were first discovered, not by studying motion in a terrestrial laboratory, but by studying the motions of the planets. If intelligent forms of life on other planets were to consider the possibilities of space travel, they would also have had to discover these same laws. The possibilities of other solar systems going around other stars mean that not only is the possibility of intelligent life in the galaxy increased, but the intellectual stimulus of trying to explain planetary motion would also have provided these life forms with the means of discovering the laws that govern space travel. Have these beings visited us in the past? Are they still visiting us today? Will they visit us in the future? Only objective scientific investigations can finally answer these questions. However, my theory of solar activity does strengthen my belief in the possibilities of extraterrestrial intelligence.

Solar Activity, Geomagnetism, Weather and Climate

Several researchers claim to have found correlations between solar activity, geomagnetism, long-term climate and our weather. One such claim seemed to show a link between the 22-year sunspot cycle and drought over the western United States. Another claimed to have found evidence for a correlation between atmospheric turbulence and the times at which the sector boundaries crossed the magnetosphere. Many of these claims need more research before they can be either accepted or dismissed.

A more convincing theory about a longer-term climatic effect rests on the evidence for a link between the sunspot cycle and the rate of production of a radioactive form of carbon, known as carbon-14, in our atmosphere. The carbon-14 in tree rings has been measured to show that solar activity was weaker in certain centuries than at other times. The use of geophysical data on climatic conditions in the past indicates that several periods of severe winters have corresponded to times when solar activity was much weaker.

Another interesting discovery, this time concerning the link between weather and the geomagnetic field, was made by Goesta Wollin. He shows that changes in the sea-surface temperature were somehow linked to changes in the geomagnetic field, and explained this as follows. The water of the oceans conducts electricity. Changes in the geomagnetic field cause currents to flow in the oceans, or affect currents already flowing. This causes changes in sea-surface temperature patterns, which in turn affect the temperature above the ocean. Wollin shows that because of the relatively sluggish response of the oceans to changes in the geomagnetic field, changes in the weather lag behind the geomagnetic changes by about 2 years. More recently he has shown that if the magnetic field changes very violently near a given magnetic observatory, then there are unusual weather conditions in the vicinity of the observatory about 5 days later.

Conclusion

In this chapter I have described my theory on how the planets control the overall direction of the solar magnetic field near the poles, and how conjunctions, oppositions and squares of the planets as seen from the Sun control the onset of violent storms on the Sun. I have also discussed how solar activity is linked to geomagnetic activity, the Northern and Southern Lights, short-term terrestrial weather and long-term climate.

In the next chapter the use of my theory in explaining astrological predictions is considered. The relationship between our reaction to the music of the spheres and other predictive techniques is then assessed.

IO

Responding to Celestial Music

'Haven't you heard of the music of the spheres?' asked the dragon. 'It's the music that space makes to itself. All the spirits inside all the stars are singing. I'm a star spirit. I sing too. The music of the spheres is what makes space so peaceful.'

Ted Hughes, 'The Iron Man'

Central to much of past and present-day practice in astrology is the idea of being able to predict the future of individuals from the positions of the heavenly bodies at birth and subsequent changes in the positions of these bodies. My theory, as explained so far, is able to show why the positions of the Sun, Moon and planets at birth, which are contained in the horoscope of the individual, can be used to identify some of the genetically inherited characteristics of a person. At first sight it does not seem to provide any basis for astrological prediction. However, this is not the case, and in this chapter I will discuss how my theory can be used to understand the possibility of predicting some general trends in the development of the individual. I will also show that links between astrology, palmistry, graphology and physiognomy are a natural consequence of my theory.

Flower Clocks and Futures

There are two ways in which the cosmos can play a part in the future development of a person for whom we have a birth chart. In this section I will describe the first method using the analogy of the flower clock. In some of the formal gardens of Europe, in the last century, one could find a flower clock that consisted of twelve flowerbeds, each bed containing a different type of flower. The flowers were carefully chosen according to when they opened or closed throughout the day. For example, the Spotted Cat's Ear opens at 6 a.m., the African Marigold opens at 7 a.m., the Star of Bethlehem opens at 11 a.m., the Scarlet Pimpernel closes at 2 p.m. and the Evening Primrose opens at 6 p.m. It was thus possible to tell time by noting which flowers were open and which were closed, to an accuracy of about one hour. The time at which a given plant would open was determined by its genes, and so its genetically inherited characteristics could be identified by noting the position of the Sun in the sky when it opened. However, once the plant had been identified, it was possible, on the basis of past experience with similar plants, to sketch out some aspects of its development. For instance, it may be possible to state how many years after the seed is first sown the plant will start to flower. It may also be possible to say at what time of year it will flower, how long the flowers will last and when the last flowers of the year are likely to appear. Similarly, it is possible that one can sketch out large-scale patterns in the life of an individual with a given set of inherited characteristics, identified on the basis of the horoscope, from a study of the patterns in the lives of individuals with similar sets of characteristics. The subsequent motions of the Sun, Moon and planets, with respect to the zodiac constellations, then, merely serve as a giant cosmic clock, and in this case there is no need for a continuing connection between the cosmos and the individual.

In order to understand the other way in which the cosmos can affect our actions after we are born, we need to make a further excursion into harmonic astrology, and we also need to see how this links up with my theory.

Our Cosmic Telephone Exchange

In Chapter 8 I discussed the use of harmonics in astrology. There I merely show that the tidal effects of the planets, due to gravitation on the magnetosphere, generate a set of notes, or 'chord', that is related to the 'planetary day' of each planet, and this chord triggers the actual birth time of individuals with a particular set of characteristics. However, further investigations in harmonic astrology revealed that, although for certain types of individual one planet plays the major role, the other planets also play a part, and in particular there are subtle angular relationships between the various planets that are also important for an interpretation of the birth chart. From this it would seem that what is important at the time of birth is the phase relationship between the various 'planetary chords'. When this is in tune with the individual, then the baby is born. In order to understand this in more detail, I will use the analogy of the automatic telephone exchange.

When dialling with a modern push-button telephone, one can hear that each number is encoded in the form of a different note. When we dial the first digit, we are selecting, by means of a ten-way switch in a bank of switches, one connection, of ten possible connections, to a second bank of switches. The next digit selects one of a possible ten connections to a third bank of switches, and so on. Thus when we dial a number, we are selecting a unique sequence of connections between six or seven banks of switches. We can picture our central nervous system as a telephone exchange. The 'planetary chord' of each planet selects one position in one bank of switches, and there will be one bank for each of the bodies of importance, i.e. the Sun, Moon, Venus, Mars, Jupiter and Saturn. The zodiac and its subdivisions, in my theory, replace the normal telephone dial with its ten numbers, and they become the cosmic dial of our internal telephone exchange. We are born when the cosmos dials our own personal telephone number.

This, however, cannot be the whole story, and in order to explain the rest I want to use another analogy. One day, our washing machine at home was not working properly. The programme seemed to have got stuck at one particular point, with water still in the machine. After following the manufacturers' instructions for getting rid of the water, I investigated what was wrong, and found that some fluff from an old blanket had got stuck in the pump that empties the machine. I also then discovered that if there is still water in the machine, this water forces air up into a pressure switch, which prevents the programming timer from going on to the next stage of the programme.

According to my theory, something similar is happening near the time of birth. The cosmos may ring our number several times before we are actually born, but until we are biologically ready, and the waters in the womb have broken, we will not be born. The ringing of our telephone number by the cosmos causes our central nervous system to co-ordinate the release of a number of hormones, and it is this release of hormones that causes the baby to push and be pushed out into the world. The waters in the womb operate the analogy of a pressure switch that will not allow the cosmos to play its role until the baby is ready to be born.

Memories of Magnetic Melodies

There is another way in which the complex symphony played on the magnetic field of our Earth by the positions and motions of the Sun, Moon and planets can directly influence the way in which we respond to given situations even after we are born. However, in order to explain this, I need first of all to discuss a theory of aesthetics. I first came across this theory in a book by the physicist H. E. Huntley, called *The Faith of a Physicist*,[1] but it is really based, as Huntley fully acknowledges, on the work of the pioneer psychoanalyst Carl Jung. According to this theory, our appreciation of any piece of music or work of art is based on the sum total of all our memories and the particular memories evoked by the music or the art. The theory states that the bedrock of all our memories is that which we share with the whole human race, such as the beauty of the sunset or a rainbow, or the rustle of leaves in the wind. This bedrock of human memories is rather like the floor of the ocean, and rising out of the ocean are continents and islands of memory that we share with those of our own race. These might be the particular colours of the vegetation of the land in which our ancestors lived, or the song of the birds that shared the ancestral homeland. Rising out of the plain of these racial continents of memory are smaller plateaux of memory that we share with those of our own family, for example, family holidays or shared festivities like Christmas. Then there are the personal memories that are very much our very own, and they are like mountain peaks rising out of the family plateau of memory.

Throughout the nine months of pregnancy we are exposed to fluctuations of the Earth's magnetic field. Even before our sense organs are able to respond to any sort of external stimulus, we have a developing central nervous system and a growing brain. According to my theory, fluctuations of the Earth's magnetic field have associated with them electric currents that can cause nerve impulses to pass along the nerve cells of this nervous system, and these impulses can leave their imprint on the brain of the foetus in the form of rudimentary memories. This nervous system is embedded in the body, and so it must reflect the general structure of the human form. This means that the magnetic aerials with which we receive changes in the magnetic field of Earth are basically similar, and, although there are differences in these fluctuations from one place to another, there are also many basic similarities, and hence there are global human similarities between the magnetic memories that are stored in our foetal brains. These would correspond, in my theory, to the basic human memories that form the ocean floor of memory.

Since there are racial differences in the physical dimensions and proportions of our bodies, the shapes of our hands and faces, and racial differences in character (which would correspond to racial differences in the way our nervous system was 'wired up'), there would also be slight racial differences in the aerial system that the foetus would present to the magnetic field of Earth. Added to this we have regional differences in magnetic fluctuations, so not only are our aerials tuned to different stations, there are also regional differences in the programmes being broadcast. Thus some of the magnetic memories would be racial and this would correspond to the racial memories that are like islands and continents rising out of the ocean bed.

Family differences in the dimensions and proportions of our bodies, the shape of hands and faces, and internal 'wiring up' of the nervous system (which is related to character traits) will give rise to fine-tuning of our magnetic aerials. Add to this the unique set of fluctuations of the field that occurs over the nine months of pregnancy, and that reflects the changing positions of the Sun, Moon and planets, and we all end up with a very personal set of magnetic memories. Our magnetic aerials thus play a dual role.

They receive a whole set of memories from the magnetic field of Earth, but they also co-ordinate the moment of birth. By playing this dual role, they are telling us something about our genetically inherited characteristics, and they are also telling us something about the magnetic memories that we recorded while still in the womb. The moment of birth is thus synchronized by a particular set of magnetic fluctuations that is unique to the individual, but it also separates the time during which we learn our own set of magnetic music from the time during which we can respond to this music. After we are born the information coming from our sense organs generally swamps the information we receive via our nervous system aerials from the magnetic field of Earth.

These ideas lead to the second way in which the cosmos could play some part in the future of individuals. The magnetic tunes recorded on our brains while we are still in the womb do become part of our earliest memories. When some of these tunes are played on the magnetic field of the Earth by the Sun, Moon and planets at a later stage in our lives, it could evoke these early memories, and hence it could influence the way we respond to a given situation. It is well known that different types of music can affect our moods and our emotional response to particular events, especially if certain pieces of music are associated with significant events in our lives, so it is quite likely that the celestial magnetic music can have similar effects. However, such effects are likely to be more pronounced when the information coming to us via our sense organs is less effective; for example, in moments of reverie or meditation, or when we are asleep. It is still likely that this recalling of the magnetic music from our memories can have some influence on our subsequent behaviour. This, then, is the second way in which the cosmos can influence our futures.

Cosmic Programming of Human Computers

The theory described above can be further clarified by using analogies based on modern household electronic equipment, such as a television set and a home computer.

The scenes from a television studio set and sound from the

speech or music are converted into electrical signals that are then converted into radio waves by the transmitter. The transmitted information is then picked up by the television aerial and passed on to the receiver (which can be tuned), where it is amplified and processed prior to activating the speaker and the television picture tube. Alternatively, the processed information can be stored on a videotape for use at a later stage. We are all familiar with interference with sound and vision on television programmes. Interference can result from lights being switched on and off in the house, or may be generated by electrical equipment in the home, or in a car. Some of this interference is conveyed via the aerial, but several of the wire connectors in the television set can also act as aerials themselves, and they too pick up interference. Interference picked up in this way will be greater if the aerial is unplugged.

Suppose several different makes of television sets are all tuned to the same channel. Although the broadcast transmission is the same for each set, the interference on each set will vary slightly, and this is because each set is slightly differently made. The type of interference picked up by the connectors will depend on their physical and electrical properties as well as the arrangement of their circuit boards. Thus different makes of set will respond to interference of slightly different frequencies. When we are watching a programme, provided interference of this kind is not too great (and this is normally the case with a good aerial system and a properly tuned set), we manage, on the whole, to reject the additional noise on the sound and the spots on the screen. This is because past experience tells us that this extra 'noise' is not part of the programme.

Various subsystems of the central nervous system concerned with our senses are similar in many respects. Each has an organ or set of organs to detect a particular sort of information. Eyes detect light; ears detect sound; tastebuds taste; noses smell; and the nerve-endings beneath the skin can collect information on the things we touch. These subsystems also have transmission systems to communicate the information to the brain, via nerve cells or neurons. Different parts of the brain are concerned with receiving, processing, interpreting, acting on and storing all the information. In this respect the system is rather like a television receiver fitted with a memory in the form of a video recorder. The stems of the neurons are rather like electrical wires covered with insulation. However, a fluctuating magnetic field can cause currents to flow in such a system. We have already discussed the evidence for the theory that fluctuations of the geomagnetic field can cause electrical currents to flow in parts of the central nervous system.

So, to return to the analogy of the television set, the entire universe may be seen as a set of broadcasting stations, but our sense organs are tuned into particular channels and collect signals from the environment around us, much as an aerial picks up a channel for a television set. However, the chains of neurons that carry the information as electrical impulses, and connect our sense organs to the brain, are like the wire connectors in the television, and in the same way as television connectors pick up interference, the neurons pick up information directly from the geomagnetic field. The information that the foetus can collect via its sense organs is strictly limited because it is sheltered in the womb from external sensory stimuli, but it is not sheltered from the influence of the geomagnetic field. Therefore, to continue the analogy, the foetus is like the television set with its aerial unplugged. Because the foetus is receiving very little information via its sense organs, the chains of neurons in its nervous system are directly susceptible to the patterns of 'interference' coming via the geomagnetic field. This 'interference', however, should not be so called, because the foetus is not yet 'tuned in' to the channels of information coming via the sense organs and therefore the electrical signals coming to the brain from the geomagnetic field are not getting in the way of other signals.

Our senses act as a sort of filter: the sensory receptors collect only certain kinds of signal, and the information they collect is limited. The brain is capable of receiving a much greater range of information, but once the sense organs are in operation they have an organizing function and limit and arrange information from the external world. Let me use the analogy of the home computer to expand these ideas.

Computers are programmed using a coded set of instructions called a language. Most home computers make use of standard English words as well as symbols and expressions used in mathematics. However, the basic central unit of a computer operates on a much more restricted set of symbols and characters called 'machine code'. The high-level languages we use to programme computers all have to be translated into machine code before our instructions can be understood by the central unit. Information coming to our sensory receptors (eyes, ears, tastebuds, etc.) is like a high-level language, which has to be translated into machine code, i.e. electrical impulses, before the chains of neurons can transmit the information to the brain.

Before a computer leaves the factory, it will have been instructed to receive and deal with information fed into it in a high-level language. In other words, a certain amount of pre-programming will have been built into the computer, and this programming will have been done using machine code. I suggest that once we are born we function largely via the high-level languages of sight, sound, smell, touch and taste, but my theory proposes that some pre-natal programming can take place via the 'machine code' fluctuations of the geomagnetic field acting on the unborn baby. This pre-natal programming from the geomagnetic field could feed information to the foetus's brain, and thus modify the brain's capacity to use the information that will later come in particular ways via the child's sensory organs. This modification will be the effect of the geomagnetic field and will be different in different people, because of differences in our genetically inherited nervous system aerials, and because of the ever-changing magnetic field of Earth that reflects changes in the solar system.

Hence the geomagnetic field will contribute something unique to the individual personality of each child. This, then, corresponds to the first way in which the cosmos can affect the future of an individual, according to my theory. To understand the second way, discussed above, we have to return to the home computer analogy. It is possible to use 'machine code' to programme our computers, even in our own homes, but in order to do so we have to learn this code. Some people who make a hobby of computing actually do this when using their computers for some advanced applications. I am suggesting that it is possible for post-natal fluctuations of the geomagnetic field to recall, via its own 'machine code', some of the pre-natal programming it fed into the brain of the developing foetus, and thus influence its behaviour in certain circumstances.

Astrology and Appearance

Over many centuries it has been claimed that there is a correlation between appearance and character, and since astrology shows that character is related to the birth chart one would expect to find a correlation between appearance and the birth chart. A great deal of work has been done in this direction. One such investigation sought a correlation between Sun-signs and appearance, but found that no such correlation existed. However, convincing evidence was found for a correlation between the positions of the planets at birth and facial appearance. The most important results in this connection come from the work of Edith Wangemann in Germany. In fact, Wangemann found that the correlation with facial appearance was so precise that it can be used to make small corrections to the birth chart, and that charts corrected in this way were found to check accurately with events.

In order to understand the work of Wangemann in a bit more detail, it is necessary to explain a few astrological concepts. The first is the idea of astrological houses. The inner circle of the birth chart is divided into twelve houses that, in the simplest of systems, the equal house system, are all of 30 degrees each. The houses are numbered in an anti-clockwise direction, with the first house just below the eastern horizon and the seventh house just above the western horizon. A cusp is the dividing line between two houses; the ascendant is the sign rising at the time of birth; the cusp ruler is the planet ruling the sign on the cusp; and an aspect is the angular relationship, as we have already seen, between two objects or points on the zodiac.

Wangemann found little or no correlation between facial appearance and the cusps of the equal house system. However, she found a correlation between certain aspects of the more sophisticated Koch house system of cusps, cusp rulers and facial appearance. The most important aspects were 0, 45, 90, 135 and 180 degrees. According to these correlations, the ascendant correlated with the bone structure of the head and forehead; the second cusp with lips, cheeks and the distribution of flesh on the face; the third cusp with lower jaw and general mobility of expression; the fourth cusp with the tip of the nose; cusp five with the middle nose; and cusp six with the setting of the eyes and the area between the eyes.

For Western Europeans, Wangemann found that the facial characteristics imparted by the Sun, Moon or one of the planets under the conditions described above were as follows: for the Sun – well-proportioned, frank and open; the Moon – round, soft and sometimes fat; Mercury reflects the sign it is in and any planet in aspect to it; Venus – pleasant, rosy, glowing, dimples and feminine; Mars – dry, muscular and masculine; Jupiter – jovial, friendly smile and photogenic; Saturn – angular, with prominent bones, yellowish, dark, thick skin; Uranus – dry, skinny, no fat, skin not thickened; Neptune – pale, puffy, shapeless, heavy jowls and neck. In 1973 Wangemann finalized a scheme that gave the following results for one of the bodies of the solar system aspected with the ascendant or the ascendant ruler. This scheme is as follows: Sun – round, well-proportioned face; Moon – round, full face; Jupiter – long face; Saturn – square face; Uranus – long face; Pluto – broad face; other planets – indefinite.

Investigations into possible correlations between general body shape have yielded much less convincing evidence.[2]

Palmistry and Graphology

Palmists claim that they can tell character from the lines on the palms of our hands. Lyall Watson argues in his book *Supernature* that this is not as fanciful as most scientists would claim it to be, and he further suggests that it may have a biological basis. He points out that the distribution of the ridges in our hands is determined by the arrangement of nerve-endings and sweat glands. This distribution is so firmly established that it is impossible to change the pattern permanently, and even after severe burns and skin grafting, the pattern will reappear as healing brings the natural skin to the surface again. These patterns form during the third and fourth month of pregnancy and then persist unchanged throughout life. In recent years specialists in genetics have become interested in these lines and ridges because they show hereditary characters. Each person has his or her own unique pattern in the palms of their hands and so it can be used as a method of identification, and has been employed in this way ever since AD 700 when the Chinese first introduced a method of classification.

One scientist who took seriously the idea that the palms of the hands could be used for medical diagnosis was Sir Francis Galton, who was a cousin of Charles Darwin. At the University of London, the Galton Laboratory has made a careful study of the relationship between congenital disorders and particular patterns on the hands. The scientists at this laboratory have been able to show that about thirty such disorders are linked to specific patterns on the hands, and that sometimes the disorder can be diagnosed by these patterns even before the disorder manifests itself in any other way. One specific example of the work of this laboratory involved mongolism. In 1959 these scientists showed that the chromosomal abnormality that produced mongolism also generated a specific line called the 'simian crease' across the top of the palm.

The smaller creases in our hands do change with time and they seem to be somehow associated with the activity of our brains. To illustrate this, Watson quoted a rather interesting story of a house painter who suffered severe concussion when he fell from a building. After one week in this condition all the creases in his hands disappeared, but, as he regained consciousness, the lines reappeared.

Watson also argues a strong case for the link between handwriting and character. One of the first books on the subject, *Treating of How a Written Message May Reveal the Nature of Qualities of the Writer*, by Camillo Baldo, was published in 1622. Since then many people from different walks of life have taken an interest in the art of graphology. These include Elizabeth and Robert Browning, Van Gogh and Freud. It now seems very likely that not only is there a relationship between handwriting and character, but that graphology may also be useful in medical diagnosis. Lyall Watson quotes from a report of the American Medical Association on the possibility of diagnosing diseases by means of handwriting: 'There are definite organic diseases that graphodiagnostics can help to diagnose from the earliest beginnings.' At the end of his section on graphology, Watson has this to say: 'The hand and its behaviour provide one of the most sensitive external measures of the working of the brain.' My theory of cosmic personality relationships is able to explain why there should be links between astrology, physiognomy, palmistry and graphology.

Astrology, Physiognomy, Palmistry and Graphology

In my theory our hands are an important part of our nervous system aerial, and so their physical dimensions and proportions, as well as the way the nervous system of the hand is 'wired up', to some extent determine the messages we receive from the magnetic field of Earth. In recent years scientists doing research on the human brain have mapped the parts of the brain that are linked to different parts of the body. Such a mapping shows that a large proportion of the brain is linked to our hands (see illus. 21). This is because of the sensitivity and versatility of these parts of our bodies. Another large proportion is linked to our faces, including eyes, ears, noses and mouths (see illus. 22). This means that our faces form another important part of the nervous system aerial. From my theory, then, it is possible to understand the correlations between character and the findings of astrology, physiognomy, palmistry and graphology. This is because every part of the nervous system is part of our magnetic aerial, but those parts of our bodies that have larger areas of the brain linked to them will be more effective in receiving information from the magnetic field of Earth. Just as the aerial system on top of the house can be used to tell us something about the programmes that the television set in the house is capable of receiving, so the patterns on our hands and the general structure of our faces can reveal something about the magnetic messages we are capable of receiving from the cosmos. It must be emphasized that according to my theory we inherit, to a large extent, the shapes of our faces and hands, and that the cosmos plays no part in influencing these genetically inherited characteristics. However, the birth chart, by giving us information on the state of the solar system and its associated geomagnetic variations at birth, tells us something about our aerial system and its responses. This means that the state of the solar system merely labels the characteristics we inherit, and tells us something about how these characteristics will interact with the cosmos in later life.

In his book *Cosmic Loom: The New Science of Astrology*, Dennis Elwell has this to say: 'Astrology is not a close relative of hand reading . . . science says that astrology can't happen, therefore it doesn't. The "can't happen" trap has caught so many savants down the years, you would think they would have learnt by now.' According to my theory, it is possible to understand, in hard scientific terms, the link between palmistry and astrology, so Elwell

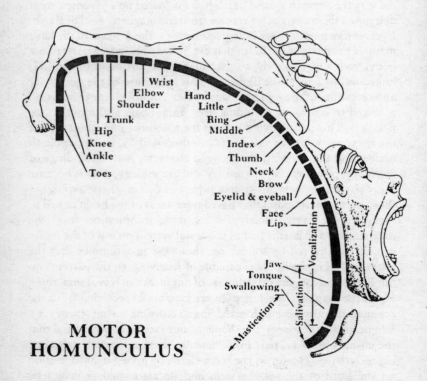

Wrist
Elbow
Shoulder
Hand
Little
Trunk
Ring
Hip
Middle
Knee
Index
Ankle
Thumb
Toes
Neck
Brow
Eyelid & eyeball
Face
Lips
Vocalization
Jaw
Tongue
Swallowing
Salivation
Mastication

MOTOR HOMUNCULUS

21 This shows, diagrammatically, the part of the brain devoted to sending nerve impulses to the body. The sizes of the parts shown are related to the proportion of the motor homunculus serving that part of the body.

falls into his own trap with his categorical denial of any such link.

Conclusion

In this chapter we looked at how the element of prediction in astrology can be understood in terms of my theory. We also saw that a natural consequence of this theory is that there should be some correlation between character analysis and the findings of

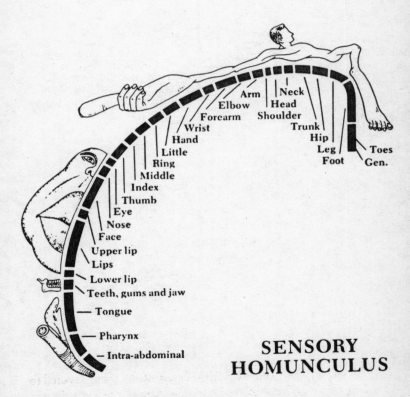

Arm
Neck
Elbow
Head
Forearm
Shoulder
Wrist
Trunk
Hand
Hip
Little
Leg
Toes
Ring
Foot
Gen.
Middle
Index
Thumb
Eye
Nose
Face
Upper lip
Lips
Lower lip
Teeth, gums and jaw
Tongue
Pharynx
Intra-abdominal

SENSORY HOMUNCULUS

22 This shows the part of the brain that receives nerve impulses from the different parts of the body.

astrology, palmistry, graphology and physiognomy. There is, how-ever, the question of how astrological prediction arose. Why did ancient civilizations relate the presence of the Moon and the planets to events on Earth? The use of the theory in explaining these developments is the subject of the next chapter.

11

The Origins of Astrology

The observation of planetary effects at birth would be a discovery of that magnitude. It would demonstrate, too, that the age-old, good-for-nothing, fossilized astrology wasn't legend after all.

Michel Gauquelin

The work of Michel Gauquelin, combined with my theory of astrology, leads me to the conclusion that the ancient founders of astrology made some very important basic discoveries about personality and the state of the cosmos at birth. The well-documented evidence does not really tell us how they managed to make these discoveries, without the advantages of the sophisticated procedures and methods of modern science, several centuries before the birth of Christ. In this chapter I discuss some of the ideas that have been put forward by various people in their attempts to explain the origins of astrology. I show that all these ideas have serious disadvantages, and that they do not explain the evidence that we have to hand. I then propose my own theory based on the ideas developed in previous chapters. This theory overcomes the difficulties encountered by historians of astronomy and astrology when they try to account for the origins of astrology.

Some Ideas on the Origins of Astrology

Derek and Julia Parker, in their book *A History of Astrology*, describe some ideas on the origins of astrology. They point out that in 235 BC an astrologer told one of his clients that 'if your child is born when Venus comes forth and Jupiter has set, his wife will be stronger than he'. To this they add their own comment that Venus is associated with indecision and laziness, whereas Jupiter is associated with kindliness and ease. These are not the characteristics that Gauquelin would list as being of paramount importance for people born under these two planets, but it is nevertheless important to notice that even at this stage in history, astrologers were associating certain types of character with the rising of specific planets.

Further along in the same book, the Parkers point out that 'astrologers argue that associations between the signs and planets and certain characteristics were empirically made . . . And certainly there is much evidence to suggest that the elaboration of the techniques of astrology came about not through psychic guesswork, or even the symbolic unconscious, but (as in science) through observation and careful record.' In other words, the Parkers claim that by the third century BC astrologers had, through the methods of empirical science, already laid down the basic principles of the subject.

John Gribbin and Stephen Plagemann put forward a similar suggestion in their book *Beyond the Jupiter Effect*. They say:

> So what is the simplest way to explain how the ancients knew that the positions of the planets affect the Sun? It is now clear that the changing level of solar activity affects the weather on Earth . . . So it is easy to imagine the wise men of an ancient agricultural community noting that certain patterns of moving lights in the sky – the planets – often heralded unpleasant weather, while other patterns seemed to be more common when the weather was good.

They add: 'We leave the debate for others to take up as they wish: the point we wish to make is just that such a scenario is far simpler, and far more plausible, than invoking the ancient wisdom of a spacefaring race, or a Velikovskian lost civilization, to account for the birth of astrology.'

In earlier chapters we mentioned the book *The Gemini Syndrome* by two astronomers, Culver and Ianna, who set out to disprove all of astrology. This book, however, puts forward some suggestions that are similar to those of Gribbin and Plagemann, although these suggestions are not put forward specifically to account for the origins of astrology. They write:

> Consider for example: if the Moon affects the geomagnetic field, which is somehow related to the establishment of certain weather patterns, which in turn somehow affect the number of ions in the air, and subsequently the level of particular hormones in the body, which may cause susceptible people to feel rotten and perhaps even commit a homicide – can you blame the Moon?

In fact, Culver and Ianna use this suggestion to demolish all of traditional astrology, with the words:

> Although we can perhaps see a vague outline of a mechanism and causal chain of physical and biochemical effects on physiological processes and their resulting behavioural consequences, a great deal of study is still required. If any conclusion is to be drawn here regarding astrology, it is that the traditional systems should be discarded.

My own theory proposes a more direct mechanism based on more substantial evidence and it also shows that some of the ideas of ancient astrology, do, in fact, have a substantial scientific basis.

Lyall Watson in his book *Supernature* also puts forward some ideas on the origins of astrology. 'It seems obvious that astrology is not the result of some sudden insight of the *"Eureka!"* kind; it never sprang fully formed from anyone's mind. So there is only one other possibility: that it evolved, like a living organism, out of the very stuff of which it is made.' To illustrate his point, Watson points to the behaviour of a termite, to be found near Darwin in northern Australia, that constructs a weirdly shaped nest. It is well known that many termites construct huge, rock-hard mounds by cementing fine grains of sand together with saliva. The particular species of termite discussed by Watson builds slabs 10 ft sq and only a few inches thick. These mounds apparently resemble large tombstones scattered across the outback of Australia. The long axes of these mounds are accurately oriented along a north–south line, and it is from this fact that the termite gets its name of *Omitermes meridionalis*, or the compass termite. Apparently the mound of this termite is so constructed that during the early morning and the late afternoon, a maximum area is exposed to the Sun so as to gather heat, but at noon, when the Sun's rays are hotter, the mound exposes a very narrow face to the Sun. Watson notes that: 'Built into every single one of the termite labourers is an awareness of the Sun's movements that leads it to construct its little bit of mound so that the whole thing relates to the cosmos in a way that expresses the needs of the society. The termitarium is literally shaped by cosmic forces.'

From this he concludes that astrology might have arisen in a similar way: 'I believe that astrology arose in this way: that an awareness of the cosmic forces predisposes man to certain ideas and patterns, and that, despite the fact that each contributing astrologer could see only his little bit of the structure, the final synthesis took on a natural and relevant form.'

Further along in *Supernature* Watson states: 'There are some mystical things about astrology, but there is nothing supernatural about the way it works. Man is affected by his environment according to clearly defined physical forces, and his life, like all others', becomes organized by natural and universal laws.' I would agree wholeheartedly with this last statement.

Problems Posed by the Above Ideas

All the suggestions that astrology arose as a result of empirically collected sets of observations must have elements of truth in them, but they do not tell the whole story. The correlation between day and night, the seasons and changes of the position of the Sun in the sky, is direct and immediate. There can be no question that these phenomena are all related. The same is true for the position of the Moon in the sky, the phases of the Moon and the ever-changing nature of the tides. However, the planets are very much fainter than these two objects and their motions are much more complex, so to claim that astrology arose purely out of empirical observations of the sky alone does immediately pose some serious problems.

In a previous chapter we saw the great difficulties that had to be overcome by the Babylonians when they tried to construct a lunar calendar that did not require an actual observation of the crescent Moon for them to start their month. They had, in fact, to work out in principle when they would be able to see the Moon so that they could start their month on that day. As we saw then, this required a detailed knowledge of the motions of both Sun and Moon with respect to the background stars, and in order to obtain this they created an arithmetical astronomy that became the basis of their astronomical and astrological predictions.

Because of the complexity of planetary motion, the faintness of the planets and interference from meteorological conditions the problem of predicting where a planet should be in the sky, even when you cannot see it, is many times more difficult than that concerned with the appearance of the crescent Moon. Yet this was a prime requisite for all of ancient astrology, and in particular for the casting of horoscopes. It was necessary to know the positions of the Sun, Moon and planets with respect to the background stars, at the time of birth of an individual, even if the sky was cloudy, or the presence of the Sun in the sky blotted out a view of the planets at the time. This means that in order to notice a correlation between the more complex patterns of planetary positions and the specific characters of different individuals, they had to have a fully developed theory of planetary motion. As has already been pointed out in a previous chapter, this was the prime motive for constructing such theories.

The problem left unsolved by the above suggestions is that they do not tell us why the ancient astronomers should have considered the planets important in the first place. The effect of the complexities of the motions of these bodies on terrestrial phenomena is by no means direct and immediate. In Chapters 7 and 8 we saw the difficulties encountered by Gauquelin when he first tried to link astrological ideas with the characters of individuals. He had the benefits of a fully developed theory of planetary motion, based on Newtonian mechanics, and very sophisticated methods of statistical analysis, that had really been developed only over the last 300 years. The ancients did not have this knowledge at their disposal.

The same type of argument applies to the correlation between planetary positions and weather, which Gribbin and Plagemann saw as a possible key to the origin of astrology. The work of Goesta Wollin on the meteorological effects of changing magnetic fields shows that as far as short-time weather effects are concerned, the changes of weather lag behind their geomagnetic causes by as much as 2 years. For the very abrupt changes of the Earth's magnetic field that do cause severe changes in weather over shorter periods, the time lag is only 5 days. However, these short-period links between geomagnetism and weather are really associated with geomagnetic storms, and whereas these are more frequent when sunspot activity is at a maximum, they are not very obviously linked to planetary positions as seen from the Earth. In order to discover such correlations one does need very sophisticated methods of analysis, and the large number of calculations involved have been possible only since the availability of advanced computers.

Also in their book *Beyond the Jupiter Effect*, Gribbin and Plagemann discuss another link between planetary positions, as seen from the Sun, and our weather. This link was discovered in 1980 by two Chinese scientists, Ren Zhenqui of the Peking Academy of Meteorological Science, and Li Zhisen of the Peking Astronomical Observatory. They found that when several of the planets were grouped within an angle of less than 90 degrees, which they called a synod, on one side of the Sun, and the Earth was on the opposite side of the Sun, then there were unusual weather conditions on Earth. They explained this in terms of changes in the actual orbit of Earth caused by the grouping of the other planets. The gravitational tug of the planets in this synod on our Earth will cause changes in the time the Earth spends in the winter and summer parts of its orbit, and thus cause slight changes in the actual lengths of the seasons, and this in turn gives rise to unusual weather conditions. However, it should be pointed out that Ren and Li made this discovery by studying ancient Chinese records that go back for more than 3,000 years, because China has the longest continuous civilization that has kept such records. This means, once again, that these correlations are not all that obvious when one is dealing with the shorter periods of time, and this must have been the case during the early years of astrology.

A theory of astrology based on the suggestions of Culver and Ianna is also beset with the same difficulties. Their mechanism is much too complex and involved to lead to some of the more simple and straightforward 'laws of astrology' discovered by the ancients, and for which my theory now provides a convincing scientific basis. How these laws were discovered, and how they provided the framework and motivation for a more detailed and systematic study of the correlation between planetary motion, personality and terrestrial events, will be discussed in more detail in the next section.

Magnetic Dowsing and Direction-finding

The discovery of links between terrestrial events and planetary motion as seen from Earth must have been based on something that was obvious, direct and immediate for the people of the ancient world. The ancient peoples of pre-recorded history used the magnetic field of the Earth for direction-finding, and dowsing, and they were aware of the celestial conditions that produced changes in their ability to use the Earth's field in this way. In other words, for them the world was like a cosmic ballet, with the changing magnetic field of the Earth providing the music and the Sun, Moon and planets as the ballet dancers, dancing to the music of the spheres.

In *Supernature* Lyall Watson writes: 'Bas-reliefs from early Egypt show figures in strange headgear carrying, at arm's length in front of them, a forked stick; and Emperor Kwang Su of China is depicted in a statue dated 2200 BC carrying an identical object. Both, it seems, were in search of water.' The finding of water must have been of vital importance to the people of the ancient world, and so developing dowsing methods must have been important to them. It has long been known that human dowsers claim that they can detect water, but they have not always been taken seriously. Watson discussed the evidence in favour of the dowsers' claim, and pointed out that this evidence showed that dowsing was somehow connected to magnetism. More recent evidence along these lines has been discussed in the *New Scientist* by Tom Williamson.[1]

Watson discussed the work of the Leningrad mineralogist Nikolai Sochevanov, who led an expedition to the Kirghiz of Russia in 1966. They set out to investigate scientifically the claims of dowsers. In their first survey they used an aircraft fitted with special magnetic measuring devices, called magnetometers, and inside the plane Sochevanov and some other dowsers used their dowsing rods to try to detect water. When they flew over the river Chu, they found that the vast amounts of water of the river itself had no effect, but all of them could feel the effect on their rods when they were near the banks of the river. Apparently, from this and other tests in different parts of the world, people respond much more strongly to places where the water is in friction with the soil than to large masses of water flowing at great speeds.

Both Williamson and Watson discuss the work of the Dutch geologist Solco Tromp. In 1949 Tromp had shown that dowsers were unusually sensitive to the Earth's magnetic field, and they would respond to changes of the field that could be measured with magnetometers. Tromp also showed that a good dowser could detect an artificial magnetic field a hundred times weaker than that of Earth, and the dowser could use his rod to chart the geometry of the field in a laboratory. Yves Rocard, a French physicist, supported these ideas in 1962, and further support came from the work of Valery Matveev, a Soviet geophysicist, in 1967. However, as was to be expected, all this work came in for a great deal of criticism from the scientific establishment.

More convincing evidence has come from the work of Gene Simmons, from the Massachusetts Institute of Technology, and Duane Chadwick of Utah State University. Simmons, a geophysicist, carried out surveys of the changes in gravitational and magnetic fields surrounding two wells near Boston. These wells had particularly large yields of water, of about 140,000 litres per hour. He found that dowsers could site both holes within a rather narrow magnetic feature only a few metres wide. Chadwick carried out controlled experiments on 150 subjects and found convincing evidence that the movements of the dowsers' rods were linked with tiny changes in the Earth's magnetic field.

Williamson also drew attention to magnetic direction-finding by animals, which was a subject I mentioned earlier in connection with bird navigation. One new piece of information that he mentioned was how whales use magnetic stripes for long-distance navigation. These stripes were produced during the geological process known as the spreading of the ocean floor.

In an earlier chapter I mentioned some experiments showing that most humans also possess the ability to find direction directly from the Earth's field, although this faculty is more highly developed in some people than in others. These experiments were carried out by Robin Baker of the University of Manchester. Baker, in one of his early experiments, drove blindfolded students by winding routes distances of 50 kilometres from the university. He found that students gave good estimates of the direction of the university while they were still blindfolded, but when their blindfolds were removed they became disorientated.[2]

In a second series of experiments Baker used a busload of blindfolded schoolchildren. He divided them into two groups: one had bar magnets attached to their heads, while the second had unmagnetized pieces of metal, similar in shape and size to the bar magnets, attached to their heads. The second group was much better at finding the direction of north than the first.

The question that arises is, how do humans and animals detect this magnetism? Baker found evidence for magnetite, a magnetic substance, in the sinus bones of human corpses, and several other researchers have found traces of this substance in magnetic bacteria, in birds and in other vertebrates that can orient themselves with respect to the magnetic field. Other mechanisms of magnetoreception have been proposed that do not require a specific magnetoreceptor organ, and this is especially true with regard to migrating birds. According to one of these proposals, the body of the bird is a weak electrical conductor, and as it moves through the lines of force of the Earth's field so, like an electric generator, an electric field is set up between its two ends. An alternative explanation involves electrostatic forces generated by friction between the bird's wings and the air, and the subsequent interaction between these forces and the magnetic field of Earth. It has also been suggested that the magnetic field of Earth can influence the movement of lymph in the lymph tubes. As pointed out by Baker, all these suggestions present some problems, one of which is that they require detection of rather small effects against a lot of background noise. One of the suggestions does not involve a special magnetic sense organ, but proposes that the detection of the magnetic field takes place in the molecules of the retina of the human eye, as a by-product of the normal process of vision.

There have also been a number of suggestions concerning the detection of the small changes in magnetic fields associated with the process of dowsing. A group of scientists from the University of Hawaii, the California Institute of Technology and the Marine Fisheries Service in La Jolla recently calculated the theoretical sensitivity of the Yellowfin Tuna. The first stage of the calculation involved estimating the number of crystals of magnetite there were in the tuna's minute sensor. They came to the conclusion that there are 85 million of these crystals arranged in chains, and that if suitable receptors could detect the movements of these chains, then the system could detect changes in the magnetic field of Earth amounting to less than 1/20,000 of the steady field. As Williamson says in the *New Scientist*, such a system in human beings could easily account for the detection of very small changes in the Earth's field by dowsers.

These arguments have been taken further by two scientists from the California Institute of Technology, David Presti and John Pettigrew. They suggested that particles of magnetite could be embedded in muscle tissue. The rotation of these particles could be recorded by receptors, called muscle spindles, that play a control-ling role in muscle movement. Their suggestion implies that the dowsing reaction does not involve the dowser's brain, but that it may be a simple reflex response.

My own theory proposes that the entire nervous system of the individual can detect very small changes in the magnetic field of Earth, because there exist loops of neurons in the system that do resemble the tuned electric circuits of a radio receiver. These circuits could well, like radio and television aerials, have directional sensitivity, and so they can be used to detect the direction of the field as well as small changes in it.

Discovering the Laws of Astrology

In an earlier chapter we saw that the Solar Department at Green-wich was established because solar activity caused deviations in the compass needle. I also showed that my theory for solar activity could account for the observations that particularly violent events on the Sun were associated with planetary conjunctions or squared aspects of the planets, as seen from the Sun. When the planets as seen from the Earth are either in opposition to the Sun or in conjunction with it, then they and the Earth will also be either in conjunction or in opposition to each other as seen from the Sun. Such a situation would give rise to violent events on the Sun. The very early watchers of the sky may well have found that such events in the sky interfered with their ability to find direction and to dowse. This I believe is the most straightforward way that this rule of astrology could have arisen.

My theory also shows that near the end of the solar cycle, 90-degree configurations of the planets Saturn and Jupiter, as seen from the Sun, would give rise to violent events like solar flares. Because these planets are much further from the Sun than we are, some 90-degree configurations of these planets, as seen from the Sun, correspond to very nearly 90-degree configurations of these planets from the Earth. This would have led to the idea that square configurations give rise to powerful astrological influences on Earth.

I further believe that the ability to detect changes in the magnetic field of Earth was more highly developed in ancient man than it is in modern human beings. This was because the finding of direction and water was part of their survival. It is just possible that people with slightly different characters 'heard' different magnetic tunes from the celestial spheres, because of genetic differences in the tuning of their nervous system magnetic aerials. Thus, for example, those of a warlike disposition 'heard' martial music, whereas those of a jovial disposition 'heard' the music of Jupiter. Thus the human ability to detect magnetic fields formed a framework into which other changes, such as the meteorological effects of changes in the geomagnetic field, could be fitted. During violent sunspot activity it is not unknown for the Northern Lights to be seen much further south. This too would thus have been associated with those times when ancient man found it difficult to dowse and find direction. I believe it was in this way that astrology arose, some time before it was more formally systematized by the work of the Babylonians and the Greeks.

Conclusion

In this chapter we have considered the origins of astrology. First of all we looked at some of the suggestions that have been made concerning its origins and then we looked at the problems posed by these suggestions. I then pointed out that the simple rules of astrology must have arisen from observations that were more obvious, direct and immediate than those involved in earlier proposals. Finally, I proposed that early human beings had a more highly developed awareness of their magnetic sensitivity than we have, because it was important to their survival to be able to find direction and dowse for water. Quite early on they must have realized that certain planetary configurations upset these abilities and thus the first simple laws of astrology were discovered. These were later expanded and systematized by the Babylonians and the Greeks. This was the origin of our planetary awareness. From these simple beginnings, there developed the highly complex astrological cultures that were dominant 2,000 years ago. In the next chapter, it seems appropriate to combine astrology and science to explain the events marking the birth of the Christian religion.

12

The Gift of the Magi

Now when Jesus was born in Bethlehem of Judaea in the days of Herod the king, behold, there came wise men from the east to Jerusalem, saying, where is he that is born King of the Jews? For we have seen his star in the east, and are come to worship him.

Matthew 2:1,2

I believe that the Magi played a vital role in the Christmas story, and that they were, in a very real sense, the founders of Christmas. This conviction is based on the concepts and ideas developed in previous chapters. The wise men, or Magi, are referred to as astrologers in the New English Bible. This is really the only sensible way of seeing these men, because astrologers were, and are, the only people who associate births with celestial events. It is not part of any purely astronomical or religious custom to link the birth of any individual with celestial phenomena, but it is very much part of a centuries-old astrological tradition. It is necessary to accept the fact that the wise men were astrologers, if one is to understand the fundamental importance of the Star of Bethlehem. In this chapter I will discuss the evidence for this assertion, the nature of the Star, which must necessarily follow from this, and the consequences for the Gospel stories. I will also discuss why the alternative explanations for the Star are really untenable.

The Star of Bethlehem

Over the years many authors and thinkers from different walks of life have suggested that the Christmas Star should be given an astrological interpretation. This suggestion has been resisted by the Church and by many scientists. It is only since the publication of the New English Bible that the Church has at least opened the door to such an interpretation by admitting that the wise men were astrologers. Scientists, on the other hand, with very few exceptions, have continued to reject such an interpretation. They have done so for two reasons. First of all, almost all scientists dismiss all of astrology simply as meaningless mumbo-jumbo. Second, as a result of the first error, they have failed to see the overwhelming symbolical significance of the factual astronomical events that almost certainly marked the birth of Christ.

Jupiter was the Star of Bethlehem – as it rose at sunset on Tuesday, 15 September 7 BC. This was the moment in time when Christ was born. We have already seen that the French psychologist and statistician, Michel Gauquelin, found convincing evidence that most great politicians, military leaders, top executives, journalists, playwrights and actors are born when Jupiter has either just risen or just passed its highest point in the sky. We also saw in previous chapters that this can be understood in scientific terms, which say that the cosmos triggers the actual moment of birth in such a way that people with a given set of inherited characteristics will be born at a given time. This means that one can understand Christ's qualities of leadership in scientific terms.

Jupiter rises at some time of every day, although, if it is too close to the Sun in the sky as seen from Earth, we do not always see it rise. This means that the rising of Jupiter is in itself not unusual. What made the rising of 15 September 7 BC, of such great interest to the Magi-astrologers were the associated astronomical events. Jupiter was very close to the planet Saturn at the time of rising, and both planets were in the constellation of Pisces. As we have seen, the appearance of two planets very close together in the sky is called a conjunction. Conjunctions of Saturn and Jupiter take place roughly every 20 years, so this too is not very unusual.

The circumstances that start to make the year 7 BC of special interest are that in that year conjunctions of Saturn and Jupiter took place three times. Such a series of conjunctions is called a triple conjunction, and for Saturn and Jupiter it takes place only once every 139 years. A triple conjunction in the constellation of Pisces takes place only once every 900 years, and Pisces also had a special significance for the astrologers.

Jupiter, in ancient astrology, was identified as the planet of kings. This is consistent with Gauquelin's scientific evidence that Jupiter is associated with the births of great military leaders and politicians. As we have already seen in a previous chapter, Saturn was the planet that ruled over Saturday, the Jewish Sabbath, so it became known as the protector of the Jews. The world known to the ancients was divided up into geographical regions, each of which was associated with a sign of the zodiac. The geographical region around Palestine was associated with Pisces. This collection of symbolism would have been interpreted by the Magi as indicating that a king of Jewish origin would be born in Palestine. We then see that to understand the meaning of the Star of Bethlehem we have to rely very heavily on astrological symbolism.

Is this approach valid? I believe that this general approach has the backing of several leading Churchmen.

In his book *The Sea of Faith*, Don Cupitt, Dean of Emmanuel College, Cambridge, says:

> As people come increasingly to feel that purely historical criticism of the Bible is yielding diminishing returns, we may soon see them turning to a more literary approach. There are those who believe that the anthropologists' ways of interpreting myth and symbols . . . may discover laws that govern the working of the creative imagination and can be used to explain literary texts. If they are right, then we may indeed gain a better understanding of what the biblical writings mean and how they work . . . for they will make it clearer that the biblical writings are products of human religious psychology functioning under certain historical conditions.[1]

Astrology was very much part of the 'historical conditions' that existed in the ancient world, and it also made inroads into many religious considerations, so to shy away from astrological interpretations of the Star is to impose on the ancient world our own scientific world view.

Astrology can also shed light on other aspects of the Christmas story. One of these is discussed by Hans Sandauer, former Vice-president of the Viennese Astrological Society, in his book *History Controlled by the Stars*.[2] On the basis of his own researches into Christ's birth, Sandauer gives this as 17 September 7 BC. He also points out that on this day the Sun was in the constellation of Virgo, and suggests that this circumstance – Christ had his Sun in Virgo – might have been the origin of the story that Christ was the son of a virgin. In view of statements made by some leading Churchmen concerning the virgin birth, this seems very plausible, especially since the Gospels were written at least one generation after the birth of Christ.

One of the first scientists to suggest that the Saturn–Jupiter conjunction of 7 BC may have been related to the birth of Christ was Kepler. We have already seen, in a previous chapter, that Kepler had an interest in both astronomy and astrology, even though, at times, he had misgivings about the validity of the latter. On 17 December 1603, just a few days before Christmas, Kepler observed a Saturn–Jupiter conjunction in the constellation of Pisces from his observatory in Prague. This conjunction fascinated Kepler, not least because he seems to have been aware of the work of Rabbi Abarbanel, who wrote a commentary on the book of Daniel in the fourteenth century. This Jewish commentator believed that Saturn–Jupiter conjunctions in Pisces had a special significance for Israel. Prompted by these circumstances Kepler worked backwards to see if a similar conjunction of these two planets could have been seen close to the time of the birth of Christ. His calculations led him to the discovery of the triple conjunction of 7 BC that we discussed earlier in this chapter. However, Kepler had formulated his own brand of astrology, in which the moment of conception was more important than the moment of birth, so he placed Christ's conception in 7 BC and the birth of Christ in 6 BC.

More recently another astronomer, K. Ferrari d'Occhieppo from the Astronomical Institute of the University of Vienna, took Kepler's suggestions a great deal further by combining modern astronomical methods of calculation with what we know of Babylonian astronomy and astrology. He believes that the Magi were Babylonian astronomer–astrologers of the Zoroastrian religion, and as a consequence he suggests that the Star should be seen in the astrological terms discussed earlier.

D'Occhieppo develops these ideas in a book called *Der Stern der Weisen – Geschichte oder Legende?*[3] published in Vienna in 1977. Some of the work that appears in this book was introduced to the English-speaking world and developed a great deal further by the English astronomer David Hughes from the University of Sheffield in his book *The Star of Bethlehem Mystery*, published in 1979.[4] My own work on the subject is a development of the work of both these men. David Hughes lists in his book the most important astronomical events relating to the Saturn–Jupiter conjunction, which occurred in the year 7 BC. Not all these events have the same importance for the hypothesis presented later in this chapter, so I will just discuss the dates of the most important events.

The first conjunction of Saturn and Jupiter, in the constellation of Pisces, took place on 27 March 7 BC, the second took place on 6 October and the third on 1 December. Yet d'Occhieppo believes that the Magi were quite convinced that Jesus was born on 15 September, so why does he settle for this date? This is because on 15 September, just as the Sun was setting in the west, Jupiter, with Saturn very close by, was rising in the east. Such a rising is called the acronychal rising, and the Magi-astrologers would have considered the effect of these planets to be greatest when this event took place.

This point of view has scientific support from my theory of astrology. According to my theory, Saturn, Jupiter and Earth would have been in a straight line as seen from the Sun, and this could well have caused an increase in solar activity, which in turn would have amplified the direct tidal influence of Jupiter on the magnetic field of Earth. Also at such a time Jupiter would be on the same side of the Sun as the Earth, and as a consequence it would be much closer to the Earth than at other times, so these circumstances mean that the Jupiter effect discovered by Gauquelin would have been most effective. As I have already pointed out, the effect linked the rising of Jupiter with the birth of great politicians and military leaders.

Another question that has to be answered is why the Magi decided to go to Bethlehem. The answer lies in the biblical prophecies of the Old Testament. Herod also made use of these after the visit of the wise men. As he was concerned with their revelation that a king of the Jews had been born, he summoned the chief priests and scribes, and asked them where Christ should be born. Their reply is contained in Matthew 2:5,6: 'And they said unto him, In Bethlehem of Judaea: for thus it is written by the prophet. And thou Bethlehem, in the land of Juda, art not the least among the princes of Juda: for out of thee shall come a Governor, that shall rule my people Israel.' I am proposing that the wise men combined their own astrological predictions with the biblical prophecies to settle on Bethlehem.

How were they led to the stable in which Christ was born? The Matthew Gospel says that the star guided them to the correct place. This is highly unlikely, as it stands. Seamen have for centuries used the stars to find position at sea, so at first sight it may appear that the wise men could have done something similar. However, even today one star cannot be used to fix a position of a ship at sea. At least two, or even better three, stars are needed to fix the position of a ship, and even today this cannot be done, using the most modern equipment and techniques, to an accuracy of less than 3–4 miles. The methods used by seamen today were not available to these Magi, so there really is no way in which the astrologers could have used astronomical methods of navigation to guide them to the infant Jesus. I do believe that the star did guide them but in a less direct sense.

In Matthew 2:7 we are told that: 'Then Herod, when he had privily called the Wise Men, inquired of them diligently what time the star appeared.' This verse provides the clue as to how the Magi found Jesus. They actually went in search of a male baby born in Bethlehem just as the Sun was setting, and Jupiter and Saturn were rising, on 15 September 7 BC. This was not at all like looking for a needle in a haystack. In a city the size of Plymouth, with a population of 250,000 people, the maximum number of births per day is about twenty-four. This means that, on average, one baby is born every hour, and half of these babies are likely to be female. The population of Bethlehem today is about 17,000, so even if one ignores the effects of modern contraceptives on the birth rate figures of Plymouth, it is very unlikely that there would have been one birth per hour in Bethlehem in the time of Christ. We also know from the Bible that a census was in progress at the time of Christ's birth – this was Joseph and Mary's reason for going to Bethlehem – so it is quite likely that the Magi enlisted the help of the people who did the census in their search for Jesus. It is well known that the people of Tibet choose for the new Dalai Lama the baby born close to the death of the old one; I am suggesting that the Magi used their astrological interpretation of the astronomical events in a similar way to help them find the new 'King of the Jews'.

As a scientist I do not believe in virgin births, neither do I believe that an angel of the Lord appeared to Mary. I believe that the first suggestion that Christ had a special destiny actually came when the Magi told Mary that her son was born to be 'King of the Jews'. As Jesus grew up, Mary told him of the visit of the wise men, and Christ combined his belief in his own destiny with his own natural abilities, revealed by his time of birth, and lived his life in a way that he believed would help him to fulfil this destiny.

Albert Schweitzer, the great humanitarian, philosopher and musician, building on the work of many great German theologians, made his own unique contribution to historical studies of the life of Christ, in his book *The Quest of the Historical Jesus*.[5] In this work he tried to sort out the myth and legend from the historical facts of the Gospels. His work was re-evaluated a few years ago by Don Cupitt, Dean of Emmanuel College, Cambridge, in *The Sea of Faith*, which was the book that accompanied a television series of the same name. Cupitt has this to say: 'Schweitzer thought that Jesus had been aware of his exalted destiny. The secret must be kept hidden for the present, but when the Kingdom came Jesus would be revealed in all his glory as the Messiah and Son of Man.'

I believe it is quite likely that it was the message of the Magi, revealed to Christ by his own mother, that was the source of this belief in his own destiny. In an earlier chapter we saw that quite often people who know something about astrology answered questions about themselves, and sometimes behaved, in a way that they believed to be consistent with their astrological chart. These effects are called self-attribution effects, and they can, as we saw, interfere with some of the experiments designed to test astrology. If this is true today, when astrology carries less weight with most people than it did in the ancient world, how much more so would it have been true for the world into which Christ was born.

Other Supporting Evidence

The interpretation of the triple conjunction given earlier in this chapter is able to explain another symbol connected with Christianity and the early Church – that of the fish. The *Oxford Dictionary of the Christian Church* says that the origin of this symbol is obscure. Since the Saturn–Jupiter conjunction took place in the constellation of Pisces, could this not be the origin of this symbol? This suggestion is, in fact, backed by some eminent scholars who are not astrologers.

Carl Jung in *Aion* argues that at least part of the connection between Christ and the Fishes has an astrological origin. He starts by pointing out that the fish was a particularly widespread symbol, so its appearance in any place at any time was not really surprising. He then goes on to say: 'But the sudden activation of the symbol, and its identification with Christ even in the early days of the Church, lead one to conjecture a second source. This source is astrology.' He then goes on to discuss Saturn–Jupiter conjunctions in Pisces and their significance for the destiny of the Jews.[6]

Gordon Strachan, a Church of Scotland minister, in his excellent book *Christ and the Cosmos*, is another scholar who links Christ with Pisces, but he does so from a slightly different point of view, while at the same time supporting the triple conjunction in Pisces and its astrological interpretation. He makes use of the astrological concept of the great year, which has its origins in the astronomical phenomenon of the precession of the equinoxes.[7]

In an earlier chapter we discussed the precession of the equinoxes in connection with the origin of the constellations. There we pointed out that the Earth's axis makes a double cone in space, so although at the moment the north end of this axis points very nearly to the Pole Star, this was not the case when the Pyramids were built. The cycle of the precession, which takes about 26,000 years to complete, also has other consequences for astronomy and astrology. On 21 March we have the spring equinox, and on this day we have equal day and night all over the world. If one could see the Sun and stars at the same time, then the Sun would be seen against the background of the constellation of Aquarius on 21 March. In 1987 the Sun would have been seen in the constellation of Pisces on the same date, so the Age of Aquarius has only just started.

Since the precessional cycle is 25,800 years long, it means that the position in the sky at which the spring equinox occurs takes about 2,000 years to move through each one of the twelve zodiac constellations. This length of time is called a great year. When systematic astrology first started in the ancient world, this position was in the constellation of Aries, and so it is still called the First Point of Aries by astronomers and astrologers. However, by the time Christ was born this position had moved into the constellation of Pisces. Gordon Strachan argues that Christ ushered in the age of Pisces, which has just ended for us, and that this provides yet another link between Christ and the Fishes.

It has long been known that the traditional date for Christmas was not the day on which Christ was born. The use of 25 December was really based on a pagan festival that also had its roots in an astronomical phenomenon. As we move from the northern summer towards winter, the Sun sets closer and closer to the south-western part of the horizon, and the days get shorter. On 21 December the Sun sets further to the south-west than on any other day of the year, and we have the shortest day in the northern hemisphere. This is called the winter solstice. However, by 25 December there is a noticeable lengthening of the day, and the point on the horizon at which the Sun sets seems to be moving back towards the west. Many people who worshipped the Sun as a god saw this day as that on which the Sun-god returned from the south, and hence for them it was a festival day. The early Christian Church adopted this day as the day on which Christ was born.

Jesus, the Astronomer–astrologer

Morton Smith wrote a very fascinating book called *Jesus the*

Magician. He is well qualified to do this: at one time he was Professor of Ancient History at Columbia University and has a doctorate in theology from Harvard as well as a doctorate in classics from the Hebrew University in Jerusalem. The essence of the book is best described in Smith's own words:

> 'Jesus the magician' was the figure seen by most ancient opponents of Jesus; 'Jesus the Son of God' was the figure seen by that party of his followers which eventually triumphed; the real Jesus was the man whose words and actions gave rise to these contradictory interpretations. 'Jesus the Son of God' is pictured in the Gospels; the works that pictured 'Jesus the magician' were destroyed in antiquity after Christians got control of the Roman empire.

Further along the Preface Smith has this to say: 'This book is an attempt to correct this bias by reconstructing the lost picture from the preserved fragments and related material, mainly from the magical papyri, that New Testament scholarship has generally ignored.'[8]

In this book he puts forward strong arguments that seem to show that Christ used magical techniques and methods for many of his miracles. At one stage in the book he says: 'Since the stories of Jesus' miracles come mainly from the magical tradition, we expect them to be full of details found in that tradition; they should share the same notions and express them in the same words. This they do, and the wealth of such details affords further proof of the magical origin of the stories.'

Since astrology was a subject with which many magicians were familiar, we might well ask if Christ knew anything about astronomy and astrology. In the Arabic Gospel of the Saviour's infancy we are told in verse 51:

> And a philosopher who was there present, a skilful astronomer, asked the Lord Jesus whether he had studied astronomy. And the Lord Jesus answered him and explained the number of the spheres, and of the heavenly bodies, their natures and operations; their oppositions; their aspects, trian-

gular, square and sextile; their course, direct and retrograde; the twenty-fourths and sixtieths of twenty-fourths; and other things beyond the reach of reason.

If Christ's destiny was first revealed to his mother by the Magi-astrologers who sought for someone who was born at the right astrological time, it is not surprising that he took a great interest in the subject.

Other Possible Explanations for the Star

In 1985, with the reappearance of Halley's Comet, the possibility that this was the Star of Bethlehem was once again revived. In particular this hypothesis was supported by James Fleming, a lecturer in Historical Geography and Archaeology at Jerusalem's Hebrew University. Fleming had discovered evidence that there was a census in 12 BC, and that Halley's Comet had also appeared in the same year, so he concluded that this was the Star, since Mary and Joseph had gone to Bethlehem to take part in a census. There are several objections to this idea. First, comets were always associated with the death of kings or with other disasters, but they were never associated with good things happening on the Earth, so why this exception? Also at this stage in history it was not realized that some comets – like Halley's – actually returned to the sky on a regular basis. This discovery was made by Halley himself, who lived between 1656 and 1742. As we have already seen, astrology was, and still is, based on using predictable events in the sky in attempts to predict the destinies of individuals. Since it was not possible at this stage in history to predict the return of comets, they were not really part of the astrologer's scheme. The final objection is that it is not possible to use a comet to fix a position on Earth or at sea, so there was no way in which a comet could have led the Magi to Palestine or to Bethlehem.

In the December 1986 issue of the American popular astronomical magazine *Sky and Telescope*, Roger Sinnott backs the conjunction of Jupiter and Venus that took place on 17 June 2 BC. In the past this possibility had been ruled out by the belief that

Herod, who was alive when Christ was born, died in 4 BC. This estimation was based on the fact that the Jewish historian Josephus recorded that Herod's death was preceded by an eclipse of the Moon. It is generally believed that this was the eclipse of 12–13 March 4 BC but Sinnott now argues that it could have been the eclipse of 9–10 January 1 BC. On this basis the Venus–Jupiter conjunction of 2 BC could have been the Star of Bethlehem. My feeling is that the Saturn–Jupiter conjunction of 7 BC still remains the most likely possibility because of its overriding astrological significance; this is something not possessed by any of the other possibilities, including the Venus–Jupiter conjunction.

An astrological interpretation also rules out another possibility that is sometimes discussed in connection with the Christmas Star. This is that the star was a nova. Novae are not really new stars, as their Latin name implies; they are stars that suddenly greatly increase their brightness over a period of days. Two novae were recorded by Chinese astronomers close to the time of Christ's birth, one in March of 5 BC and one in April 4 BC. Once again this is not a predictable event, even today, so this was not part of the astrologers' scheme.

Conclusion

The combination of astrology and science leads to the inevitable conclusion that there was a unique conjunction of cosmic factors present about the time of the birth of Jesus. It was knowledge of these factors that enabled the Magi to play their part in defining the future of Christianity.

13

Astrology and Magnetic Astrology

The question of all questions for humanity, the problem which lies behind all others and is more interesting than any of them, is that of the determination of man's place in nature and his relation to the cosmos.

T. H. Huxley

The theory I have proposed in this book makes use of knowledge derived from a wide variety of disciplines. In this chapter I want to bring the strands of the theory together, so that the links between the different aspects become more apparent and the theory can be seen as a unity. I also discuss how my theory is related to some more traditional concepts in astrology, and the directions in which it can be developed further.

There are three main links in the causal chain of my theory. Each link is a unity in itself in that it can be subjected to scientific tests that are independent of those applied to the other links. However, once we have fully tested all the links we can then make further tests on the strength of the whole chain. In this chapter I also examine the present state of the information on which the theory and its individual parts rest.

The three parts of the theory are: the planetary-solar connection; the solar-lunar-Earth connection; and the Earth-human-life connection.

The Planetary-solar Connection

The first link in the chain is the effect of the planets on the Sun. Contrary to popular belief, the Sun is not fixed at the centre of the solar system. The planets, especially the large outer planets like Jupiter, Saturn, Neptune and Uranus, move the Sun very slightly around the common centre of mass of the solar system. I am proposing that changes in this movement result in changes in the overall pattern of heat convection in the Sun. The convective motions are responsible for the generation of the solar magnetic field, and the changes in these motions result in a change of direction of this magnetic field. This aspect of my theory is consistent with the work of Paul José, which was discussed in Chapter 9.

Since the Sun's equator is moving faster than the rest of it, the magnetic lines of force get wound up into structures that resemble magnetic canals at the later stages of the sunspot cycle. These canals make it possible for all the planets in turn to have an effect on violent outbursts of magnetic energy on the Sun. They do so because as the lines of force are stretched, so their periods of vibration change, and they are successively in tune with each of the tidal frequencies (due to the gravitational tug of the planets) of one of the planets, starting with Mercury and ending with Neptune. In other words, the magnetic canals resonantly amplify the tidal tug of the planets, but the dominant planet at each stage in the solar cycle will be different. If the tuning of the solar magnetic field lies between the periods of two planets, then square configurations of these two bodies will give rise to violent activity on the Sun. At other times conjunctions or oppositions will give rise to similar events. This work is consistent with the findings of Blizard, which was also mentioned in Chapter 9. It also deals very well with the objections raised by John Addy, and described by Culver and Ianna. Addy's objections are based on the equilibrium theory of the tides, and are not applicable to my use of the resonant canal theory of the tides applied to magnetic fields on the Sun.

Magnetic activity on the Sun modulates the solar wind, and this modulation causes corresponding changes in the magnetic field of the Earth.

The Solar-lunar-Earth Connection

We could, if we wished, draw a graph of how much sound intensity we got out of our radio receiver as we moved the tuning control from one end of the frequency (or wavelength) scale to the other. The sound level would be very low between stations but high every time the receiver was tuned to a local or national station. The response would be quite sharp when the frequency corresponded exactly to that of a particular station, and on our graph the response would look like a very narrow line. It is well known from atomic physics that the atoms of each element 'broadcast' at a specific number of 'lines' (mostly as light waves), and the spacing between these lines is characteristic of the type of element. Thus, from an examination of the spectra that an element will emit or absorb, we can identify its physical properties and chemical characteristics. The magnetic field of Earth vibrates with a wide range of frequencies (or periods) ranging from several years to fractions of a second. On top of this wide spectrum there has also been detected a number of fairly sharp 'lines', some of which correspond to the solar day and its harmonics, the lunar day and its harmonics, and the year and its harmonics.

Many researchers have noted the effect of the variation of sunspot numbers on the behaviour of the geomagnetic field. The most important work in this area, with regard to my theory, is that of Robert Curry. Using a special mathematical technique called the Minimum Entropy Method, he was able to show that many of the long-term variations of the field were related to the solar cycle and its harmonics. Just as the sound waves in a radio studio are used to modulate the very high-frequency radio waves used to transmit information, so the long-term variations of the Earth's field modulate the short-term variations that result from the spinning of the Earth and the motion of the Moon around the Earth. This means that the lines corresponding to the solar and lunar daily magnetic variation are flanked by lines, very close by, corresponding to the year and to the solar cycle and its harmonics. This was first noted in 1965 by Edward Bullard in his Harold Jeffreys Lecture, 'Electromagnetic Induction in the Earth', where he has this to say:

In fact, most of the information has been obtained from the daily period and its first three harmonics of 12, 8 and 6 hours ... The amplitude of the terms varies with the season of the

year and with the sunspot cycle: it might . . . be more convenient to regard these changes not as changes in the amplitude
of a term with a single frequency but as beats between a
group of terms with slightly different frequencies.[1]

This suggestion is consistent with the general mathematical theory
of amplitude modulation. Bullard also notes that 'it is a curious
fact that no attempt seems to have been made to resolve this fine
structure by the methods of power-spectrum analysis'. This situation has improved slightly in recent years because of the work of
F. de Meyer of the Royal Meteorological Institute in Brussels. He
was able to show that some of the terms of the solar daily magnetic
variation did indeed have such a fine structure.[2] However, the
mathematical methods of analysis we have at the moment are
refined enough to reveal only the structure associated with the
year. Further improvements are needed before we can detect those
associated with the solar cycle and its harmonics. This deals with a
point Henbest makes in his *New Scientist* review of this book's
first edition: 'Indeed, if there are effects that the foetus can perceive,
why do they not show up on magnetometer traces?' The magnetometers used at geomagnetic observatories simultaneously record *all
the fluctuations associated with the geomagnetic field, since they
are in no way tuned to do anything else*. It is the refinements in
mathematical techniques, due largely to modern high-speed computers, that have made it possible to detect the different variations
in geomagnetic records. This point is well made by S. Malin, an
internationally recognized authority on the mathematical analyses
of geomagnetic data.

Just as starlight can be analysed into its component frequencies by a spectroscope, and shown to have regions of greater
and lesser intensity together with discrete spectral lines, so
the geomagnetic variations can be considered as a spectrum
. . . The optical analogy can be taken further: there are
broader bands present (e.g., one at around one cycle per 11
years) and many show fine structure (e.g., the one-cycle-per-
day line is accompanied by others that differ from it in
frequency by multiples of one cycle per year). Unlike starlight,

magnetic data do not arrive conveniently packaged for instant spectral analysis, but have to be acquired over a long period by patient observation. There is no simple device corresponding to a spectroscope (unless a computer can be considered as such) and the spectrum has to be deduced from the mathematical analysis of series of equispaced observations.[3]

However, the mathematical analysis needs to be improved further before we can detect the variations required by my theory. I am also proposing that the foetus responds resonantly to specific fluctuations of the geomagnetic field, and ignores all others to which it is not tuned.

The solar cycle modulation of the solar daily magnetic variation means that the solar daily magnetic variation and its harmonics already contain information on the relative heliocentric positions of the planets (including Earth), since the planets have the overall influence on solar activity. Yet to be explained is why the direct influence of the planetary tides on the magnetosphere of Earth should phase-lock some of the vibrations of the geomagnetic field, which must be dealt with if the theory is to explain the results of Gauquelin. I am proposing this arises in the following way.

The lines of the solar daily magnetic variations and the fine structure lines flanking them do have a finite width, produced as follows. The daily distortion of the magnetosphere by the solar wind can be considered to be a special type of magnetic wave (called a transverse Alfven wave) propagating around the Earth and concentrated mainly in the ionized gases of the Van Allen radiation belts. Since these belts resemble doughnuts, they have a finite thickness, with different inner and outer radii. Since the Alfven speed (the speed with which these waves travel) depends on magnetic field strength and density, and since both these quantities change with distance from the surface of Earth, the angular speed of these waves will be spread about the angular speed with which the Earth is spinning with respect to the Sun. This will give rise to a finite width for the basic solar daily magnetic variation, for each of the harmonics associated with this variation and also for the side lines that flank these and that are related to longer-term modulations of the solar daily magnetic variation. Since the mean planetary days are very close to the mean solar day, some of the many waves propagating through the Van Allen radiation belts will have the same angular speed as the planetary tides (due to gravitation), and as a result will become phase-locked to these tides. I like to think of this as the magnetospheric equivalent of a laser. The distortion of the magnetosphere by the solar wind is doing the pumping, whereas the planetary tides are causing coherent phase-locking of some of the Alfven waves.

The Moon gives rise to the lunar daily magnetic variation. This is done via the tidal tug of the Moon on the ionized gases of our upper atmosphere. This causes changes in pressure, giving rise to winds, which generate electric currents, and these produce an additional magnetic field. The lunar daily magnetic radiation has been studied in great detail, and its mechanism is relatively well understood. However, the lunar day differs from the solar day by almost one hour, so it will not cause the type of resonant phase-locking of Alfven waves that we have just discussed. Some other points Henbest makes in the *New Scientist* review of my book should now be mentioned.

He writes: 'Let's first put the lunar daily magnetic effect into proportion. The compass needle does not swing wildly at moonrise; its position changes by 1/100 of a degree . . . Even then, the effect is masked on most days by changes in the magnetosphere that are caused by the buffeting of the solar wind.' When putting something into proportion, I always understood that it is necessary to quote not only the value of one quantity but also the value of the other with which you are comparing it. So this is what I will do. The peak of the solar daily variation [due to the buffeting of the magnetosphere by the solar wind] occurs at about noon on each day, and this peak is about five to six times that of the lunar daily magnetic variation, the peaks of which will coincide with that due to the Sun on about four occasions out of fifty-six in one lunar month. This is because they have different periods. However, it is necessary to compare like with like, and really the solar daily magnetic variation consists (as we have already seen) of about three to four different harmonics (this varies with position on Earth). The basic harmonic has a period of 24 hours, the next one of 12 hours, and so on. The basic harmonic of the lunar daily magnetic variation is 12 hours, 24 minutes, and so the 12 hours of the second harmonic of the Sun is the only one that is close to the basic harmonic of the Moon. When one compares these two, which still have different periods, then the one due to the Sun is about three to four times that of the Moon.

The experiments of Frank Brown of Northwestern University in the States provide strong evidence that many marine organisms have two biological clocks: one tuned to magnetic variations due to the Sun and one tuned to magnetic variations due to the Moon. These organisms could become phase-locked to these variations far from the coastline, even in the high-frequency magnetic environment of a modern biology laboratory.

Henbest also claims with regard to the lunar daily magnetic variation that: 'It's such a small effect that you can detect it only with sensitive magnetometers sited well away from electromagnetic interference.' The reason why geomagnetic observatories are sited well away from urban areas is not that given by Henbest. Geophysicists are interested in the whole range of fluctuations associated with the geomagnetic field, including very short-period fluctuations called micropulsations. However, the equipment that they use to record these fluctuations does so with no selective tuning whatsoever, and the search for these fluctuations is then undertaken by subjecting the entire magnetic record to mathematical analysis using computers. The interference from electrified railways does swamp the shorter-period variations of the geomagnetic field; this interference can be picked up by the recording equipment and is also difficult to filter out using mathematical analysis. The magnetic department at the Royal Observatory at Greenwich moved out to Abinger in 1925 because of the electrification of the Southern Railway. By 1937 the continuing extension of the Southern Railway caused disturbances that were noticeable at Abinger. The Astronomer Royal, Spencer Jones, wrote in 1939:

The removal of the magnetic observations to another site has become a necessity. The observations made at Selsey in March have shown that the site selected should be at a distance of not less than 8 miles, and preferably of at least 10 miles, from any electrified railway. As a safeguard against the probable extension of railway electrification in the future, the essential condition for a new site is that it should be at least 10 miles from any railway line.[4]

There are two reasons why electrified railways present such a threat to magnetic observatories. The first is the strength of the currents used; the second, more important reason is that the magnetic field that results from long straight electrical conductors becomes weaker much more slowly with distance than is the case with domestic equipment. If you double the distance from a long straight conductor, then magnetic field strength is weakened by a factor of four, whereas if you double the distance from a heater or fridge, then the strength of the magnetic field is weakened by a factor of eight.

Henbest also claims that 'A pregnant woman in a modern household will experience much stronger magnetic fluctuations from the washing machine and the food processor. The regular rhythm of the storage heaters will swamp the weak lunar signal.' The strength of magnetic fields is measured in Teslas. This is defined in the following way. If an electric conductor, 1 metre in length and carrying a current of 1 amp, is placed in a uniform field of 1 Tesla, then the force acting on it will be 1 Newton. We can use this to examine the validity of Henbest's last statement. In 1987 the World Health Organization published *Environmental Health Criteria 69: Magnetic Field*. On p. 34 of this document we have the following statement: 'The naturally occurring time-varying fields in the atmosphere have several origins, including diurnally varying fields of the order of 3/100,000,000 Tesla associated with solar and lunar influences on ionospheric currents.' On p. 36 in Table 5 are listed the 60 cycles per second magnetic fields associated with some household equipment at varying distances from the source. The worst offender in this respect is the electric can-opener, which has a maximum field of 2/1,000 Tesla 3 centimetres from the opener, a maximum field of 3/100,000 30 centimetres away and a field of 1/1,000,000 Tesla 1 metre away. Most other household equipment has fields of about 5/100,000,000 Tesla (similar to that of the solar and lunar daily magnetic variation) at 1 metre from the source, and this is further reduced by a factor of eight at 2 metres from the source. This means that the fields at more than 2 metres from most sources are actually less than that associated with the lunar daily magnetic variation. What completely invalidates Henbest's argument is that a magnetic biological clock, resonantly tuned to responding to the lunar daily magnetic variation of two cycles per lunar day, will not respond to fifty cycles per second because it is 2 million times greater!

In another part of the review, Henbest says: 'The Earth's ocean tides can be amplified as they travel up an estuary, so perhaps there are "magnetic bays" in the Earth's magnetosphere. Perhaps. But the magnetosphere is extremely squishy, and as far as we know it contains no permanent features that could amplify anything in this way.' Here Henbest again seriously misrepresents geophysical facts. On p. 31 of my book *Cosmic Magnetism* is a schematic representation of the main features of the magnetosphere. The ionized gases, or plasma, of the magnetosphere are indeed 'squishy', but the lines of force that form the organizing field of the magnetosphere are embedded in the Earth, and the electrical properties of the Earth's crust prevent any rapid changes (of less than a few months) taking place near the surface. The lines of force from the magnetosphere do converge on particular points on the surface of Earth, so they become more and more permanent as they approach the surface, and this is why it is possible to use magnetic compasses for direction-finding on land, sea and in the air. As they converge on Earth, they concentrate the magnetic energy that originates in the outer reaches of the magnetosphere, and thus, like the bays of the coastline, can, and do, amplify disturbances that have their origin in the magnetosphere. The persistence of these lines of force, their resemblance to bays close to the Earth's surface, and their consequent ability to focus magnetic waves generated thousands of miles away, are convincingly demonstrated by the phenomenon of whistles. Most of us will have experienced a whistling interference on some radio channels; this is technically called a whistler and arises in the following way. The lines of force that emerge from the interior at a specific place on the Earth diverge into the magnetosphere, arching hundreds of miles above the surface at the place where they re-enter the surface. If there is a lightning or thunder storm at any one of these two places, then this storm generates magnetic waves that travel along the lines of force; these waves will converge on the other place, causing whistling interference. The lines of force are thus able to act as lenses that focus magnetic energy from one part of the magnetosphere to the other. This also holds true for energy generated elsewhere along the lines of force – and not only at the surface of the Earth. Most of the short-period changes at the surface, ranging from a few minutes to a few months, arise in this way.

The Van Allen radiation belts are also largely permanent features of the magnetosphere, and they can act as canals that, with solar pumping, can give rise to a wide range of frequencies, some of which may become phase-locked to the planetary tides. The knowledge we have at present can neither confirm nor deny this possibility. On p. 38 of *Cosmic Magnetism* I give a series of schematic diagrams showing the changes that take place in the outer parts of the magnetosphere during a magnetospheric substorm. These storms are of short duration, lasting about 2 hours, and they do have effects on the Earth's surface. One effect is to increase the amplitude of both the solar daily magnetic variation and the lunar daily magnetic variation. They are also more frequent during periods of high sunspot activity, and since these are, according to my theory, controlled by the relative movements of the planets, they also carry information on these movements.

The tides of the ocean have very little effect on marine life in the open ocean. It is on the coastline that they have the greatest influence, especially in bays and estuaries. Most pregnant mothers spend the major part of their pregnancy close to the surface of Earth, where the magnetic field does resemble bays and estuaries, so once again Henbest's arguments are without foundation in fact.

Biological Consequences of Geomagnetic Variations

Many researchers, including A. P. Dubrov, Frank Brown, James Gould and Robert Becker, have investigated the effects of the geomagnetic field on living organisms. A discussion of some of this work is to be found in Dubrov's book *The Geomagnetic Field and Life.*[5] I would just like to add to this a few comments made recently by Western scientists. Brown says that the ability of many animals to know the time of the tides, the time of day, the phases of the Moon and the time of year cannot all be explained in terms of light cues, but he feels that the geomagnetic field (and he produces considerable experimental evidence to support this view) is actually talking to many different species of animal. In an interview on the BBC *Horizon* programme called 'Magnet Earth', he states the matter slightly differently. He says that all organisms have magnetic fields because of their electrical activity. These fields pervade both the organisms and the space around them, thus becoming intertwined and tangled. He goes on to say that the organisms are not actually sensing the field in the way we sense light or sound, but 'riding the field'. Gould says on the same programme that it might well turn out that the magnetic field of Earth is second only to the Sun and sky in helping animals to know the time, where they are and which direction is which.

Becker, once nominated for the Nobel Prize in Medicine for his work on the use of electrical fields in bone regeneration, suggests a mechanism for this interaction between the geomagnetic field and life. Starting with the well-known fact that electrical potential differences exist between the various parts of a living body, he goes on to suggest that this potential is the controlling influence of the activities of a living body. He further suggests that the direct current potential system is frequency sensitive, responding to certain frequencies and not to others. He concludes by proposing that over the aeons the body of every living organism had, in a sense, become phase-locked to specific pulsations of the geomagnetic field, since all of life had evolved in this field. The work of Dubrov, Brown and Becker is discussed in more detail in a recently published book, *Electromagnetic Man*, by C. W. Smith and Simon Best.[6] Its main thesis is that coherent electromagnetic oscillations exist in living organisms and that these are used for long-range interactions between molecules within cells. They discuss the consequences of this idea for a wide range of phenomena, from alternative medicine to the possible harmful effects of living close to power lines.

A Model for Gauquelin's Planetary Effect

The history of theoretical physics provides one with many interesting insights into the trials and tribulations that have to be faced by those who seek to give mathematically quantifiable descriptions of natural phenomena. Our increased understanding of atomic physics provides a very relevant specific example. J. Fraunhofer, G. R. Kirchhoff and R. W. Bunsen laid the observational and experimental foundations of atomic spectroscopy, which enabled scientists to identify chemical elements by the spectral lines they emitted or absorbed. It was soon after this that George Stokes, William Thompson, Belfour Stewart, Kirchhoff and others suggested that certain resonant frequencies characterized each element. This idea was further developed by the Dutch theoretical physicist, H. A. Lorentz. Although at this time scientists had virtually no idea about atomic structure, it was known that electric current was made up of charged particles. He applied the theory of damped simple harmonic motion to these particles, and thus was able to explain some of the basic properties of the interaction between electromagnetic radiation and the atoms of specific elements. In this connection I would like to quote from *Introduction to Theoretical Physics* by J. C. Slater and N. H. Frank:

> In optics, the theory of refractive index and absorption coefficient is closely connected with resonance. As is shown by the sharp spectrum lines, atoms contain oscillators capable of damped simple harmonic motion, or at any rate they act as if they did: the real theory, using wave mechanics, is complicated but leads essentially to this result.[7]

We thus see that Lorentz's simple theory provided a basis for identifying atoms from the spectra, thus enabling their physical and chemical properties to be empirically deduced, long before Bohr, Sommerfeldt, Heisenberg, Schrodinger and Dirac developed quantum mechanics, which allowed us to understand these characteristics in terms of the electronic personalities of atoms. I believe the work of Gauquelin points to a resonant interaction between the geomagnetic field, which is linked to the movements of the Sun, Moon and planets, and the internal personality of the individual, which can be used to label some of the characteristics of the person. In the historical development of astrology, his work is comparable to that of Fraunhofer, Bunsen and Kirchhoff in the historical development of atomic spectroscopy. Although we are not at the moment able to deduce 'the electronic structure of personality' from this response, I think we can take similar steps to those taken by Lorentz, and propose a mathematical model of the Gauquelin birth clock based on the theory of resonance. In doing so, I am making use of some ideas put forward by A. J. Winfree in his book *The Geometry of Biological Time*: 'From cell division to heartbeat, clock-like rhythms pervade the activities of every living organism. The cycles of life are ultimately biochemical in mechanism but many of the principles that dominate their orchestration are essentially mathematical.'[8] I also make use of some of the ideas discussed by F. C. Hoppensteadt in his book *An Introduction to the Mathematics of Neurons*: 'Neurons . . . are the basic timers in our bodies. They also play a central role in storing and processing information in our brains. As timers, neurons drive higher-level biological clocks in much the same manner as an alternating electric current drives an electric clock.'[9] Most of the attempts to describe the electrical behaviour of the neuron have been based on electrical circuit analogies and their associated mathematical models. My proposal is that the influence of the geomagnetic fluctuations on the neural network as a whole can be described in similar terms.

Anthony Garrett's review of my book cannot really be described as completely independent, since he quotes several of the erroneous points from Henbest's review that have already been discussed. However, he does make some points that Henbest does not. For example: 'How are neurons tuned to cycles lasting many hours? We know how to calculate resonance frequencies of organic molecules, and they are typically millionths of a second. Analogy with the daily cycle is misleading at the level of the neuron.' This clearly shows that Garrett is not aware of the work on biological clocks, and that he overlooks the fact that it took several decades to go from atomic spectroscopy to a stage where we can, in principle, calculate the resonant frequencies of organic molecules. In fact, the calculations are so difficult for the more complicated organic molecules that they have not been carried out for many of them. Chemists working in these areas quite often use empirical data rather than the calculations. He also fails to point out that the larger the molecule the lower the frequency with which its vibrates, and the frequency of vibration of a molecule, which is made up of many atoms, is much lower than the frequencies associated with the individual atoms. The periods of oscillation of large neural loops are much longer than those of individual neurons. He also denies other branches of theoretical science the right to go through the same stages of development that atomic spectroscopy had to go through.

In this model I propose that the internal linkages between the various neural loops of the central nervous system are to some extent inherited, and that this linking determines not only the personality of the individual, but also the way in which the nervous system acts as the co-ordinator of the birth process in response to specific changes in the geomagnetic field. I further propose that an electrical circuit can be the model for the behaviour of the central nervous system when acting as the count-down to the birth clock. This circuit consists of a coil of wire (called an inductance), a capacitance (which can store electric charge) and a resistor (which offers resistance to electric current). The coil of wire has a soft iron bar passing through it, which is suspended on one arm of a balance. When the current flowing through the system is sufficiently large, the soft iron bar is drawn into the solenoid and trips the switch that opens the gate. The electric power for this circuit is provided by the changes of the geomagnetic field that threads its way through the circuit. However, only those fluctuations that are resonant with the natural frequency of the circuit will produce a large enough current to open the birth gate, and this has to be built up over several cycles, as required by the theory of resonant circuits.

In order to clarify the model further, I want to use the analogy of the magnetic mine that was used in the Second World War. This was detonated by a device triggered by the magnetic field of a passing ship. In such a mine there would be, in addition to the magnetic trigger, a timing device that would arm the bomb some time before it was triggered by a magnetic field. Thus mines could be safely placed without being triggered by the fields of the ships laying the mines. If we see birth as an explosion, the biochemical and biophysical energy of mother and child as the explosive, and the other biological processes in child and mother (including the breaking of the waters) as the timer that arms the bomb, then the nervous system is the magnetic aerial that detonates the explosion. This, then, constitutes my complete model of Gauquelin's planetary effect.

Resonant phenomena play a vital part in a very large class of natural phenomena, ranging from the nuclei of atoms, through large engineering structures and the tides of estuaries, right up to the dynamics of Saturn's rings and the asteroid belt. Gauquelin's work has shown us that cosmic links with human personality are another facet of this effect. An important point to note is that although the physical details change from one member to another, the mathematics of resonance remain essentially unchanged and are largely independent of the physics. The progress of science will no doubt change some of the basic details of the model presented here, but the basic mathematical features are likely to remain unchanged as long as we have the Gauquelin data as the prime source of evidence in this area.

Update on the Data Debate

The debate on the validity of data that support, or do not support, some astrological ideas has, of course, continued. Here I will consider some recent developments that have occurred since the first edition of this book was published.

Garrett in his review of my book has made some contribution to the debate, which I will now examine:

> There has been only one double-blind test of astrology [by Carlson] conducted with the co-operation of astrologers, and this is therefore of the utmost importance. It concluded that 'the experiment clearly refutes the astrological hypothesis'. Consequently it is disturbing to observe Seymour dismissing this in two paragraphs ... The failure of perspective here is so great that one might reasonably conclude Seymour has an axe to grind.

I did not give much weight to these findings (see pp. 92–3), since they basically compared personality traits as predicted, subjectively, by astrologers from the birth chart with personality traits found from the use of a standard personality test. Since they involved the subjective intervention of the astrologer, they merely showed that traditional astrologers were not able to predict personality traits from birth charts; they in no way refute 'the astrological hypothesis', which, in its broadest sense, merely implies some link between personality characteristics and the state of the solar system at the time of birth. The work of the Gauquelins, Eysenck, Nias, Dean and Mather, some of it undertaken more than 10 years ago, had already established that traditional astrology, as practised by most astrologers, was unable to do what it was supposed to do. As we will see in a moment, I choose an aspect of Gauquelin's work that represents the most objective data in the field to date. However, I would like to quote from a letter, written by Eysenck, to *Correlation* (the journal of research into astrology) in June 1986; it concerns Carlson's double-blind test.

A recent article by a young physicist, Shawn Carlson, in *Nature* (vol. 318, 1985, pp. 419–25) described a very carefully conducted experiment on the validity of astrology. The negative outcome of this study has been quoted many times and seems particularly impressive when it is realized that the whole plan of the experiment was welcomed by the astrologers who took part in it. In actual fact the experiment illustrates the danger of carrying out psychological experiments (and any experiment using personality variables in its design must be a psychological experiment) without having psychologists with experience in this field directing the relevant portions of the research design. The absence of experienced psychologists is noticeable both in the list of people who advised the author and in the ranks of the astrologers who approved the design.

Eysenck also criticizes the personality test used:

The CPI [California Personality Inventory] is a well-known and widely used personality test, but it was constructed *a priori* and not on the basis of a proper correlation and factor-analytic analysis. Such analyses, carried out more recently, indicate that most of the variance of the test items is carried by two factors: neuroticism–stability and extroversion–introversion, as is the total validity of the test in predicting various types of behaviour. Thus there is a defect in the test itself which may be crucial.

Eysenck goes on to discuss how the test was carried out:

If the CPI had to be used, then a lengthy period of training should have been given to the participating astrologers and the students; without this period of training they would be as incapable of reading the results as would a novice looking through a microscope without having received any instruction! Indeed, the way the whole experiment was designed, and approved by astrologers, indicates clearly that both sides regarded psychological expertise as a negligible quantity, and felt that anybody can do as well as a trained psychologist in choosing, interpreting and evaluating results of the application of personality inventories. This may be a widespread belief but it is an erroneous one, and we must be grateful to Carlson and the participating astrologers for making the point so clearly that psychologists should always be involved in experiments using psychological material.

It is quite clear that Garrett was unfamiliar with this and other criticisms of Carlson's work.

Garrett continues his review with these words: 'By contrast Seymour places great store in the findings of Michel Gauquelin. Gauquelin's results are controversial and quite beyond detailed evaluation here.'

Garrett's review of my book was preceded by an article entitled 'Astrology and Gauquelin', which appeared in the September–October 1988 issue of the *British and Irish Sceptic*. In this article he says: 'It is also worth asking how Gauquelin came to select this particular profession and planet, and these particular birth sectors ... Alternatively, a secret hunt for correlations between planets and sectors of sport stars could have led to the choice of Mars, and of sector.' He continues: 'These suggestions involve fraud. I am not suggesting Gauquelin cheated; he could perfectly well have found results by chance, and have been mystified by their cause. But the sceptic, sensibly, will want to check this.' He concludes: 'We should also ask: on what grounds does Gauquelin posit a correlation between sporting abilities and the Mars effect? He is adamant about this. What secret information led him to suggest it? These questions demand answers.'

Garrett is a physicist, and as far as I have been able to ascertain through literature searches, he is not a specialist in the application of statistics to the human sciences. I am not either, but I have taken the trouble to hear the debate from both sides and to keep up to date with the literature on statistical tests concerning astrology. I have also taken the trouble to look at the original papers and documents published by Gauquelin and others, and have not been content merely to read second-hand criticisms of his work or his own semi-popular writings. In recent months Heather Couper has also commented on Gauquelin's findings. Couper is a former president of the British Astronomical Association, and is well known for her media coverage of astronomical matters. In an article in the *Observer*, she writes: 'The attitude of astrologers to Gauquelin is particularly fascinating. He has spent hours comparing detailed personality profiles with planetary aspects, and has found no correlation whatsoever. He has, however, unearthed a curiosity in the birth chart data of top achievers.'[10] After describing his results briefly, she goes on to say, 'No one else has managed to duplicate Gauquelin's findings, and – as he himself points out – they are not generally applicable to the populace at large.' Couper is obviously not aware of the replication of these results carried out by the Committee Para in Belgium. She also does not mention the fiasco that surrounded efforts by the Committee for Scientific Investigations of Claims of the Paranormal.[11] She also omits any mention of Gauquelin's work on planetary heredity, which was carried out on samples in no way restricted to eminent individuals but taken from the populace at large.

Let us take a look at some of the comments made on Gauquelin's work by some specialists in the appropriate fields. One of the few astronomers who actually acquainted himself with Gauquelin's work was G. O. Abell, a distinguished American astronomer well known for his work on observational cosmology. He writes: 'Gauquelin's findings represent an anomalous result that remains unconfirmed to the degree necessary to be accepted as scientific fact' and adds 'I strongly suspect that in the end Gauquelin's results will turn out to be spurious. But if by any (to me) miraculous chance they should be even partly correct, it would be a tremendous milestone in establishing cosmic influence on man.'

In 1988 some of Gauquelin's early writings in French were published in English under the title *Written in the Stars*.[12] Gauquelin ends the first appendix to this work with the following words: 'At the moment, there is no longer any doubt about the validity of my methodology, as three members of the Committee for Scientific Investigation of Claims of the Paranormal, Professors Abell, Kurtz and Zelen, eventually acknowledged in 1983, in an article which caused a considerable stir: "Gauquelin adequately allowed for demographic and astronomical factors in predicting the expected distribution of Mars sectors for birth times in the general population."'

In April 1989 I attended the First International Conference on Geocosmic Relations. Held in Amsterdam, it was attended by astronomers, geophysicists, meteorologists, physicists, chemists, biologists, physicians and psychologists. At this conference I was able to hear the latest assessment of the work of Gauquelin, by Suitbert Ertel of the Institute for Psychology at Georg-August University in Göttingen, Germany. He kindly sent me a copy of his paper, which will be published in the conference proceedings. Here he first addresses himself to a reanalysis of a replication study performed by the sceptics Abell, Kurtz and Zelen between 1979 and 1980. This is the only study so far that supposedly contradicts Gauquelin's Mars effect. He makes use of his own largely objective method of grading eminence, based on a count of the citations that the various sportsmen had received in a number of publications. From this he concludes: 'the sample collected by Kurtz, Zelen and Abell was indeed mediocre and did not well serve its replication purpose. The result of their study cannot throw suspicion on Gauquelin's Mars effect.' He continues: 'The present procedure has the advantage of not presupposing any astronomical or demographic assumption, it circumvents thus all difficulties which former Gauquelin critics had regarded as severe: including astronomical [Committee Para] as well as demographic factors [Zelen].' Applying these methods to an extended Gauquelin sample, collected by himself, Ertel 'concurs' with the findings of Gauquelin.

When I started my work, I was well aware of the debate on Gauquelin. This is why I decided to concentrate on his work on planetary heredity. In Chapter 8 of the first edition of this book (on p. 113) I say, with regard to this aspect of his work: 'These particular results of Gauquelin's are the most important of all his findings, as far as my theory is concerned. This is because they are based on objectively measurable quantities, like planetary positions and birth times, but they also indicate quite clearly that a physical agency is involved, and that this agency is the magnetic field of the Earth.' I might also add that these results apply to ordinary as well as eminent individuals, and so are not subject to the same criticisms that have been raised against Gauquelin's other work. Most of his critics never get this far in an evaluation of his contribution.

Recently doubt has been cast on his earlier work on planetary heredity by no less a person than Gauquelin himself. His book *Planetary Heredity*[13] has recently been translated into English, and the 1988 version carries information on his failure to replicate his results on planetary heredity. Gauquelin carried out this experiment on three different occasions: first in 1966, then in 1976 and 1984. Although the first two gave positive results in favour of the planetary heredity result, the last one did not. This is Gauquelin's account of his findings:

It took me and my collaborators – Geneviève Artru, Maryse Damiens, Valérie Loizance and Geneviève Martichoux – three years of hard work to gather 50,942 birth data from five separate areas, four from Paris and one from Lille in the north of France. It includes 33,120 parent–child comparisons, almost as many as in the two previous experiments combined ... Sadly, the results of this huge new experiment showed only slight agreement with those of the previous two experiments. This time, except perhaps at the rising zone, there is almost no tendency for parents born with a significant planet in rise-culmination zones to have children with the same planet in the same zones ... The distribution of the birth times is normal and shows no evidence of medical interference, so if planetary heredity is real, then the data should show it ... The results for both parents born with the same planet in rise-culmination zones are a little more encouraging, but the effect remains nonsignificant and is much weaker than before. The results of geomagnetic activity are also encouraging, and tend to support the hypothesis, but again they are not significant ... There is no doubt that these observations constitute a setback that is hard to reconcile with the significant and consistently positive results that I had observed over 25 years of work, especially in view of a recent comparison of planetary heredity between two samples from the same *arrondissement* of Paris. The samples were for 1923–31 and 1931–9 respectively: each consisted of nearly 12,000 birth comparisons, and each was checked by the same people. The samples seemed identical in every way, yet the first gave results strongly in support of the hypothesis, while the second gave results almost as strongly against the hypothesis. Puzzling indeed!

Although this may seem to be a blow to the planetary heredity hypothesis and to my theory, this is not the case. Gauquelin apparently expected the planets to have a direct influence on the time of birth of babies with certain personality characteristics. In my theory there is an intermediary, the magnetic field of Earth, which can introduce a phase-lag between the tide due to a particular planet and the actual position of the planet in the sky. What is more, the geometry of the geomagnetic field where it enters the Earth is known to vary with time, on a time scale of a few years, and this variation is known to introduce a time-varying phase-lag between the position of the Moon in the sky and the peak of the lunar daily magnetic variation. It is also known that the phase-lag changes according to one's position on the surface of Earth, and so a further weakening of the effect will occur if parents are not born in the same place. I had already discussed this possibility at the Fifth International Astrological Research Conference in London in 1986, and it is described in my monograph, *A Causal Mechanism for Gauquelin's Planetary Effect*:

> Several people have commented on the fact that Gauquelin's planetary-eminence link is rather a weak effect and it does not increase with the size of the sample used. The same is also true for planetary heredity. I believe there are three possible causes that can explain this weakness. The first involves a spread in frequencies to which the nervous system is tuned. As far as planetary heredity is concerned, people with similar, but not the same, personality are likely to have a small spread about the central frequency associated with that particular set of character traits. This would lead to some weakening of the result in a large sample . . . The planetary heredity effect is also likely to be affected by a phase shift between lunar and planetary tides and rising and transit times. The next diagram shows the average lunar daily magnetic variation, for one month, at two different geomagnetic observatories: one in Batavia and another in Huancayo in Peru. The two graphs show an obvious phase shift between lunar transits, rising and setting of the Moon, and the peaks and troughs associated with the lunar daily magnetic variation. This is because the phase does depend on the local geometry of the field. A similar situation arises in the tides along the coastline, where the phase at a particular port is dependent on the shape of the coastline at that particular point. The geometry of the magnetic coastline is undergoing continual changes due to what is called the secular variation of the geomagnetic field. These are of internal origin and they occur over periods of a year or more. Any faster changes of internal origin are damped out by the conductivity of the Earth's crust. This means that over the time period that elapses between the births of parent and child there could well have been phase shifts in the lunar and planetary magnetic variations and rising and transit times. There could also be additional phase shifts if the parent and child were not born in the same place.

The effect (of weakening) should disappear, according to my theory, if one had to compare, not rising and transit times, but the peaks and troughs of the lunar variation in particular, and the planetary variations, when they are discovered![14]

This question is also discussed on pages 122 and 123 of the first edition of this book. The question may well be asked why the planetary heredity effect is evident in some of Gauquelin's samples and not in others. This is because the secular shifts in the geo-magnetic field, which result in the phase shifts, do not occur in a regular and systematic way; they can happen faster at certain times than they do at other times, and the samples used by Gauquelin do cover different periods of time. Unfortunately, we do not at the moment have sufficiently detailed data on the variations of the geomagnetic field at the places at which parents and children were born and at their respective times of birth. These data are what is needed to test my theory.

My Theory and Traditional Astrology

As will be quite clear by now, my theory was originally conceived to explain the work of Gauquelin, with particular reference to his work on planetary heredity. It does, however, also shed some light on other areas of astrology.

Aspects

To start with, let us consider what it has to say about planetary aspects. This is a rather difficult field of astrology in any case, and many astrologers disagree about the significance of the various aspects. John Addey draws attention to this in his book *Harmonics in Astrology* when he says: 'Even the resourceful Michel Gauquelin has declared, after making studies of traditional aspects, that he can find no scientific foothold in the astrological doctrine of aspects.' Dean and Mather also discuss this point in *Recent Advances in Natal Astrology*: 'Some workers use geocentric positions.

Others use heliocentric. The question arises, which is best? For the most important aspects (i.e., those between the outer planets) the maximum time difference between heliocentric and geocentric exactness is only a few weeks. This is insufficient for a distinction to be made, especially as several aspects operate simultaneously.'

According to my theory, heliocentric aspects, including our Earth with the other planets, are the important ones to use. They are likely to give rise to violent events on the Sun which will in turn give rise to disturbances in the geomagnetic field, thus enhancing the effect of the planetary tides on our planet. In my theory Jupiter, Saturn, Uranus and Neptune give rise to the movement of the Sun about the common centre of mass of the solar system, and they have control over the direction of the Sun's magnetic field. As the Sun's field is tuned by the solar rotation, so each planet in turn will play a dominant role in giving rise to solar activity, and the aspects that are important will vary with the relative positions of the planets as the cycle progresses. Thus, at the start of the cycle, squares between Mercury and Venus will be important, but oppositions and/or conjunctions between Venus and the other planets will also play a part. If the tuning of a magnetic canal lies between the angular speed of any two planets, then the squares between those two will be important, and conjunctions and/or oppositions between the outer planets will contribute. This tuning will gradually shift from the inner planets to the outer planets as the cycle progresses. At the end of the cycle it will be conjunctions and/or oppositions that have the most influence. I have yet to discover when the changeover in dominance of each of the planets occurs, so although the basic theory has been developed, the final theory, as with all new theories, must still be fine-tuned. However, as it stands it does not provide support for angular aspects of 30, 60, 120 and 150 degrees. At the moment these aspects also have no empirical support, although some astrologers claim that experience has taught them that these should be considered.

Prediction in Astrology

Prediction has always been a part of astrology, and my theory allows us to understand how this might occur. I have already discussed this in some detail in Chapter 10, but here I want to briefly relate these ideas to some traditional astrological methods of prediction.

The major methods of predicting the future of individuals from their birth or natal charts are: directions, progressions and transits. In this section I will rely heavily on the definitions of these concepts given in *The Dictionary of Astrology* by Fred Gettings. He writes, 'the art of making "directions", as of interpreting them, is the most important part of "Predictive Astrology", and is involved with studying the future configurations of planets and angles in regard to a radical chart, with a view to learning something about the native.'

In Chapter 10 I said that there were two possible ways in which my theory can be used to understand astrological prediction. The first is that we can use the positions of the planets at birth to identify the inherited personality characteristics of the individual, and from past experience of the development of people with these characteristics, we can sketch out future trends in their lives. In this way there is no continuing effect of the geomagnetic field on the individual after birth, and the movements of the planets are then just the hands of a vast cosmic clock used to identify certain stages in that individual's development. To return to the analogy of atomic physics used earlier in this chapter, the birth chart is rather like the spectrum of an atom, which can be recorded at a single instant of time. However, once recorded we can use it to identify the type of atom, and after this is done we can identify the physical properties of the atom and make some predictions as to how it will react to the atoms of other chemical elements, and also how it will behave under specific physical conditions. But if the physical conditions included the exposure of the atom to specific types of radiation, this could well alter its physical and chemical behaviour. Should the atoms of one chemical element go into chemical combination with atoms of other elements, then the molecules of the combined resulting compound will have a different response to radiation from that of the response of the individual atoms. This analogy can be used to understand the second way we can understand the links between planetary motions and positions, and the post-natal development of the individual. In doing so, it sheds light on how we can, perhaps, understand progressions and transits in terms of my theory.

As pointed out by Gettings, there are several systems of progressions used by astrologers. I will just mention one in fairly common use. This is known as the Day for a Year system. According to this method, 'a progressed horoscope is cast for a given number of days after birth equal to the number of years elapsing from birth time to the time under scrutiny, and the two charts (radical and progressed) are linked schematically by arcs denoting planetary and nodal movements'. The relationship between the two can then be used to make a new set of predictions on the future development of the individual. Transits can also be used to understand the developing influences on the life of an individual. Gettings says 'that branch which was concerned with the study of the actual transits (movement across) of planets over emphatic points in a radical chart was itself called "transits"'. Further along he writes, 'Practically this means that if an astrologer wishes to establish by means of transits the influences playing on the life of someone born in say 1937 in the fiftieth year of that person, he will study the transits over the radial chart of 1937 which occur in the year 1987.' Both transits and progressions imply that our response to planetary influences evolves with time.

In the Introduction to this book, I wrote:

> However, the womb is no hiding place from the all-pervading magnetic field of Earth, so the tunes of the magnetic symphony of the solar system that we receive can become part of our earliest memories. It is here that some of the magnetic music of the spheres becomes etched on our brains. When the orchestra of the solar system plays our tune on the magnetic field of Earth at a later stage of our life, it evokes these memories, and our response can influence the way we react to a given situation.

When stated in this rudimentary way, the theory implies a very simple straightforward response to the evocation of these memories in later life. However, it is possible to see how the theory can be developed further. To return to the analogy of atomic spectroscopy used earlier, it is possible to say that the birth chart gives us information on the astrological atomic elements of personality. As the body grows and the nervous system develops, personality develops in parallel with these changes. Thus we can think of the 'atomic elements' forming into more 'complex molecules' that form the 'astrological compounds of our personality'; these compounds will react to the magnetic music in more complex ways, so our response to changes in the magnetic field of Earth will change with time. This, then, is one possible way in which we can understand the evolving response we have to cosmic influences on our personality that is implied by progressions and transits.

Conclusion

The theory I have proposed in this book is the first stage in the development of a more complete theory for the links between the cosmos and personality. We are now in a position to see the basic ideas that underlie 'astrological spectroscopy' and to formulate the rudiments of a theory, just as Lorentz did for spectroscopy at the turn of the century; but with the knowledge and the data available at the moment we cannot proceed to the formulation of a 'quantum theory of astrology' from which we can begin to deduce the 'electronic structure of personality'. This, then, is very much in keeping with the nature, history and development of science.

The nature of the scientific endeavour is very well captured in a story told by Olive Schreiner in her book *The Story of an African Farm*. Once, a hunter glimpses the reflection of the Bird of Truth in the still waters of a pool, and after that he devotes his life to finding and holding this beautiful bird. On the way he meets Wisdom, who gives him some instructions on how to find Truth:

> The mountains of stern reality will rise before him: he must climb them: beyond them lies Truth ... He will never see her, never hold her ... Some men have climbed on those mountains ... some have chanced to pick up from the ground, one white silver feather, dropped from the wing of

Truth. And it shall come to pass ... that, when enough of those silver feathers shall have been gathered by the hands of men, and shall have been woven into a cord, and the cord into a net, that in that net Truth may be captured. Nothing but Truth can hold Truth.

Near the end of his long quest the hunter says:

I have sought ... for long years I have laboured; but I have not found her ... Where I lie down worn out other men will stand, young and fresh. By the steps that I have cut they will climb; by the stairs that I have built they will mount ... At the clumsy work they will laugh; when the stones roll they will curse me. But they will mount, and on my work; they will climb, and by my stair! They will find her, and through me ... If Truth had appeared above him in the clouds now, he could not have seen her, the mist of death was in his eyes ... Then slowly from the white sky above, through the still air, came something falling, falling, falling. Softly it fluttered down, and dropped on the breast of the dying man. He felt it with his hands. It was a feather. He died holding it.

I believe that this is all we can really expect from the scientific quest, but that does not make it any less exciting – it is the excitement of this ongoing quest that sustains us.

Notes

Preface to the Arkana Edition

1. Nigel Henbest, *New Scientist*, 12 May 1988
2. Adrian Berry, *Daily Telegraph*, 16 July 1988
3. Jacqueline Mitton, *Journal of the British Astronomical Association*, October 1988
4. Anthony Garrett, *British and Irish Sceptic*, November/December 1988
5. Nick Herbert, *Quantum Reality*, Rider, 1985

Introduction: Astronomy versus Astrology – the Age-old Debate

1. Patrick Moore in the *Daily Express*, 14 November 1984
2. Fred Gettings, *The Dictionary of Astrology*, Routledge & Kegan Paul, 1985
3. John Addey, *Harmonics in Astrology*, Fowler, 1976
4. Hans J. Eysenck and David Nias, *Astrology: Science or Superstition?*, Temple Smith, 1982
5. T. G. Cowling, 'Astrology, Religion and Science', *Quarterly Journal of the Royal Astronomical Society*, vol. 23, 1982
6. R. B. Culver and P. A. Ianna, *The Gemini Syndrome*, Pachart, 1979
7. Otto Neugebauer, *A History of Ancient Mathematical Astronomy*, Springer-Verlag, 1975
8. Thomas S. Kuhn, *On the Structure of Scientific Revolutions*, Chicago University Press, 1962
9. Thomas S. Kuhn, *The Copernican Revolution*, Princeton University Press, 1957
10. 'Objections to Astrology', *Humanist*, vol. 35, no. 5, September–October 1975
11. Carl Sagan, 'Reader's Forum', *Humanist*, vol. 36, no. 1, January–February 1976
12. Paul Feyerabend, *Science in a Free Society*, New Left Books, 1978

13. Michel Gauquelin, *Cosmic Influences on Human Behaviour*, Futura, 1976
14. Geoffrey Dean and Arthur Mather, *Recent Advances in Natal Astrology*, Analogic, 1977

1 Getting to Know the Cosmos

1. Interested readers can find further details in: Percy Seymour, *Adventures with Astronomy*, John Murray, 1983; R. Hanbury-Brown, *Man and the Stars*, Oxford University Press, 1978; J. K. Beatty, B. O'Leary and A. Charpin (eds.), *The New Solar System*, Cambridge University Press, 1982; R. Giovanelli, *Secrets of the Sun*, Cambridge University Press, 1984; and B. W. Jones, *The Solar System*, Pergamon, 1984
2. G. O. Abell and P. J. E. Peebles (eds.), *Objects of High Redshift*, Reidel, 1980

2 The Influence of Cosmic Belief

1. Derek and Julia Parker, *A History of Astrology*, André Deutsch, 1983
2. Seyyed Hussein Nasr, *Islamic Science: An Illustrated Study*, World of Islam, 1976
3. J. Needham, *Science and Civilization in China*, Cambridge University Press, 1962
4. J. Needham, *The Shorter Science and Civilization in China* (an abridged version of reference 3 above edited by C. A. Ronan), Cambridge University Press, 1978
5. J. E. S. Thompson, 'Maya Astrology' in F. R. Hobson (ed.), *The Place of Astronomy in the Ancient World*, Oxford University Press, 1974
6. Derek and Julia Parker, *The New Compleat Astrologer*, Mitchell Beazley, 1984
7. Edward FitzGerald, *The Rubáiyát of Omar Khayyám* (ed. Reynold A. Nicholson), A. & C. Black, 1978
8. Peter Brookesmith, *The Occult Connection*, Orbis, 1984
9. Quoted by Judson Bennett in the *Western Evening Herald*, 25 January 1985

3 From Calendars to Horoscopes

1. R. A. Parker, 'Ancient Egyptian Astronomy' in F. R. Hobson (ed.), *The Place of Astronomy in the Ancient World*, Oxford University Press, 1974
2. ibid.
3. R. H. Allen, *Star Names: Their Lore and Meaning*, Dover, 1963
4. M. W. Ovenden, 'The Origin of the Constellations', *Philosophical Journal*, vol. 3, 1966
5. A. E. Roy, 'The Lamps of Atlantis', lecture delivered on the island of Samos in June 1980 as part of the Aristarchus of Samos Symposium, private communication

4 From Astrology to the Mechanical Universe

1. Thomas S. Kuhn, *The Copernican Revolution*
2. J. D. Bernal, *Science in History*, Penguin, 1969
3. Jeff Mayo, *Teach Yourself Astrology*, Hodder & Stoughton, 1984
4. Arthur Koestler, *The Sleepwalkers*, Hutchinson, 1959
5. T. G. Cowling, *Isaac Newton and Astrology*, Leeds University Press, 1977

5 Science and Astrology

1. Lyall Watson, *Supernature*, Sceptre, 1986
2. Shawn Carlson in *Nature*, 5 December 1985
3. Magnus Pyke in the *Sunday Mirror*, 24 February 1985
4. Dennis Elwell, *The Cosmic Loom: The New Science of Astrology*, Unwin Hyman, 1987
5. Michael Shallis, *On Time*, Pelican, 1982
6. Carl Jung, *Synchronicity*, Routledge & Kegan Paul, 1985
7. John Addey, *Harmonics in Astrology*

6 Cosmic Earth

1. R. R. Ward, *The Living Clocks*, Collins, 1972

2. F. A. Brown, 'Evidence for External Timing of Biological Clocks' in J. D. Palmer, *Human Biological Rhythms*, Biology Readers, 1983
3. Dennis W. Sciama, *Modern Cosmology*, Cambridge, 1971
4. Nigel Calder, *The Violent Universe*, BBC Publications, 1975
5. Fred Hoyle and Jayant Narliker, *The Physics–Astronomy Frontier*, Freeman, 1980; Paul Davies, *Space and Time in the Modern Universe*, Cambridge University Press, 1977
6. John Barrow and Frank Tipler, *The Anthropic Cosmological Principle*, Oxford University Press, 1986
7. Fred Hoyle, *The Intelligent Universe*, Michael Joseph, 1983

7 The Magnetic Music of the Spheres

1. Percy Seymour, *Cosmic Magnetism*, Adam Hilger, 1986
2. J. A. Jacobs, *Reversals of the Earth's Magnetic Field*, Adam Hilger, 1984
3. A. P. Dubrov, *The Geomagnetic Field and Life*, Plenum, 1978; M. F. Barthnothy (ed.), *The Biological Effects of Magnetic Fields*, Academic Press, 1965 (vol. 1) and 1969 (vol. 2)
4. Michel Gauquelin, *The Truth about Astrology*, Hutchinson, 1984
5. F. C. Hoppensteadt, *An Introduction to the Mathematics of Neurons*, Cambridge University Press, 1986

8 The Magnetic Midwifery of the Planets

1. Edwin Hubble, *Surveying the Universe: Discovering Physics*, Open University Press, 1982
2. A. P. Lightman, W. H. Press, R. H. Price and S. A. Teukolsky, *Problem Book in Relativity and Gravitation*, Princeton University Press, 1975

9 The Tides of the Sun

1. John Gribbin, *The Strangest Star*, Athlone, 1980
2. J. B. Blizard, *Long-range Solar Flare Prediction*, NASA Contractor Report, CR 61316, 1969

3. George B. Airy, Section 6, Encyclo, Metrop, 1845
4. John R. Gribbin and Stephen H. Plagemann, *The Jupiter Effect*, Fontana, 1977

10 Responding to Celestial Music

1. H. E. Huntley, *The Faith of a Physicist*, Bles, 1960
2. Geoffrey Dean and Arthur Mather, *Recent Advances in Natal Astrology*

11 The Origins of Astrology

1. Tom Williamson in the *New Scientist*, 19 March 1987
2. Robin Baker, *Physics in Technology*, vol. 15, 1984

12 The Gift of the Magi

1. Don Cupitt, *The Sea of Faith*, BBC Publications, 1984
2. Hans Sandauer, *History Controlled by the Stars*, Prisma/VVA, 1979
3. K. Ferrari d'Occhieppo, *Der Stern der Weisen – Geschichte oder Legende?*, Herold Verlag, 1977
4. David Hughes, *The Star of Bethlehem Mystery*, Dent, 1979
5. Albert Schweitzer, *The Quest of the Historical Jesus*, A. & C. Black, 1911
6. Carl Jung, *Aion, Collected Works*, part 2, vol. 9, Routledge & Kegan Paul, 1981
7. Gordon Strachan, *Christ and the Cosmos*, Laborum, 1985
8. Morton Smith, *Jesus the Magician*, Aquarius, 1985

13 Astrology and Magnetic Astrology

1. Edward C. Bullard, 'Electromagnetic Induction in the Earth', *Quarterly Journal of the Royal Astronomical Society*, vol. 8, 1967
2. F. de Meyer, 'Solar and Lunar Geomagnetic Variations at Dourbes', *Journal of Atmospheric and Terrestrial Physics*, vol. 42, 1980

3. S. Malin, 'Historical Introduction to Geomagnetism' in J. A. Jacobs (ed.), *Geomagnetism*, vol. 1, Academic Press, 1987

4. A. J. Meadows, *Greenwich Observatory*, vol. 2, Francis & Taylor, 1975

5. A. P. Dubrov, *The Geomagnetic Field and Life*, Plenum, 1978

6. C. W. Smith and Simon Best, *Electromagnetic Man*, Dent, 1989

7. J. C. Slater and N. H. Frank, *Introduction to Theoretical Physics*, McGraw-Hill, 1933

8. A. J. Winfree, *The Geometry of Biological Time*, Princeton University Press, 1985

9. F. C. Hoppensteadt, *An Introduction to the Mathematics of Neurons*

10. Heather Couper, 'Pie in the Sky', *Observer*, 1 January 1989

11. A detailed discussion of these matters can be found in Carl Sargent, 'Parapsychology and Astrology', in S. and C. Modgil (eds.), *Consensus and Controversy*, Falmer Press, 1985

12. Michel Gauquelin, *Written in the Stars*, Aquarian, 1988

13. Michel Gauquelin, *Planetary Heredity*, ACS Publications, 1988

14. Percy Seymour, *A Causal Mechanism for Gauquelin's Planetary Heredity Effect*, Plymouth Polytechnic, 1986

Index

PENGUIN

ARKANA

NEW AGE BOOKS FOR MIND, BODY & SPIRIT

With over 200 titles currently in print, Arkana is the leading name in quality books for mind, body and spirit. Arkana encompasses the spirituality of both East and West, ancient and new. A vast range of interests is covered, including Psychology and Transformation, Health, Science and Mysticism, Women's Spirituality, Zen, Western Traditions and Astrology.

If you would like a catalogue of Arkana books, please write to:

Sales Dept. – Arkana
Penguin Books USA Inc.
375 Hudson Street
New York, NY 10014

Arkana Marketing Department
Penguin Books Ltd
27 Wrights Lane
London W8 5TZ

PENGUIN
ARKANA

NEW AGE BOOKS FOR MIND, BODY & SPIRIT

A SELECTION OF TITLES

Weavers of Wisdom: Women Mystics of the Twentieth Century
Anne Bancroft

Throughout history women have sought answers to eternal questions about existence and beyond – yet most gurus, philosophers and religious leaders have been men. Through exploring the teachings of fifteen women mystics – each with her own approach to what she calls 'the truth that goes beyond the ordinary' – Anne Bancroft gives a rare, cohesive and fascinating insight into the diversity of female approaches to mysticism.

Dynamics of the Unconscious: Seminars in Psychological Astrology II
Liz Greene and Howard Sasportas

The authors of The *Development of the Personality* team up again to show how the dynamics of depth psychology interact with your birth chart. They shed new light on the psychology and astrology of aggression and depression – the darker elements of the adult personality that we must confront if we are to grow to find the wisdom within.

The Myth of the Eternal Return: Cosmos and History   Mircea Eliade

'A luminous, profound, and extremely stimulating work … Eliade's thesis is that ancient man envisaged events not as constituting a linear, progressive history, but simply as so many creative repetitions of primordial archetypes … This is an essay which everyone interested in the history of religion and in the mentality of ancient man will have to read. It is difficult to speak too highly of it' – Theodore H. Gaster in *Review of Religion*

The Second Krishnamurti Reader   Edited by Mary Lutyens

In this reader bringing together two of Krishnamurti's most popular works, *The Only Revolution* and *The Urgency of Change*, the spiritual teacher who rebelled against religion points to a new order arising when we have ceased to be envious and vicious. Krishnamurti says, simply: 'When you are not, love is.' 'Seeing,' he declares, 'is the greatest of all skills.' In these pages, gently, he helps us to open our hearts and eyes.

PENGUIN

ARKANA

NEW AGE BOOKS FOR MIND, BODY & SPIRIT

A SELECTION OF TITLES

Meeting Life Krishnamurti

In the last teachings before his death in 1986, Kirshnamurti suggests that we solve our problems most effectively when we let go of everything we know and purport to be, and meditate – which entails no more than dropping our hurts, fears, anxiety, loneliness, despair and sorrow on the spot. 'That is the foundation, that is the first step, and the first step,' he insists, 'is the last step.'

GAIA: The Growth of an Idea Lawrence E. Joseph

Many cultures use the figure of Mother Earth to express the idea that the Earth is a *living creature*; with the Gaia Hypothesis, the idea has now attained the status of science. In this immensely readable book the author describes how James E. Lovelock came to formulate the hypothesis, how it was developed and how it has subsequently been acclaimed and argued over by an international array of scientists.

Tertium Organum P. D. Ouspensky

First published in 1912, *Tertium Organum* was the first major work to re-examine the ancient and still largely unresolved philosophical problem of the nature of consciousness. In it Ouspensky conducts a fascinating post-Kantian inquiry into many of the major issues that have preoccupied generations of Western philosophers – an inquiry that bridges the gulf between Wetern rationalism and Eastern mysticism.

Saturn: A New Look at an Old Devil Liz Greene

Liz Greene draws on the depth psychology of Jung to go beyond the simplistic view that we are controlled by our stars. The way Saturn moves through the different houses, she suggests, can reveal much about a person's conscious and unconscious impulses; but it is up to us to travel along the roads to fulfilment the Initiator planet offers. 'As deep and thorough as Saturn himself' – Cherry Gilchrist

PENGUIN

ARKANA

NEW AGE BOOKS FOR MIND, BODY & SPIRIT

A SELECTION OF TITLES

The Dreambody in Relationships Arnold Mindell

All of us communicate on several levels at once, and Mindell shows how much of our silent language conflicts with overt behaviour. He argues that bringing all the hidden parts of ourselves to awareness as they affect us is important for the well-being not only of our relationships but also of the community – indeed, the world – in which we live.

Buddhism Geshe Kelsang Gyatso

Tibetan Buddhism has in many respects preserved the original teachings of the Buddha. Here they are presented with great wisdom and the paths towards liberation and enlightenment mapped out with painstaking care. For those seeking spiritual awakening, peace and serenity, this excellent book will open up a world of new possiblities.

Be As You Are Sri Ramana Maharshi

'The ultimate truth is so simple.' This is the message of Sri Ramana Maharshi, one of India's most revered spiritual masters whose teachings, forty years after his death, are speaking to growing audiences worldwide. 'That sense of presence, of the direct communication of the truth so far as it can be put into words, is there on every page' – *Parabola*

In Search of the Miraculous: Fragments of an Unknown Teaching P. D. Ouspensky

Ouspensky's renowned, vivid and characteristically honest account of his work with Gurdjieff from 1915–18. 'Undoubtedly a *tour de force*. To put entirely new and very complex cosmology and psychology into fewer than 400 pages, and to do this with a simplicity and vividness that makes the book accessible to any educated reader, is in itself something of an achievement' – *The Times Literary Supplement*

NEW AGE BOOKS FOR MIND, BODY & SPIRIT

CONTEMPORARY ASTROLOGY

Series Editor: Erin Sullivan

The ancient science of astrology, founded on the correlation between celestial movements and terrestrial events, recognizes the universe as an indivisible whole in which all parts are interconnected. Mirroring this perception of the unity of life, modern physics has revealed the web of relationships underlying everything in existence. Despite the inevitable backlash as old paradigms expire, we are now entering an age in which scientific explanations and models of the cosmos are in accord with basic astrological principles and beliefs. In such a climate, astrology is poised to emerge once again as a serious tool for a greater understanding of our true nature. In readable books written by experts, Arkana's *Contemporary Astrology* series offers all the insight and practical wisdom of the newest vanguard of astrological thought.

Titles already published or in preparation:

The Gods of Change: Pain, Crisis and the Transits of Uranus, Neptune and Pluto Howard Sasportas

Character and Fate: The Psychology of the Birthchart Katharine Merlin

Chiron and the Healing Journey: An Astrological and Psychological Perspective Melanie Reinhart

Working With Astrology Michael Harding and Charles Harvey

Saturn: A New Look at an Old Devil Liz Greene

The Karmic Journey Judy Hall

Neo-Astrology: A Copernican Revolution Michel Gauquelin

Saturn in Transit Erin Sullivan